Post-Souvenir City
Mediterranean Urban Intensity
And New Tourism Practices in Alicante

Intensidad urbana mediterránea
y nuevas prácticas turísticas en Alicante

ポスト・スーヴェニア・シティ：地中海都市アリカンテの活力と新しい観光

Measuring the Non-Measurable 05

| Measuring the Non-Measurable 05

Post-Souvenir City
ポスト・スーヴェニア・シティ

Mediterranean Urban Intensity and New Tourism Practices in Alicante
Intensidad urbana mediterránea y nuevas prácticas turísticas en Alicante
地中海都市アリカンテの活力と新しい観光

PREAMBLE / PREÁMBULO / はじめに

Prologue — 006
Prólogo
プロローグ
Darko Radović | ダルコ・ラドヴィッチ

Crossing Points of Two Noises — 010
Lugares de paso de dos ruidos
二つの物音の通り道
José María Torres Nadal | ホセ・マリア・トレス・ナダル

INTRODUCTION / INTRODUCCIÓN / イントロ

Alicante: Tourism and Urban Identity — 014
Alicante: turismo e identidad urbana
ツーリズムと都市アイデンティティ：アリカンテを例に
Jorge Almazán | ホルヘ・アルマザン

PART I   ESSAYS / ENSAYOS / エッセイ

Tourism, Territory, Identity — 026
Turismo, Territorio, Identidad
ツーリズム、テリトリー、アイデンティティ
José Oliver | ホセ・オリベール

Costa Blanca: Public Space and Perceived Image as Key to Tourism Competitiveness — 036
Costa Blanca: Espacio público e imagen percibida como clave de competitividad turística
コスタ・ブランカ：観光競争力強化の鍵としての公共空間と知覚イメージ
Rosario Navalón | ロサリオ・ナバロン

Benidorm. Esplanades and Ordinary Urbanities — 046
Benidorm. Paseos marítimos y urbanidades ordinarias
ベニドルム海浜遊歩道と平凡な都市性
Miguel Mesa del Castillo | ミゲル・メサ・デル・カスティジョ

Commons-based Urbanism: Can Alicante Be a Case Study? — 058
Urbanismo de los comunes: ¿puede ser Alicante un caso de estudio?
「コモンズ」型都市計画：アリカンテはケーススタディの対象となり得るか？
Enrique Nieto | エンリケ・ニエト

The Street : A Celebration of Transformative Architectural Installations 068
La calle: una fiesta de instalaciones arquitectónicas transformativas
街路：変移的建築装置の祝賀
Mio Suzuki | 鈴木美央

Toward Building a "Healthy" and Sustainable Urban Identity 074
Hacia una identidad urbana "saludable" y sostenible
"健全"で持続可能な都市アイデンティティの構築に向けて
Yukino Tairako | 平子雪乃

PART II URBAN EXPERIMENT / EXPERIMENTO URBANO / 都市的実験

Collective Urban Drift 084
Deriva urbana colectiva
集団的都市の漂流

Jorge Almazán, Mio Suzuki, Yukino Tairako, Shun Kawakubo, Gaku Inoue
ホルヘ・アルマザン、鈴木美央、平子雪乃、川久保 俊、井上 岳

Cross-cultural Debates 104
Debates transculturales
異文化間討論

Jorge Almazán, Yukino Tairako, Mio Suzuki, Milica Muminović, Gaku Inoue, Shun Kawakubo
ホルヘ・アルマザン、平子雪乃、鈴木美央、ミリッツァ・ムミノヴィッチ、井上 岳、川久保 俊

Urban files	01	Mercado Square	114
	02	Ereta Park	115
	03	Postiguet Beach	116
	04	Marvá, Soto and Gadea Boulevards	117
	05	New Square	118
	06	Castaños, San Ildefonso Crossing	119
	07	Calvo Sotelo Square	120

EXTRODUCTION / EXTRODUCCIÓN / エクストロ

Toward a Post-Souvenir City? 121
¿Hacia una ciudad post-souvenir?
ポスト・スーヴェニア・シティをめざして？
Jorge Almazán | ホルヘ・アルマザン

Postiguet Beach (September 2013)

Prologue

Prólogo
プロローグ

Darko Radović | ダルコ・ラドヴィッチ

The *Post-Souvenir City* was conceived and edited by Jorge Almazán, Keio University academic and a member of the Measuring the Non-Measurable — Mn'M core research team. The book brings together a series of essays and investigations, written by architects, urbanists and other specialists from Spain and Japan, in which they address various dimensions of tourism industry.

Research presented in the *Post-Souvenir City* the focus is on Spain, whose tourism is among the most visible in the world, and which has experienced both the excitements and the lows of tourism-fueled growth. Recently, Spain was among the countries which suffered most in the global economic downturn. The overall unemployment rate in the country has reached 26%, with youth unemployment getting close to 60%. That was, in a significant degree, due to drastic deregulation, an accordingly permissive development legislation, and high exposure to speculative and extremely damaging practices of what some theorists labeled "toxic neoliberal economic policy cocktail". The dominant, environmentally and culturally unsustainable, pseudo-economic development has, first, spectacularised, then consumed and, eventually, all but abandoned the most attractive places of Spain. During the rule of Debordean Spectacle, "the globalisation of the false" has, indeed, caused "the falsification of the globe".

In order to change development patterns which glorify irresponsible growth, we need paradigm-breaking research and innovation. That can happen only within broader, much needed paradigm shift, which would include the return and renewal of the rightful aura of authenticity, and redefinition of the value system, so that it can recognise the difference between precious, rooted cultures and superficiality of banal Disneyification. That is where Almazán places work presented in this volume, and opens its themes to public. His book both theorises and illustrates some of the possible alternative development scenarios, from the perspective of a very unique culture, with many and diverse experiences in tourism.

The primary focus of Mn'M project is at two systems of urban phenomena which resist quantification — culture and sustainability. In that context tourism is particularly interesting. It is, by definition, about culture and environment and, inevitably, about measurement. In tourism, the resource on sale is decidedly of non-measurable kind and, most importantly, non-renewable. Investigations how to get the things right in tourism may provide significant clues for broader, environmentally, culturally and economically responsible development.

Darko Radović
Head of the Mn'M Research Project
Tokyo, 8.2.2014

Post-Souvenir City ("La ciudad post-souvenir") ha sido concebida y editada por Jorge Almazán, profesor en la Universidad de Keio y miembro del equipo de investigación del proyecto Measuring the Non-Measurable – Mn'M ("Midiendo lo no-medible"). El libro compila una serie de ensayos e investigaciones escritas por arquitectos, urbanistas y otros especialistas españoles y japoneses, en los que abordan varias dimensiones de la industria del turismo.

La investigación de Post-Souvenir City se centra en España, país cuyo turismo es uno de los más visibles del mundo, y que ha experimentado tanto la euforia como la desolación de un crecimiento alimentado por el turismo. Recientemente España ha sido uno de los países que más ha sufrido la recesión económica global. La tasa de desempleo ha alcanzado el 26%, con la tasa de paro juvenil acercándose al 60%. Esto ha sido causado, en gran medida, por la drástica desregulación, una legislación urbanística igualmente permisiva, y una alta exposición a prácticas especulativas y altamente nocivas que algunos teóricos han catalogado como un "cocktail tóxico de políticas económicas neoliberales". Este modelo dominante de desarrollo pseudo-económico, insostenible desde el punto de vista ambiental y cultural, ha sometido los lugares más atractivos de España a un proceso sucesivo de espectacularización, consumo y finalmente de práctico abandono. Bajo el dominio del espectáculo debordiano "la globalización o mundialización de lo falso" ha provocado de hecho "la falsificación del mundo".

Para cambiar estos patrones de desarrollo que glorifican el crecimiento irresponsable, necesitamos investigación e innovación que rompan con los paradigmas existentes. Esto sólo puede ocurrir dentro de un cambio de paradigma más amplio, que incluiría el retorno y renovación del aura de autenticidad legítima y la redefinición del sistema de valores, de tal forma que se reconozca la diferencia entre las culturas, enraizadas y de valor inconmensurable, y la superficialidad de la disneyficación banal. Este libro teoriza e ilustra algunos de los posibles escenarios de desarrollo alternativos, desde el punto de vista de una cultura muy singular que ha tenido muchas y muy diversas experiencias con el turismo.

El foco de atención primordial del proyecto Mn'M está en dos sistemas de fenómenos urbanos que resisten cuantificación – la cultura y la sostenibilidad. En ese contexto el turismo es particularmente relevante, ya que por definición, está ligado a la cultura y al entorno, e inevitablemente, a su cuantificación. En la actividad turística, el recurso en venta es definitivamente no-medible, y más importante aún, no renovable. La investigación sobre cómo hacer las cosas bien en el campo del turismo puede aportar pistas e indicios significativos para el objetivo más amplio de conseguir un desarrollo responsable, desde el punto de vista ambiental, cultural y económico.

Darko Radović
Director de Proyecto de Investigación Mn'M
Tokio, 8 de Febrero de 2014

観光産業のさまざまな側面を扱う本書『ポスト・スーヴェニア・シティ』は、慶應義塾大学で教鞭を執り「Measuring the non-Measurable – Mn'M」研究チームのコアメンバーのひとりであるホルヘ・アルマザン氏の企画・編集により、スペインと日本を拠点とする建築や都市計画などの専門家が執筆した一連のエッセイと研究論文をまとめたものである。

『ポスト・スーヴェニア・シティ』に収められた論文は、いずれも、世界で最もツーリズムが盛んな国のひとつであり、観光に支えられた経済成長がもたらす高揚とその副作用を味わった国、スペインに着目する。近年、グローバル経済低迷の深刻な影響を蒙ったスペインは、労働人口全体では26%、若年層では60%近くに及ぶ失業率に苦しめられている。この破綻を導いた大きな要因は、一部の学者によって「新自由主義経済政策の毒カクテル」と名づけられた一連の行為、すなわち乱開発を促すような法制度を伴った急激な規制緩和であり、投機的できわめて破壊的な産業のあり方であった。環境的にも文化的にも持続不能な擬似経済成長が席巻する中、スペインでも特に魅力的な場所が次々とスペクタクル化され、消費され、そして最終的に放棄されてしまった。ギー・ドゥボールのいう「スペクタクル」が社会を支配するなか、〈偽物の地球規模化〉が〈地球の偽造〉を現実のものとしたのである。

責任なき成長を美化する開発のあり方を変えるために、現代社会はパラダイムを打ち破るような研究とイノベーションを必要としている。こうした変化は、オーセンティシティーが復権してそれに相応しいアウラを再び放つようになり、価値体系が刷新されるような、大規模なパラダイム転換によってのみ実現可能であろう。

そこではじめて、深く根を張った価値ある文化と、ディズニーランド的な陳腐で表面的な事象とが峻別されるのである。この発想の転換こそ、アルマザン氏が読者諸兄と共有せんとする本書の主題であり、編者は本書において、豊富で多様なツーリズム経験を持つスペインという一文化の視座から、従来の開発のあり方とは異なった手法の具体例を検討し、その可能性を理論化することを目論む。

さてMn'Mプロジェクトの主たる関心である文化と持続可能性の二点は、いずれも定量化に抗する都市現象体系であるが、この文脈上、ツーリズムはとりわけ興味深いテーマである。なぜならそれは本質的に、文化と環境についての行為であり、また必然的に、計測についての行為でもあるからである。ツーリズムにおいて、売りに出される資源は明らかに計測不可能な類のものであるが、さらに重要なことは、それが更新不可能であることだ。したがって、ツーリズムにおける物事の正しい配し方の研究は、環境・文化・経済に対する責任ある開発のあり方という、より一般的な命題についても、きわめて重要なヒントを与えてくれるであろう。

ダルコ・ラドヴィッチ
Mn'Mリサーチ・プロジェクト代表
2014年2月8日、東京

Calvo Sotelo Square (September 2013)

Crossing Points of Two Noises

Lugares de paso de dos ruidos
二つの物音の通り道

José María Torres Nadal | ホセ・マリア・トレス・ナダル

1. The city-making, the city-becoming

The city as backdrop. Listen: the noise of an incessant MOVEMENT, without interruption. In that noise there are always two REGISTERS. The one produced by the event of the CITY IN ITSELF, and the one produced by them, woman and men, by making the city, by living the city. To act upon one. To act upon the other: How then not to REVISE then the subject and object of our model so that the noises go riding together?

2. Inspiration is more architectural than imagination

More or less like this: the democratic and mobilizing thrust which gives voice and takes care of the small objects, the small communities, the everyday situations, has permitted us to recognize the officially *non_codified_non_sponsored* immense field of facts. THAT transformative power, which, for Federico García Lorca, was like going from a FACT of architecture (*noise 1*), to a STATE of architecture: an (inspiring) action in which architecture has HUMAN LOGIC (*noise 2*). [[The END of an end: architectural practices based on imaginative unfolding of invented realities BY/FOR the discipline. Useless for their critical inefficacy and for their lack of political commitment]].

3. Urban microclimate

Post-Souvenir City aims to: >EXPLAIN>enquire>>penetrate >>>PERFORATE >>>>in that black box, that place so scholastic and hidden, which has been the practice of teaching on the city. To be with whom one loves and to think of something else. To be in ALICANTE (Tokyo) and to think in TOKYO (Alicante). Or vice versa. But not producing more and more architectural information that always ends up becoming forms of fantasy. In favor of SITUATIONS of intense POLITICAL meaning for an emotional architecture, feasible, close, amicable. Can the work of the architect be as passionate as the complex everydayness of HUMAN RELATIONSHIPS?

1. Hacer la ciudad. El hacerse de la ciudad

La ciudad como telón de fondo. Escucha: el ruido de un MOVIMIENTO incesante, sin solución de continuidad. Hay en ese ruido siempre dos REGISTROS. El que produce el acontecimiento de LA CIUDAD EN SI, y el que producen ellos y ellas al hacer la ciudad, al vivir la ciudad. Actuar sobre uno. Actuar sobre otro: ¿cómo no REVISAR entonces el sujeto y el objeto del modelo para que los ruidos cabalguen JUNTOS?

2. La inspiracion es más arquitectónica que la imaginación

Más o menos así: el impulso democrático y movilizador que da voz y atiende a los pequeños objetos, a las pequeñas comunidades, a las situaciones cotidianas, ha permitido reconocer un inmenso campo de hechos *no_codificados_no_patrocinados* oficialmente, ESA potencia transformadora, que, para Federico Garcia Lorca, era como pasar de un HECHO de la arquitectura (*ruido 1*), a un ESTADO de la arquitectura: una acción (inspirada) en la que la arquitectura tiene LÓGICA HUMANA (*ruido 2*). [[El FINAL de un final: prácticas arquitectónicas basadas en despliegues imaginarios de realidades inventadas POR/PARA la disciplina. Inútiles por su incapacidad crítica y por su falta de compromiso político]].

3. Microclimas urbanos

Post-Souvenir City intenta:>EXPLICAR>Indagar>>adentrarse >>>PERFORAR >>>>en esa caja negra, ese lugar tan disciplinar y tan oculto, que han sido las prácticas docentes sobre la ciudad. Estar con quien se ama y pensar en otra cosa. Estar en ALICANTE (Tokio) y pensar en TOKIO (Alicante). O viceversa. Pero no produciendo más y más informaciones arquitectónicas que siempre acaban siendo formas de fantasías. A favor de SITUACIONES de intensa carga POLÍTICA para una arquitectura emocional, factible, cercana, amigable. ¿Puede ser tan apasionado el trabajo del arquitecto como la compleja cotidianeidad de las RELACIONES HUMANAS?

1. 都市をつくること、都市がつくられること

背景としての都市。聞け：ひと連なりの、絶え間ない「運動」の音色を。その音にはいつもふたつの「音域」がある。「都市そのもの」の物音と、彼ら彼女らが都市をつくり、そこに生活する際に生まれる物音、前者が後者に、また後者が前者に、重なり合う演奏：であるならば、ふたつの物音が「共に」主役となれるよう、都市モデルの主体と客体を「再検討」しようではないか。

2. 直感は想像力よりも建築的である

それはだいたいこのようなこと：人を動かす民主的な衝動が、小さな対象、小さなコミュニティ、日常的状況などに着目し、その声を拾い上げ、〈体系化されていない〉無数の非公式な事実のフィールドを認識することを可能にした。その変化のエネルギーは、詩人フェデリコ・ガルシア・ロルカにとっては、建築の「事実」（物音1）から建築の「状態」（物音2）への推移であった。後者は、そこで建築が「人間的論理」を持ちうるような（直感的な）行為と言い換えることもできよう。[[ある終末の終末：建築という学問分野による、それ自身のためだけに捏造された架空の展開に基づく建築的実践。批判精神と政治責任の欠如による無用の長物。]]

3. 都市微気候

ポスト・スーヴェニア・シティが＞説明＞研究＞＞潜入＞＞＞「貫通」＞＞＞＞することを試みるのは、都市についての教育活動という、学問的であり隠匿された場所、ブラックボックスである。愛する人と共に居ながら他のことを考える。「アリカンテ」（東京）にいながら「東京」（アリカンテ）に想いを馳せる。といっても建築的情報をひたすら生産し続けることはしない。それはいつも幻想というかたちで終わるから。感情的で、現実的で、身近で、親しみを感じさせる建築のために、強い「政治性」に彩られた「状況」を支持する。建築家の仕事は「人間関係」の複雑な日常性ほど夢中になれるものだろうか？

Mercado Square (December 2013)

Introduction
Alicante: Tourism and Urban Identity

Alicante: turismo e identidad urbana

ツーリズムと都市アイデンティティ：アリカンテを例に

Jorge Almazán | ホルヘ・アルマザン

El turismo es un arma de doble filo. Dinamiza la economía pero también trastoca el equilibrio socio-ambiental del territorio. Muchas ciudades costeras españolas experimentan esta dualidad desde la irrupción del turismo de masas en los años 1960. Tendencias turísticas recientes, sin embargo, revelan la aparición un turismo más sensible a los entornos locales. Este libro se centra en esas tendencias y plantea la hipótesis de una ciudad *post-souvenir*. Una ciudad turística donde el espacio urbano no es tratado como mercancía de consumo turístico, sino como el escenario donde residentes y visitantes conviven de una forma más creativa e interactiva. Ponemos a prueba la hipótesis en el caso paradigmático de la ciudad de Alicante. Su centro urbano compacto y funcionalmente diverso, su clima benigno, playas, gastronomía e intensa vida urbana, atraen masas de turistas nacionales e internacionales desde los años 1960. Pero esta afluencia también ha afectado a los ecosistemas y ha propiciado una economía poco competitiva. ¿Cuál es el papel del espacio público urbano ante esta situación? El libro aborda esta cuestión en dos partes. La primera contiene ensayos sobre urbanismo en Alicante y su relación con el turismo. La segunda resume un experimento llevado a cabo por residentes y visitantes japoneses para evaluar el sesgo cultural en la evaluación del público urbano. La libertad ensayística y el rigor investigador, dos aproximaciones igualmente necesarias, facilitan una reflexión poliédrica que aspira a superar modelos turísticos obsoletos y poco sostenibles. Para ello no recurrimos a la frecuente demonización del turismo. Más bien al contrario, identificamos desarrollos dentro de la propia actividad turística que refuerzan la imaginación social y la intensidad urbana.

ツーリズムは両刃の剣である。地域経済を活性化する一方、社会や環境のバランスを乱すからだ。1960年代におこったマス・ツーリズムの急速な普及以降、スペイン沿岸部の多くの都市がこの二重体験をしてきた。しかし近年、地域のあり方に即した新しい観光のかたちが登場しつつある。本書ではこうした観光の新しい傾向を取りあげ、「ポスト・スーヴェニア・シティ」の可能性を検証したい。観光によって消費される商品ではなく、住民と訪問者とが創造的かつ双方向的なかたちで共存する舞台となる、「ポスト・スーヴェニア・シティ」の都市空間。本書ではその典型例としてアリカンテ市を取り上げ、新たな観光都市モデルが成立しうるかを検証する。温暖な気候、ビーチ、食文化、そしてコンパクトで多機能な市街地中心部と活発な都市文化により、アリカンテは1960年代以降、国内外から大量の観光客を惹きつけてきた。しかし観光客の大量流入は生態系に影響を及ぼし、また経済的競争力強化の足かせともなってきた。このような状況で、都市公共空間の果たす役割とは何か？本書は二部構成でこの命題を扱う。まず前半には、アリカンテの都市計画や、都市と観光との関係について扱ったエッセイを収録した。後半では、文化的バイアスが都市空間評価に及ぼす影響をはかるため、アリカンテの住人と日本からの訪問者によって実施された実験の結果をまとめた。自由な評論と厳密な研究調査という2つの異なる、しかし共に重要なアプローチから多角的考察を行うことで、肥大化し持続困難となった観光モデルを超えるために何をすべきかが浮き彫りとなるのではないだろうか。本書は、安直なツーリズム悪玉論によらず、むしろ社会的想像力と都市活力とを強化するような、ツーリズムそのものの進化の様相を解明せんとするものである。

Learning from the existing landscape is a way of being revolutionary for an architect.
   —Robert Venturi, Denise Scott Brown and Steven Izenour, *Learning from Las Vegas*

Mixed blessing

Mass tourism is a mixed blessing for cities. It vitalizes the urban economy, but it degrades the living environment of local residents. Touristic developments in coastal regions, in particular, become powerful economic engines of urban transformation. But those same developments unleash a process of self-consumption of natural ecosystems and social capital. Landscapes that once attracted visitors end up so deeply transformed that they repel those same tourists. Local economies become gradually dependent on a low-cost, low-wage, undemanding tourism industry that does not provide incentives for more innovative development. Since the introduction of mass tourism in the early 1960s, many Spanish cities on the Mediterranean coast have experienced this dual nature of tourism, and their landscapes and social structures have been radically transformed. In 2008 this self-consumption process stopped abruptly when the speculative bubble burst and the Spanish financial crisis started. Since then the limits and dangers of this production model have become obvious.

Place identity and micro-urbanism

Together with climatic, natural, and cultural assets, the idea of an "urban identity", the distinctness of a city, has become a highly valuable asset. Cities are now increasingly encouraged to specialize and compete with one another to be more attractive to visitors and tourists. While competition often means the recovery of degraded historic centers, revitalization of former industrial sites, or enhancement of areas for cultural use, it often leads to a homogenization of cities and consequently to a loss of place identity and a decline in quality of life for its inhabitants. In cities exposed to mass-tourism, like those on the Spanish Mediterranean coast, this erosion of local identity has accelerated, resulting in polarized territories that segregate areas catering to visitors from those that are still part of local everyday life.

Touristic overdevelopment can be considered as a paradigmatic case of an imbalance in the so-called "triple bottom line" of sustainability: the simultaneous consideration of the environmental, social, and economic consequences of development. Macroscopic parameters, such as nature conservation, resource recycling, and industrial and financial vitality, are essential to achieve this balance. However, the micro-scale, such as public urban spaces, ordinary streetscapes, and the perception of the city from the point of view of the user, are equally important. Especially in relation to place identity, the livability, the character of the place, and the attachment of citizens to their city depend directly on everyday urban spaces. For visitors too, the image of a city is the image of its streets, the activities seen and the experiences afforded in publicly accessible urban spaces.

The city as souvenir

The city and province of Alicante are prototypical examples of the double-edged nature of tourism. Touristic overdevelopment and the sprawling urbanization of second houses along the coast are criticized as the cause for the destruction of natural landscapes and resources. The dependence on a perceived undemanding tourism is seen as an economic weakness in an international context that valorizes competition through technological innovation

016 | 017   Introduction | Jorge Almazán

Three urban development models in Alicante province – the cities of Alicante (top), Benidorm (middle) and Villajoyosa (bottom).

Alicante seen from the sky. Photograph by Luis F. Caballero Jurado

and differentiation. This criticism must be acknowledged. However, as the essays of this book will suggest, tourism also contains the potential to enhance urban intensity, to trigger sustainable social and spatial practices. This book therefore sheds a positive light on tourism, analyzes its transformation, and offers ideas to identify potentials in the everyday life urban space.

These ideas will be tested in Alicante, as our study case, but the conclusions aim to be applicable to other touristic regions. Through this study case we explore the limits of tourism models that exploit the city and the territory as a product, neglecting its social and environmental ecosystemic complexity. Models that commodify urban spaces and transform them into stereotyped objects, or "souvenirs" for easy touristic consumption. The standardized tourist resorts, the urbanization by stereotypical "Mediterranean" houses, and the segregated areas only used by tourists along Alicante province's shores are examples of the *city-as-product* logic.

Like souvenirs, these touristy spaces do not express actual culture. Rather they are designed to match the perceptions, expectations, and stereotypes that tourists bring along from their home countries. Souvenirs are often kitschy, unsophisticated merchandise, banal and in "bad-taste". But they are also charming and humorous cultural artifacts that encapsulate the clichés and stereotypes of the buyers. Based on recent trends in tourism, in this book we propose a "post-souvenir city", a city remembered not only by the artifacts bought at the souvenir shop but also by the intensity of its everyday urban life. A city where, unlike theme parks, events are not staged but real. Where tourist are not only passive consumers but active producers. The *post-souvenir-city* is, however, not a rejection of the world of banality, the culture of the souvenir. Rather it is a call to acknowledge the new role that tourism can play. Oversimplifications and stereotypes, positive or negative, are part of the global perception of cultures, and are one of the multiple overlapping contexts to which cities need to respond.

Collective narratives

Early research on the issue of urban identity, place identity, or place character applied phenomenology to the study of place, focusing on the individual subjective experience of place (Relph, 1976). In architecture theory, in a similar phenomenological approach, Norberg-Schulz (1980) proposed the *genius loci* view of place.

Rather than this early approach, which can be considered as subjectivist and essentialist, this book is theoretically framed in a vision of place identity, as *relational* (rather than subjective) and *dynamic* (rather than essential) quality. Hague (2005:7) puts it as follows: "the interpretative notion of identity is that 'essentials', 'authenticity', and 'distinctiveness' only become identity through interpretation, communication, and action within a context, and not in isolation." And he explains the implication of his view for planning (2005.10): "We interpret planning for place identity as a process of developing a discourse, even writing a narrative. It is a selective way of *imagining, acting* and *communication* about a place" (emphasis added).

Academic framework and book structure

How should such an intangible concept as "identity" be approached? This question was framed within a wider investigation carried out in Keio University under the title "Measuring the Non-measurable". Urban identity seems one of the intangible, non-measurable qualities of places. Can we measure, evaluate or represent the identity of place, its vitality or beauty? In this book we combine two approaches to tackle this issue. The first approach is a series of free reflections by specialists in the form of essays. The second is an urban experiment based on psychological research techniques. The aim here is go beyond the confirmation of our different subjectivities, the mere acknowledgement of cultural relativity. The goal

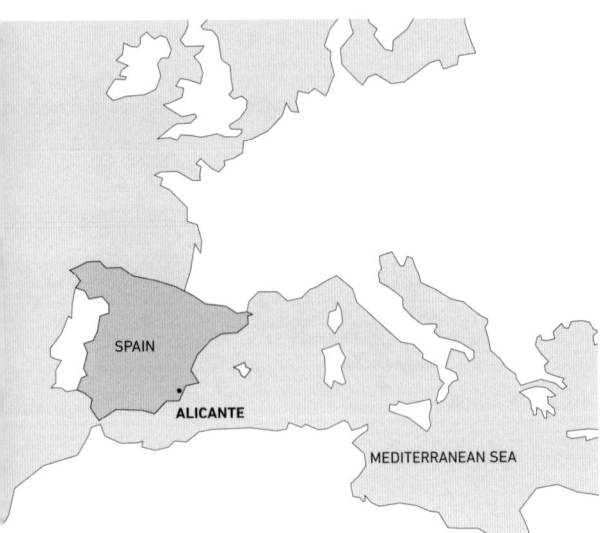

Location of Alicante, capital of the province of Alicante

is to explore the very structure of that relativity in order to, through discussion, explore our capacity to achieve a certain inter-subjective agreement, a minimum synthesis, even if partial and limited, as a necessary preliminary step for collective action. Our conclusions might be erroneous or inaccurate. But the risk of error becomes an opportunity to be amended, to generate debate, and hopefully to achieve more valid conclusions.

The two approaches mentioned above correspond to the two parts of this book and take the city and province of Alicante as a study case. Part I is a series of essays addressing tourism and how it affects urban space in Alicante. Part II compiles the results of a cross-cultural participatory urban experiment realized by local residents and Japanese visitors on the evaluation of public space. We combine essaystic freedom with rigorous research as two complementary, equally necessary perspectives to address urban complexity.

Part I starts with an essay by José Oliver. He addresses socio-economic changes in the province of Alicante brought about by two decisive historical events. First, the defeat of Alicante in 1939, as the last republican city in the Spanish civil war. Secondly, the massive influx of tourists since the 1960s, the subsequent accelerated urbanization of the territory, and the construction of new infrastructure. Oliver also explains the recent emergence of a new kind of tourist, who rejects standardized tourist facilities, personalizes his trips, and looks for cultural authenticity. He sees this new tourism as a stimulus for a renovated model of the territory that overcomes administrative micro-subdivisions to build a hyper-connected urban domain.

In the second essay, Rosario Navalón continues the examination of the provincial scale. From her point of view of Tourism Studies, she points out the challenges posed by new types of tourists, new motivations and habits, together with changes in information technology and

The souvenir does not express local culture but the tourist stereotype. Flamenco is not from Alicante, but from the region of Andalusia in southern Spain. Nevertheless, all kind of flamenco dolls are on sale in Alicante's souvenir shops.

the global economy. Navalón sees in urban space a key spatial element to respond to these transformations and to guarantee the sustainability of tourism in the province of Alicante.

In the third essay, Miguel Mesa examines the city of Benidorm, an extreme case within the province of Alicante. Often denigrated as an urban planning disaster, or as a cheap beach resort full of bad-taste giftshops and nightclubs, Mesa shows Benidorm in a positive light by exposing the points of view from which the city achieved a successful balance of the economic, cultural and ecological dimensions. He includes a detailed comparative analysis of the two main esplanades in Benidorm in order to show the role of urban design in creating a unique and lively waterfront.

In the fourth essay, Enrique Nieto focuses his analysis on the city of Alicante itself. He aims to overcome the reductionist views of the city that underlie both modern urban planning and the so-called "smart city" movement. He describes the city as an urban assemblage of heterogeneous multiplicity that works as a laboratory of controversies. Among the urban agents contributing to these controversies, Nieto mentions tourists and social activists, two types of urban agents usually considered as disconnected, who are described here as sharing a creative capacity and a decisive role in the production of the city.

The fifth essay, by Mio Suzuki, draws on one of the controversies found in the urban experiment of Part II. Are graffiti art or vandalism? From this controversy about the evaluation of public space in the city of Alicante, she reviews the opinions that support the importance of the street space to build urban identity. As an example she exposes the case of East London, where graffiti are not only tolerated but have become one of the attractors for tourism. Suzuki emphasizes the neglected role of small artistic and architectural actions, like graffiti, or street markets, to transform urban space and empower citizens to actively engage in their physical environment.

In the last essay, Yukino Tairako makes a reflection on the urban experiment explained in the Part II. From her perspective as a psychologist, she draws an analogy between urban identity and what is considered a "healthy" personal identity in psychology. In both cases, she explains, the key is on the integration of the self-perception and the social context. Applied to urban identity, it means a lack or reduction of discrepancy between how residents see their own city and how it is seen by visitors. She explains the methodological design followed in the urban experiment of Part II, which precisely had the aim of comparing the perceptions of locals and Japanese visitors in Alicante.

Part II contains two urban experiments in cross-cultural perception. It was conducted in March 2012 during a joint workshop between the University of Alicante and Keio University of Tokyo. Impressions and opinions of locals were compared with those of a sample of Japanese first-time visitors. We consider the Japanese cultural perspective on the city as particularly relevant, because Japanese visitors tend to have a greater interest in culture, art, gastronomy, etc., the kind of cultural shift that Spanish authorities are trying to implement in order to diversify the current tourist offer too centered on the so-called *sol y playa* (literally "sun and beach"), a tourism almost limited to *sun, sand and sea*. Cultural difference itself is not the object of the research of Part II. Cross-culturality is here a tool, a mirror to reproduce the images that foreigners perceive and how locals explain themselves. The aim of this Spain-Japan cross-cultural study contained in Part II is neither to provide definitive solutions nor to unveil cultural differences. Rather, we aim to methodologically facilitate a reflection on the cultural bias that affects judgment of urban quality, and on the complexity of building an identity in a context of great exposure to foreign visitors.

The city of Alicante

The Spanish city of Alicante (or Alacant in the Valencian language) is the capital of the province of the same name. The city is located in the south of the Valencian region and the population proper was 334,329, estimated as of 2011, ranking as the second-largest Valencian city (INE 2011). The coast along the province of Alicante is known in the tourism industry as *Costa Blanca* (literally "White Coast"): over 200 kilometers of Mediterranean coastline developed for the tourist industry since the late 1950s. It is a major *sun, sand and sea* spot, popular both for domestic and British and German tourists. It includes the major tourist destinations of Benidorm, Alicante, Dénia and Xàbia.

Unlike other coastal cities along the Costa Blanca, such as Benidorm or Villajoyosa, in the city of Alicante the search for an urban identity does not seem to have found any clear direction. Within the same context of mass tourism demanding sun, fun, low prices, and beaches, Villajoyosa has a clear policy of keeping its traditional morphology of Mediterranean small-scale compact and colorful building blocks, while Benidorm has radically opted for verticality, becoming the 'Manhattan of the Mediterranean'. Both Benidorm and Villajoyosa clearly depend on tourism, while Alicante is also an industrial, commercial, and administrative center. This seems to have polarized places in Alicante: those catering to visitors and those catering to locals. Many locals do not identify with specific places of Alicante, because they are too 'touristy' and, conversely, many places are ignored by visitors. The polarization of places is only one of the negative consequences. The city of Alicante has also seen how the economic force of tourism leads to the above-mentioned self-consumption of natural, cultural, and social capital. Urban overdevelopment has eroded ecological and aesthetic assets of the landscape, and tourist-oriented businesses have undermined the perceived authenticity of the city.

As a city highly exposed to mass tourism since the 1960s from North European countries, Alicante is engaged in a continuous effort to communicate and develop an attractive identity for visitors. Its dense and mixed-use Mediterranean urban fabric, in itself a sustainable asset, together with an urban beach, good weather, and cultural elements such as gastronomy and nightlife, become strong attractors for domestic and international visitors. These elements, enjoyed by locals and residents, seem to be the key in the search for an urban identity that overcomes the polarization between the "authentic" and the "touristy". The goal of this search is not to find a new slogan or logo. The idea of identity as a bottom-up process of collectively building a narrative is far from the reductionism of city branding. Rather this book hopes to add momentum to collective self-reflection, not by demonizing tourism again, but by finding the inner forces within tourism that can enhance a new way of imagining Alicante.

References

Hague, C. 2005. Planning and place identity. In Place *Identity, Participation and Planning*, ed. C. Hague and P. Jenkins. London: Routledge.

INE, Instituto Nacional de Estadística. 2011. Official population figures: Municipal Register.

Norberg-Schulz, C. 1980. *Genius Loci : Towards a Phenomenology of Architecture*. London: Academy Editions.

Relph, E. 1976. *Place and Placelessness*. London: Pion.

Venturi, Robert, Denise Scott Brown and Steven Izenour. 1977. *Learning from Las Vegas*. Cambridge: MIT Press, 1972.

Urban Evolution Of Alicante / Evolución urbana de Alicante
(Source: Ramos Hidalgo, Antonio, 1983, *La evolución urbana de Alicante*, PhD thesis, Universidad de Alicante, Facultad de Filosofía y Letras, June 1983)

before 16th century
ant. siglo XIV

A the Rock
B walled precinct
C arab city
D city wall
E medieval city

1 mosque / Holy Mary
2 Ferrisa gate
3 fish market
4 St. John the Baptist hosp.
5 St. Nicholas

A el Macho
B recinto amurallado
C ciudad árabe (?)
D muralla (?)
E ciudad medieval

1 mezquita / sta. Maria
2 puerta Ferrisa
3 lonja de Caballeros
4 hosp. s. Juan Bta.
5 s. Nicolás

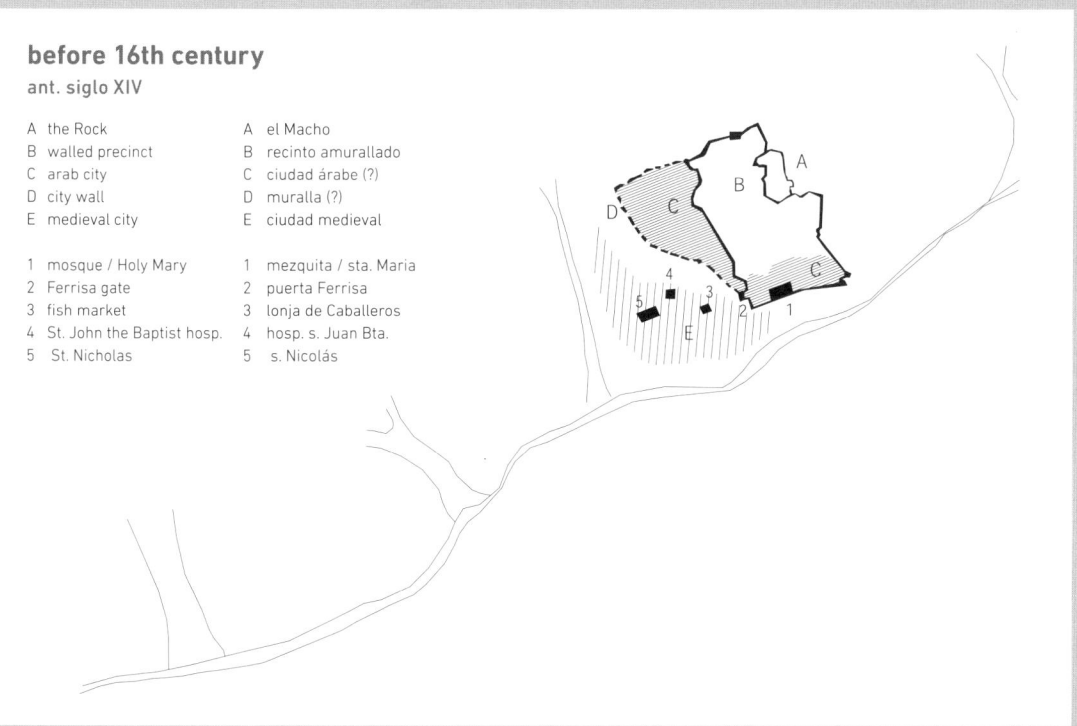

16th to 17th Centuries
Siglos XVI-XVII

A St. Barbara castle
B city wall (1558)

1 Socorro shrine
2 Asegurada
3 St. Roch shrine
4 El Carmen convent
5 St. Augustine convent
6 first Jesuit residence
7 city hall
8 St. Nicholas
9 Dominican convent
10 King's house
11 Franciscan convent
12 Capuchin convent

A castillo de sta. Bárbara
B muralla (1558)

1 ermita del Socorro
2 la Asegurada
3 ermita de s. Roque
4 convento del Carmen
5 convento de s. Agustín
6 primera residencia de jesuitas
7 ayuntamiento
8 s. Nicolás
9 convento de dominicos
10 casa del rey
11 convento de franciscanos
12 convento de capuchinos

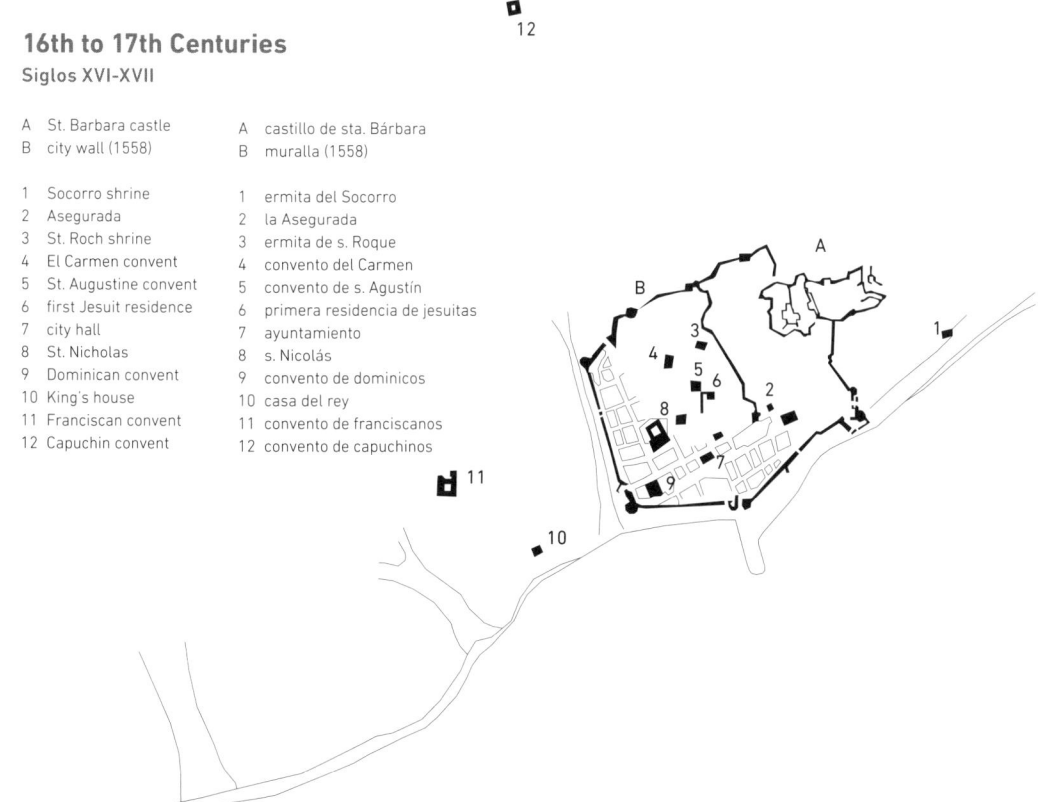

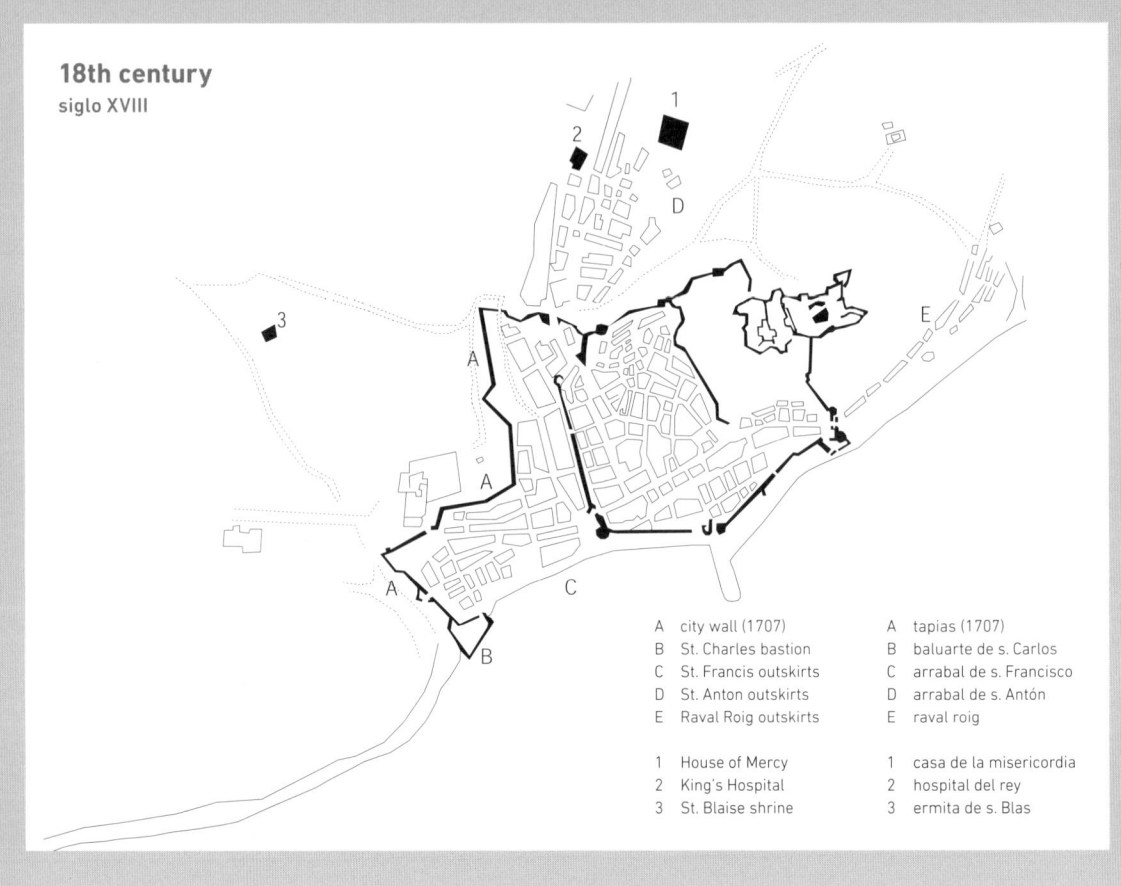

18th century
siglo XVIII

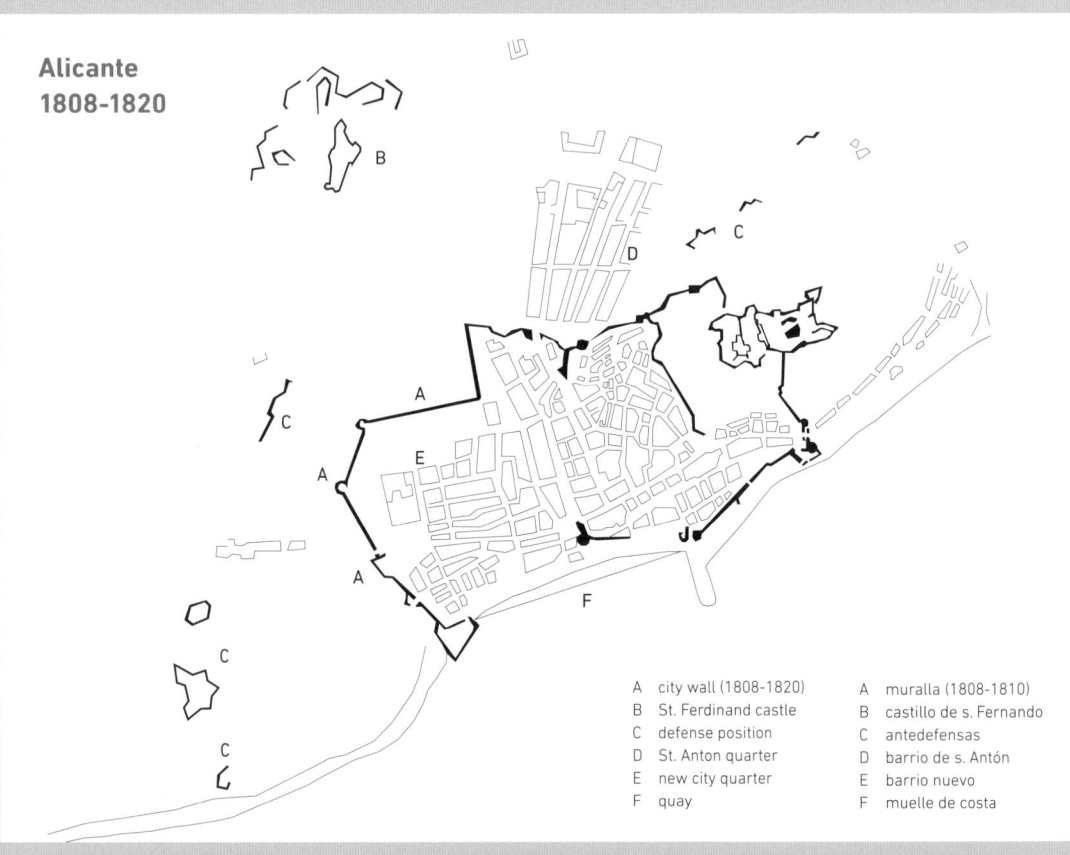

A	city wall (1707)	A	tapias (1707)
B	St. Charles bastion	B	baluarte de s. Carlos
C	St. Francis outskirts	C	arrabal de s. Francisco
D	St. Anton outskirts	D	arrabal de s. Antón
E	Raval Roig outskirts	E	raval roig
1	House of Mercy	1	casa de la misericordia
2	King's Hospital	2	hospital del rey
3	St. Blaise shrine	3	ermita de s. Blas

Alicante
1808-1820

A	city wall (1808-1820)	A	muralla (1808-1810)
B	St. Ferdinand castle	B	castillo de s. Fernando
C	defense position	C	antedefensas
D	St. Anton quarter	D	barrio de s. Antón
E	new city quarter	E	barrio nuevo
F	quay	F	muelle de costa

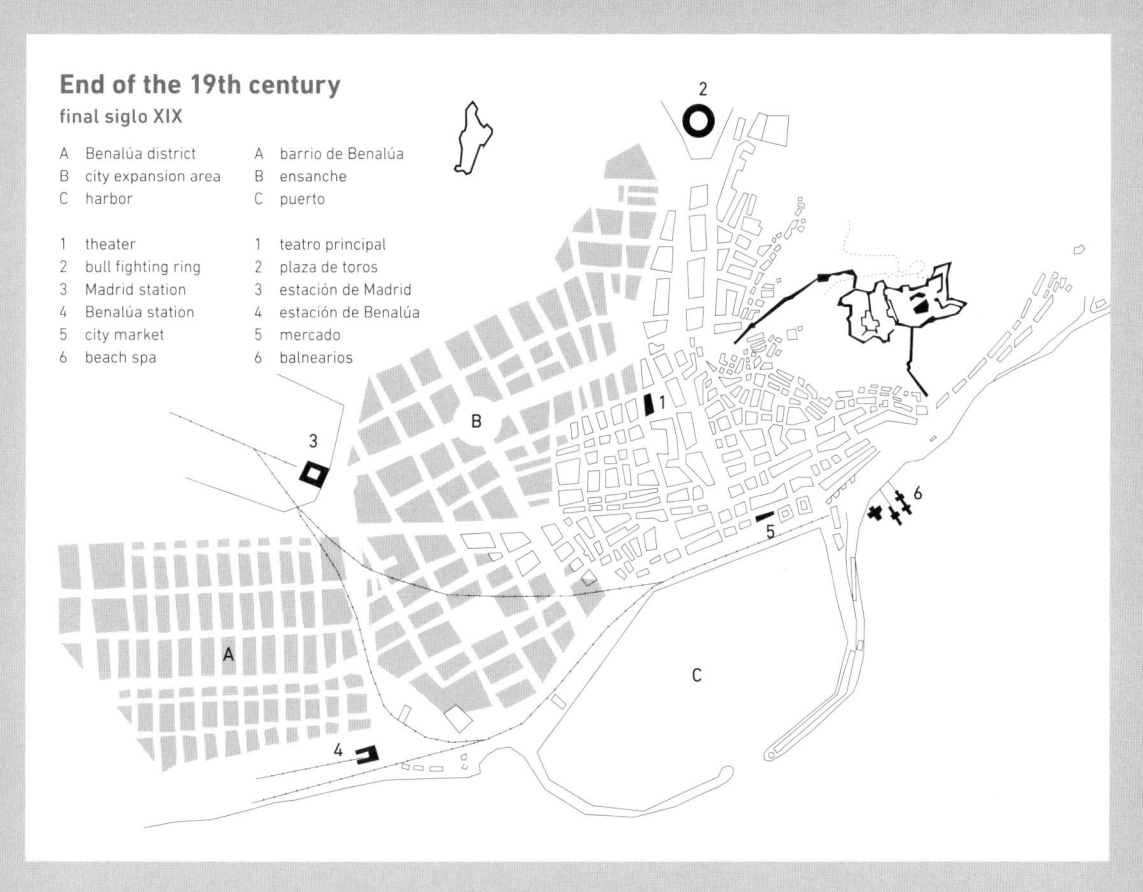

End of the 19th century
final siglo XIX

A	Benalúa district	A	barrio de Benalúa
B	city expansion area	B	ensanche
C	harbor	C	puerto

1	theater	1	teatro principal
2	bull fighting ring	2	plaza de toros
3	Madrid station	3	estación de Madrid
4	Benalúa station	4	estación de Benalúa
5	city market	5	mercado
6	beach spa	6	balnearios

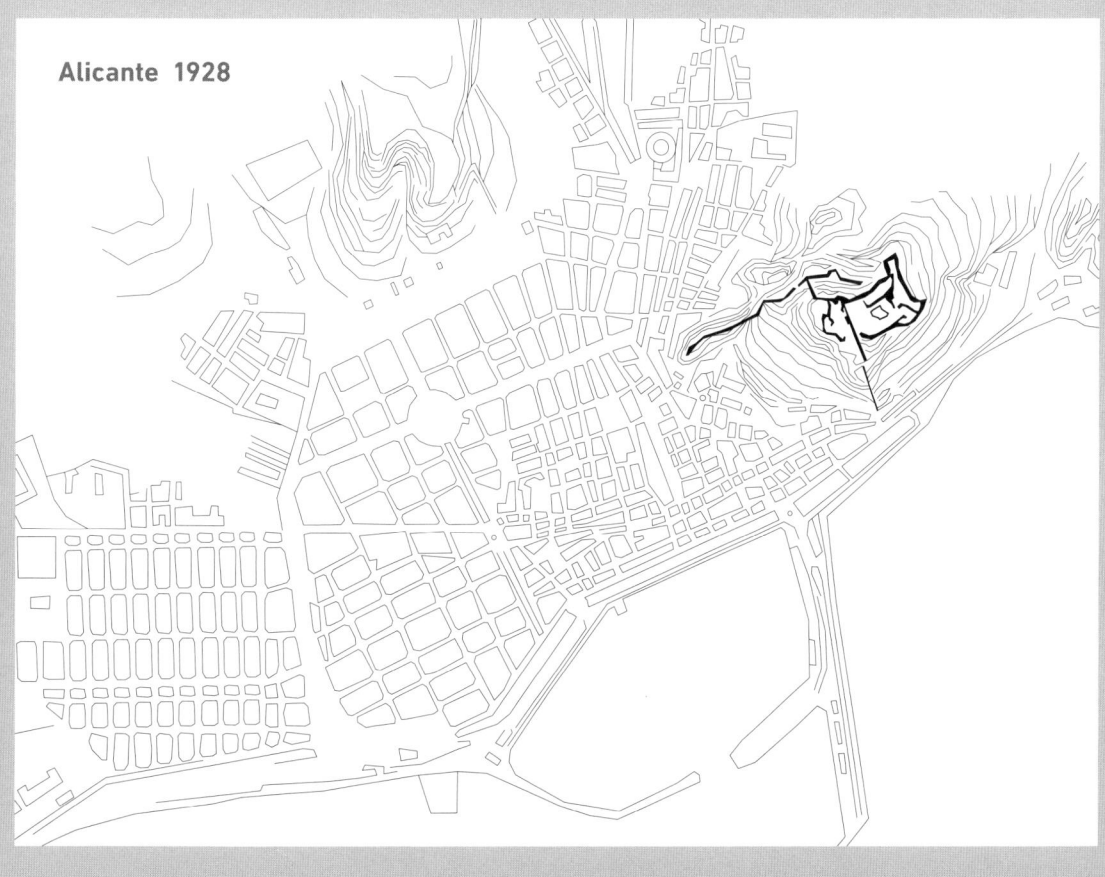

Alicante 1928

PART I
ESSAYS
ENSAYOS
エッセイ

Tourism, Territory, Identity

Turismo, Territorio, Identidad

ツーリズム、テリトリー、アイデンティティ

José Oliver | ホセ・オリベール

La transformación que los procesos vinculados al turismo ha propiciado la costa de la provincia de Alicante, es profunda y observable en diferentes aspectos. El más evidente es el físico, el que afecta a pueblos y paisajes: varias agencias medioambientales llaman desde hace años destrucción a la construcción generalizada de gran parte de este territorio. La confrontación entre estos dos términos opuestos nos sugiere que los procesos que consideramos contienen una gran carga de violencia, que queremos expresar situando el origen de nuestra reflexión justamente en esa destrucción sistematizada que fue la Guerra Civil, y las consecuencias que esa devastación tuvo justamente en esta parte del estado. Consecuencias como decimos físicas, pero no sólo. Nos interesa igualmente apuntar también cómo estos procesos no pueden comprenderse sin considerar las profundas transformaciones sociales que implican, y que nos permiten considerar conceptos como el de identidad, intensamente condicionado por una actividad cuyo objeto comercial es precisamente vender el lugar.

ツーリズムと結びついた諸々のプロセスがアリカンテ県の海岸線に引き起こした変容は、甚大である。それはさまざまな局面において観察することができるが、もっとも明白なのは村々や風景がこうむった物理的な変質であろう。この地域の広い範囲で一般化している建設事業が、複数の環境保護団体によって破壊行為と呼びならわされるようになって久しい。こうした建設／破壊プロセスに少なからぬ暴力性が含まれていることは、上記ふたつの対義語間の対立関係からも明らかであるが、まさにこのような暴力性を特徴とする体系的破壊行為であったスペイン内戦、そして内戦による当該地域の荒廃を、本論文では考察の出発点としたい。いっぽう、建設-破壊行為がもたらした変容は、物理的なものにとどまらない。社会全体が蒙った大きな変容を考慮しなければ、一連のプロセスを十分に理解したことにはならないであろう。本論ではこうした社会的側面についても言及し、まさに「場所を売る」ことを目的とした商業的活動である観光業が、その活動に強く依存するアイデンティティといった概念にどのような影響を及ぼしたかを考察する。

fig.1: 1939. The Stanbrook in the Port of Alicante. The boat departs for Oran, carrying close to 3,000 republican refugees.

In March of 1939 there was no longer any hope for the government of the Republic to succeed, but a final and terrible act had still not occurred within the context of the Spanish civil war. And it was precisely in the city of Alicante where it would take place.

Tens of thousands of refugees hoping to be evacuated had been congregating in the port of Alicante. Only a few were able to leave, however, embarking on an aged coal freighter, the *Stanbrook*. Loaded to capacity with evacuees, it left for Africa fortuitously avoiding the Italian army's bombs (Martínez Lea 2005). The destiny of these refugees was Algeria, a place which decades later would become the origin of migratory movements back toward Alicante. Such a movement contributed to a profound transformation of the area, in a sort of a historic boomerang that has over time turned out to be quite familiar.[1]

The large majority who could not escape were to observe first-hand how the fascist troops led by Franco and the Italian legionnaires entered the city, the last provincial capital still under the rule of the Republic. The ensuing desolation provoked suicides and other scenes of desperation that took place in the port, the last frontier, which after Franco's entry was transformed into a concentration camp.

The reality is that this tragedy was taking place in exactly the same location that just a few years earlier had in turn been transformed due to the massive arrival of another type of multitude: the thousands of tourists attracted by the temperate climate and sea bathing. In fact, wooden seaside "bathing platforms" had been erected on the El Postiguet beach every summer since 1854. And they soon became permanent. In 1890, a Regatta Club was cobbled together in a shed at the port, and in 1892 the inauguration of the so called "tren botijo" or "Botijo Express"[2] allowed hundreds of summer vacationers to arrive in Alicante from Madrid, on what was the first rail line connecting the capital with the Mediterranean coast. And these virtually festive transformations of the urban space in Alicante and the surrounding coast, which had been taking place up to only one decade before the end of the war, would put an end as well to the rest of the processes of change that the phenomenon of tourism had contributed throughout the roaring twenties (AAVV 2003).

The end of the war left much more than a destroyed city. Unlike other moments of recent history in which Alicante had been devastated – prior to the *Aviazione Legionaria* dropping their bombs, the French had massively bombarded the city as well, during the War of Succession, destroying it almost completely (Ramos 1991) – the physical rupture of the city at that moment was accompanied by the conviction that the Resistance had been in vain: Alicante itself demonstrated the very expression of defeat. It is interesting indeed to consider this context, as we have indicated, since the need for more than just a physical rearrangement turned out to be a crucial objective for this part of the Mediterranean coast. And it would be precisely in the violent and suntanned transforming processes associated with tourism where the energy was found to restore cities, societies and economies at a frantic pace, so that everything up to that point would seem like no more than a mere legend.

The phenomenon of tourism, thus, as an agent of massive reconstruction, encounters a very interesting condition for stimulation in this region: the lack of prejudices. We can say that the physical and moral damage that had framed the city of Alicante brought about arguments, referring neither to the landscape, nor to the architectural heritage, nor even to what can be referred to as the social construction, that raised suspicions about these transformations in one way or another. In this profoundly desolate region anything was possible, because in all actuality everything earlier had failed: the city of Benidorm, an almost cosmopolitan and fantastic metropolis that grew with urgency in the Mediterranean without seeming to be an invasive species, or perhaps as an expected invasive species, can only be

fig.2: Bathing platforms on the beach at El Postiguet, tourist facilities around the Port of Alicante in the 1930s.

understood from the perspective of the opportune tolerance that imposed this violence.

Now is perhaps the appropriate time to be precise. As is obvious, this is not about arguing that the devastation we have described is an important factor in understanding the phenomenon of the transformation brought about by tourism. What we propose in this essay is to consider how in this region in particular, the condition of being the final bastion of democratic resistance against Franco's rebellion, and the terrible ensuing defeat, can help us understand the depth and naturalness with which the changes tourism involved were accepted. We propose in brief the idea that Benidorm is possible precisely in this location – socially, architecturally and as regards the landscape – from the conviction of that greatest of failures.

Transformations

It is true that all of these processes would not begin to occur until two decades after the end of the civil war. In the 1950s, the dictatorial regime of Francisco Franco was asphyxiated from years of self-governed isolation. The only solution it had to address this reality was to allow a cautious opening to the outside world, and the direction of this political move had been proposed in an initial stage by the industrial sector.

Thus, it was finally in the 1960s when mass tourism was chosen as the new hope for the economic re-launching of the country. The exploitation of the favorable characteristics that a great part of the national territory had to offer was negotiated to serve that end. And within the geography of the Spanish state, this part of the Mediterranean coast was particularly favorable due to the climatic conditions (more than 300 days of sun per year) and due to its beaches. In such a fashion, and relying on the slogans with which the regime hoped to transmit an optimistic and relaxed image, a model of development was constructed. It was based fundamentally on these two premises, sun and beaches: the idea of "The Happy East" (*Levante Feliz*) was added to the classic "Spain is different". This new slogan aimed to define a form of Promised Land where everything was possible, where everything was definitely pleasurable (Preston 2001).

These decisions aspired, therefore, to take advantage of a new social phenomenon: the figure of the summer holidaymaker, a sort of part-time nomad able to temporarily move his full-time residence to a destination that, as we shall see, promises a life in large measure foreign to his daily existence (Martínez and Oliva 2010). As one can easily imagine, the scenery needed to construct this fiction is a city in large measure different from the "natural" surroundings of this type of individual. Consequently one can easily understand why it is possible to observe in these cities for summer holidaymakers a field of architectural experimentation that is not frequently found in the inland capitals. Here, on the coast, dizzyingly modern and carefree landscapes are established, quite cinematographic in effect; places in which the real and the imagined coexist, mutually astonishing each other, something that some experts have summed up as the *relaxed style* (Ramírez 1987).[3]

Hence, on the one hand and in spite of being located in a context far removed from the cultural foci that dominated the Spanish panorama (or perhaps precisely because of this), the development from the 1960s on in the towns located on the coast of Alicante takes on, with surprising naturalness, architectural trends typical of modernity. In this manner, a refurbished country is in some way

fig.3: 1950. Tourist posters of "Spain is different".

displayed, and so, one distant from the clichés that linked it to a permanent backwardness (Martínez 2003).

On the other hand, however, as we indicated earlier when alluding to Juan Antonio Ramírez, we observe as well how these modern principles are combined with unprejudiced freedom. The less strict the elements, the more enjoyable. Chalets, apartments, campgrounds, gas stations, hotels, any type of construction no matter how modest becomes at a determined moment an icon in this type of informal counterculture which seems simply kitsch to some. We believe that it can also be understood from the perspective of pop culture due to its correlation to the popular. In a sense, we have the impression that architects in this region behaved in a fashion similar to the summer holidaymakers themselves: they did on the coast what they couldn't do inland.

Elements

Up to this point, we hope to have outlined the conditions for the general context that we think facilitate an understanding of the processes of territorial transformation that was produced in this part of the province, which are linked to tourism. As has been shown, we have identified tourism as the most crucial agent of change. Nevertheless, these processes can only take place from the very moment in which the conditions permit them. It is here that we want to highlight two of these conditions.

The first is related to the role of the infrastructure of transportation. We have previously mentioned that at the end of the 19th century Alicante became the endpoint of the first rail line to connect the capital of Spain with the coast (Aguilar 1988). The role played by this infrastructure was extremely important with respect to the objective of this research effort. Since the construction of the rail line coincided with the rise in "sea bathing", this became one of the principal attractions sought out by visitors to the city.

But, since we are dealing with a means of communication or travel within the same country, the societies that were coming into contact with each other – with all the ensuing nuances – were culturally the same. Therefore, although we are talking about an initial investment that without a doubt is important when constructing the idea of Alicante as a tourist destination, promoting the summer vacationing of inland residents of the Iberian Peninsula on this coast resulted in consequences that on other levels were less important.

The construction of the AP7 freeway is perhaps an element of greater importance. This freeway, with its high capacity for motor vehicles, extends along the peninsula's entire Mediterranean coast, from southern Spain to the French border. The first sections were inaugurated at the end of the 1960s, a fact which takes for granted a direct element of communication with the foreign, one which permitted the massive arrival of French, Dutch and German tourists who came to spend the summer in the region. In addition to Alicante, other major tourist towns were located along this route: San Juan, Campello, Benidorm and Villajoyosa. The impact of this infrastructure on the region is evident, for in the areas along which this freeway passed there appeared hotels, motels, campgrounds and other features all unknown in the area up to that point. This was not the only impact. As we mentioned earlier, unlike the rail connection this was one of the principle roads that tourists from Central Europe used en masse. Above and beyond the economic impact that this influx of outsiders had, it was precisely the encounter of a mindset so far removed from the morals imposed by national Catholicism that brought about a jolt in the local society. And it was rife with bewilderment

fig. 4: 1960. A Campground on the Costa del Sol. The expression the "relaxed style" provides the title to a book of the same name published by the Malaga College of Architects in 1987. (Image taken from that book.)

and most undoubtedly scandal. Those Nordic women who exhibited their bodies were not only not embarrassed by their femininity, they also revealed themselves to be free and self-assured.[4] It is entirely possible that the most probable reaction of a society that had remained virtually isolated in the preceding decades, with their customs regarding meals, time schedules, personal relationships or tolerance, was mainly one of mistrust, rejection or perhaps fascination.

The cinema exploited these situations in which the locals, generally middle-aged men, normally unattractive and uneducated, unhappy in any event, came into contact with stunning young women whom they both desired and feared, overwhelmed by their incomprehensible laughter and by their zest for life.

This situation progressed with, more than anything, the building of the International Airport of El Altet. Not only did this strengthen the infrastructure of the region, but it had a sizeable impact as well. The airport was built between the two largest cities of the region, Alicante and Elche, in an area influenced by a high-density population. Thus, it had a great capacity to become the backbone of the province (Vegara 2001). Inaugurated in 1967, its role in relation to the massive arrival of tourists was essential, particularly after the increase in charter flights: as is well known, these flights are promoted by wholesalers of tourist packages, organizing lodging, transfers, activities, etc., all sold as a fixed product. By the beginning of the 1960s, the United Kingdom, the country that sent the highest number of tourists to the region, had established a service center between Alicante and Valencia. This city is located some 180 kilometers to the north of Alicante. Back then, tourists arrived at the airport in Valencia and were transported by bus to the south of the region (Matarredonda 1993). Nevertheless, as we have mentioned, at the end of the 1960s this same service could be furnished directly from Alicante. Thus, we see how the El Altet airport is linked from its origin

fig.5: Luis García Berlanga's film "Vivan los novios". The final scene of a funeral party on the beach. By arranging the people in the shape of a spider, the director expresses in one way the moral state of society at the close of the 1960s.

to the international charter activity: just five years after its inauguration, the destination of 10% of the total number of tourists who flew to all destinations in Spain was the city of Benidorm (Ivars and Menor 2008).

This arrangement enabled travel and a summer-long holiday to be purchased at a very economical price, thus opening the possibility for a large, potential market of middle and lower-middle class people to vacation. The product that was offered was clear: sun and beach seemed more than enough, and millions of people began to regularly visit the so-called Costa Blanca. Nowadays, the phenomenon of charter flights has been replaced by a boom in low-cost flights, connecting the province of Alicante with the rest of Europe at minimal cost. It is possible that this new format has points in common with the charter flights, but we also have the impression that the consequences of the low-cost flights in the province are not the same. While these impacts should continue to be studied,[5] we will propose a partial analysis further on.

The truth is that in the 1960s, the travel infrastructures we are discussing, particularly the airport, contributed to an enormous influx of visitors that need to be lodged and attended to. The local towns transformed themselves to take advantage of this new manna. These transformations were possible thanks to a second element, which we want to mention in this summary: the legislative conditions. It is appropriate to mention here that in 1956 the first Land Use Act (Ley del Suelo) was approved. The provisions of this law established legal coverage for the massive transformation of non-urban land into urban building lots. As previously mentioned, we have the impression that it was at this point that a physical reconstruction became urgent. It is quite possible as well that this physical reconstruction concealed the defeat of the civil war, substituting for it the happiness that was attributed to the eastern coastal area by the regime, thus preparing the ideal conditions to make the most of these legal provisions. In this way, the search for the maximum exploitation of land, at the lowest cost and at the greatest speed, opened the way to urban development that in the face of any social reflection or environmental precaution turned out to be nothing less than exotic.

Within this context, the city of Benidorm is one of the most significant cases. From the 1960s on, a decisively vertical development takes place, proposing an urban expansion that took advantage of a legal framework that functioned with three basic parameters: a maximum FAR of 300% (maximum quantity of buildable square meters 3 m^2/m^2), a minimum lot size of 1000 m^2, and a minimum setback from the property boundary of 7 m, with no height limitations (Jaén 1999). As can be seen in fig. 6, the town quickly abandoned its physical condition as a fishing and agricultural village to become a metropolis geared toward vacationing pleasure, practically multiplying its population by six in just under a decade. As significant as this transformation was, the truly relevant notion was that the number of inhabitants in the city could shrink and grow to both extremes depending on the tourist season. A true artifact perfectly adapted to the summer holidaymakers, some authors indicate that right now the city is able to multiply its inhabitants even up to 700% during the summer season, without, by the way, creating any particular tensions.

The result of this entire process is the Spanish city with the greatest number of skyscrapers, a truly unusual fact amongst European cities that are not capitals. Today, we find some 30 buildings higher than 100 meters, the highest residential building in Spain (at more than 200 meters) counted among them. And these freestanding towers rise along the two beaches between which, like a sort of relic, sheltered on the cape that separates the two, lies the historic city center with its small-scale buildings and unsymmetrical streets (Martínez 2001). This situation emerges as so significant that it suggests the proposal for a new reflection.

fig.6: Benidorm before (left) and after(right) tourist development. The historic city center is seen between the two beaches.

Identity

We have up to this point established how, in a society that had suffered a deep isolation from the rest of the world (Spain was readmitted to the UN in 1955) as well as a very severe indoctrination, the presence of a large influx of people from other European countries had an evident impact. Suspicious of *sinful* habits, the local society proudly maintained its traditional customs. These were often evident in popular celebrations, for the most part rooted in the Catholic religion. The new visitors observed these exotic traditions as part of the surprising charm of this country, which, like the Galapagos Islands, seemingly had developed in isolation, on the margins of the post-war evolution that other European countries had experienced: Spain, definitively, was *different*. The pleasant climate and the nature of the Mediterranean people had historically determined that these local traditions took place in the street, in the public sphere, with a festive participation on the part of all of society. In this fashion they are perceived by the foreign visitor as expressions that exemplified the *authentic* local culture, and they begin to form yet another element which the project of tourism offered. The *fiesta* is associated, thus, with an idea through which the country identifies itself, constructing an external image, which persists even today.

But these traditions turned out in many cases to be much more complex, even incomprehensible to those who had not participated in them since childhood. They could even appear to be exclusive to those not in the know. The necessity to "sell" them as part of a tourist package contributed to their modification; they were made more easily digestible for a non-specialized audience. And this process is observed in expressions of traditional culture as well as in historical architecture itself. Thus, elements that might blur a "cliché" image, are removed. As we have previously mentioned, the speed with which these processes are adapted seems to form part of the touristic transformation, and the visitor doesn't have enough time during the short summer holiday to delve into cultural manifestations. A process we could refer to as "*parquetematizacion*", or "theme-parkification" takes place, one through which one expects massive and effective consumption of something that one *hoped* to perceive (Solá Morales 1998). In the long run, the tourists are given what we think will satisfy their expectations, but as a result a doubt arises: Is this *authentic*?

Of course the question regarding authenticity takes us back to a debate that is not new, especially in architecture, but one which may be interesting to reposition here, since it is intimately related to the question of identity. Are the paellas which combine fish, meat, olives and vegetables real, considering in addition that they are served 24 hours a day? Is the historic city center of Benidorm authentic? The one that survives and is also preserved (or fossilized) in the miniscule cape situated between the two beaches replete with skyscrapers? In other words, is the historic city center where the origin of Benidorm lies, more Benidorm than the vertical metropolis that tourism built? The fiestas, the food, the way people enjoy themselves all adapt to the daily routines, the flavors and the sounds of what a sort of new dictatorship establishes: the image of the touristic product. Does this process imply a loss of identity? We might have the impression that the *authentic* becomes unfamiliar, in other words, it becomes something no one understands. The "real" is nothing more than a close-minded whim. There are housing developments along the coast where the "Spanish" is expressed through white masses, tile roofing, porches and balustrades. But the models for such buildings are not actually traditional structures from that area: they imitate the cinematographic images, which many years earlier Hollywood had defined as the *Spanish* style (Ramírez 1992). The real and the imagined become muddied in such a profound way that the question posed doesn't have an obvious answer: the *British paella* is as authentic as the one we can eat today for the price of gold – the price of the presumably genuine – in a traditional establishment. It is quite possible that the *authentic* identity of Benidorm is the one which each of its visitors desires to purchase.

The topic is fitting, however, because truth be told, this situation seems to perplex a certain type of visitor

who does not represent the prototype of the summer holidaymaker, whom we have earlier described. This visitor has only recently emerged. More akin to an explorer than to a wholesale summer vacationer, this type of traveler has begun to arrive more and more frequently thanks to the phenomenon of *low-cost* airlines. These flights allow travel at a minimal price, and are not sold as a package with fixed lodging as they were with charter flights. The *low-cost* travelers, thus, accept a certain amount of adventurous uncertainty since they do not know where they will stay. In any event, they are not part of a fixed program of activities. Thus, while summer holidaymakers are searching for a closed, lively experience, one in which even the surprises are expected because a product adapted to their expectations has been sold to them, the low-cost traveler hopes for a different scenario: she takes advantage of the freedom of her conditions to explore the authentic. Considering herself a non-tourist, she believes she is encountering a lost reality in the places she visits, ones outside the most frequented itineraries.

Interest, then, is taken in residual places, those with difficult access or those apparently marginal. Spaces in which identity or the authentic seem to have taken shelter. The experiences sought out in this fashion relate to interacting with the local inhabitants, who due to their foreignness to the newly arrived exhibit an exoticism not softened by consumption. *Friction* is definitely the experience that characterizes this other kind of tourism, compared with the smoothness of the all-inclusive package. The consequences we might intuit for the city based on these experiences can be interesting. If the phenomenon of massive tourism transformed the city in such a way that its consumption was simple, the friction explorer tries to bring these embarrassments to light. Everything that had not been publicized in the transaction, i.e. the discard pile, is transformed from the point of view of the other not only into a protagonist, but also into a reservoir of a dramatic legacy: that of authenticity. Because of these experiences, we are in *all actuality* what we do not wish to show. Perhaps *Levante* is not so happy after all.

fig.7: The paella as a tourist performance

Metalocus

The reflection we have just suggested about this new-type user of tourism is surely incomplete: we could equally have considered the importance of other social profiles and this most likely would have given way to complementary proposals. The truth is that by taking this type of nomad with pretensions as a reference, someone capable of overcoming certain limits, of leaving the beaten path, able to mix with, or at least think he can mix with the locals, presents for us a unique interest, which we will outline below. In some way it forces us to consider the hypothesis that the urban planning that came about due to charter flights and closed tourism, the all-inclusive package, can be revised. And this revision could be considered not, as we may have initially suspected, from the point of view of the parameters which that type of planning ignored at that time. It is not about questioning urban planning from the point of view of its environmental logic, from its energy efficiency, or from its social efficiency, for example. It is about evaluating it precisely from the fundamental element that was considered, from its inception: from the point of view of the client. And from this point of view, we can pose the question today as to the way in which the development of the region as a product has been managed, because the model of the client today could be very different indeed.

Thus, we take this *boundless* user into consideration. The strategies that would seem more timely would be ones that stem from the approach of the global metropolis. Here, edges would be blurred by virtue of being unnecessary; there would be no sense in talking about centers of interest or about the periphery. From this conception of a network, one can approach a region in which the hubs have much less transcendence than the connections that are established between them.

This allows us to propose two conclusions. On the one hand, the traditional coordination of the region through independent town governments becomes obsolete. In other words: the planning tools which have heretofore been used, those based on incomplete planning documents on a local scale, become ineffective in order to resolve the supra-municipal condition that characterizes the new user. We have the impression that in this manner, the definition of a continuous super-city could be a much closer modeling of the complexity of today's reality than other more incomplete simplifications.

And on the other hand, on this super-city coast, the needs of the consumer – within this context this may be the word that most precisely describes the inhabitants whom we have earlier described – unavoidably require a hyper-connection. That is to say, we understand that it is a priority to establish as a strategic element absolute inter-modality between the different means of transport. With this objective, any type of movement becomes more viable, any type of destination, from any type of route. The uselessness of preconceiving any particular itinerary, for the above mentioned reasons, allows us to approach the region as a continuum in which field, street, building, square, empty lot or corner have, in all actuality, the same qualitative importance, because they are all of equal importance to the client. And those places, therefore, should all be accessible in the same fashion. In this way, the airport, first and foremost, but also the intermodal centers of trains, streetcars, private vehicles, etc., are not simply the means that allow us to reach a destination, they are the destination.

As we can see, even from the simplification of considering only one of the profiles of the possible user, the conclusions seem to be valid in any given case. In reality, the truly revealing part of the argument is proving how an outside, curious gaze at our reality allows us to reconsider this reality. And in a region where location, landscape and society all seem to be for sale, we surely cannot postpone this reflection.

Notes

1. The pieds noirs who fled from the war in Algeria took up residence in the region of Alicante (some 30,000), building a large part of the Serra Grossa and la Albufereta for use in tourism.
2. "Botijo" is the name given to a ceramic jug, which was used in Spain to keep drinking water cool and fresh. The expression "tren botijo" referred to the first trains that connected Madrid to the coast. The name alludes to the fact that they were popular trains, and the people that traveled them carried all sorts of things with them, among them the ever-present "botijo" which provided fresh drinking water during the long voyage.
3. Juan Antonio Ramírez proposed this expression in his studies on the architecture of the Costa del Sol.
4. For example, in the northern Spanish city of Santander, the habits of university students from the rest of Europe and the United States who came to the Universidad Internacional in the 1960s, such as going to the beach in bikinis, caused such an impact in the city that the beach, from that point on, was called "Bikini Beach," a name still in use today.
5. The growing importance of this phenomenon is such that at the very University of Alicante, courses such as The Economy of Globalization, have been dealing with the topic for years now.

References

AAVV. 2003. *Sunland architecture*. Barcelona: COA Catalunya.

Aguilar Civera, Inmaculada. 1988.*La estación de ferrocarril. Puerta de la ciudad*. Valencia: Generalitat Valenciana.

Ivars, Josep Antoni and Mariano Menor. 2008. El impacto de las compañías aéreas de bajo coste en la actividad turística del área de influencia del aeropuerto de Alicante, *Rev. Estudios Turísticos* 175-176:89-104.

Jaen, Gaspar et. al. 1999. *Guía de arquitectura de la provincia de Alicante*. Alicante: Instituto de Cultura Juan Gil-Albert.

Martínez Lea, Juan. 2005. El Stranbrook. Un barco mítico en la memoria de los exiliados españoles. *Rev. De Historia Contemporánea* 4:65-81.

Martínez Medina, Andrés. 2001. Arquitectura en la frontera. *Rev. Canelobre* 44-45:26-31.

Martínez Medina, Andrés. 2003. Formigó diví, llum humana. Religiositat i modernitat en les esglésies d'estiueig del sud valencià (1959-1974). *Rev. Aiguaits* 19-20:97-128.

Martínez Medina, Andrés and Justo Oliva. 2012. Las otras ciudades: planeamiento y arquitectura para el turismo. El caso del Mediterráneo español (1945-1975). Barcelona: International Forum of Urbanism.

Matarredona, Enrique. 1993. El aeropuerto de El Altet y sus perspectivas de futuro. *Rev. Investigaciones Geográficas* 11:223-235.

Preston, Paul et al. 2001. D*e la revolución liberal a la democracia parlamentaria*. (1808-1975). Valencia: Biblioteca Nueva.

Ramírez, Juan Antonio. 1987. *El estilo del relax*. Málaga: Colegio de Arquitectos de Málaga

Ramírez, Juan Antonio.1992. *Arte y arquitectura en la época del capitalismo triunfante*. Madrid: Visor.

Ramos, Antonio. 1991. Origen, desarrollo y problemática espacial de la ciudad de Alicante. *Rev. Investigaciones Geográficas* 9:19-32.

Solà Morales, I. 1998. Patrimonio o parque temático. *Rev. Loggia* 5:30-35.

Vegara, Alfonso. 2001. El triángulo Alicante-Elche-Santa Pola. *Rev. Canelobre* 44-45:52.

Costa Blanca: Public Space And Perceived Image as Key to Tourism Competitiveness

Costa Blanca: espacio público e imagen percibida como clave de competitividad turística

コスタ・ブランカ：観光競争力強化の鍵としての公共空間と知覚イメージ

Rosario Navalón | ロサリオ・ナバロン

Los destinos turísticos tradicionales del litoral español se enfrentan a profundas transformaciones debidas a varios factores, entre los que se encuentran cambios notables en el comportamiento de la demanda y un intenso crecimiento de la competencia a todos los niveles, que puede poner en duda la pervivencia del modelo de desarrollo de estas áreas maduras. Lejos de ser una excepción, la situación que se describe para la Costa Blanca es extrapolable a otros destinos turísticos en otras regiones y en ámbitos urbanos, que se enfrentan al reto de incorporar nuevas estrategias de renovación, diversificación y reestructuración de su tejido urbano y turístico, como clave de reorientación de su ciclo de vida.

A partir del estudio del caso de la Costa Blanca, pero con una vocación globalizadora, se tratan a continuación argumentos referidos a los cambios en la demanda turística y de ocio cotidiano, y cómo ello afecta a la necesidad de intervenir de un modo distinto en el diseño y gestión del tejido urbano que perciben los visitantes y residentes. Se percibe de forma clara que se ha de trabajar de un modo distinto tanto la escena urbana como el territorio turístico a partir de la potenciación de valores diferenciadores: por una adecuada intervención urbanística en los espacios públicos con acciones capaces de distinguir al destino de sus competidores, por la incorporación de nuevos elementos de atracción e innovación urbana, o por una gestión más eficiente de los servicios y las funciones urbanas de los destinos turísticos.

A partir de varios indicadores se demuestra que la competitividad de los destinos tradicionales, sean áreas costeras o ciudades, ya no sólo reside en sus recursos patrimoniales, litorales o climáticos, sino que su valor diferenciador se vincula también a la calidad urbana percibida y a la capacidad de incorporar en las acciones de futuro las nuevas necesidades de residentes y visitantes, cada vez más exigentes e impredecibles.

スペイン沿岸部に点在する伝統的な保養地はいま、重大な岐路に立たされている。需要行動の明白な変化や競合他者のあらゆるレベルでの急成長など、さまざまな要因によって、これらの成熟した行楽地の成長モデルが存続の危機にさらされているからだ。本論でとりあげるアリカンテの保養地の状況というのは決して例外的事例ではなく、他の地方の行楽地や都市型の観光地についても当てはまる。いずれの地域も、そのライフサイクルのあり方を転換する足掛かりとして、都市構造や観光機構を刷新・多様化・再構築する新戦略の策定という難題に取り組んでいるからだ。

本論は、ケース・スタディとしてコスタ・ブランカを扱いつつも、観光需要や日常的余暇活動の変化について、グローバルな展望を射程に入れながら考察する。またこうした変化を受けて、訪問者と住民が日々知覚している都市構造のデザインとマネジメントに対して、これまでとはどう異なったかたちで取り組む必要性が生じているかについても論じる。論中では、都市域においても、またツーリズムの領域においても、従来とは異なった地域運営のあり方が求められていることが明らかとなる。すなわち、公共空間に対して適切な都市整備を実施すること、人を惹きつけ都市構造を刷新するような新たな要素を積極的に取り入れていくこと、あるいは観光地の都市サービスや機能をより効率的に運営すること等により、当該地域を競合する他地域から差別化することが、ますます重視されるようになっているのである。

さまざまな指標が示しているように、沿岸部であれ都市部であれ、伝統的保養地の競争力が、もはや歴史的遺産・海岸・気候という資源だけに存するのでないことは明白である。これらの観光地を差別化する価値は、知覚される都市の質と深い関わりを持っており、また日増しに水準が上がりますます予測不能になっている訪問者と住民の新しいニーズを汲み取り、それを今後の活動に組み込んでいく能力にも関係しているのである。

fig. 1: Sprawl in urban planning for tourism is a generalized reality in the Costa Blanca region. It imprints a commonplace and undifferentiated character on the destination, which barely highlights the cultural and natural values the region enjoys. Panorama of the town of Calp. Photograph: R. Navalón 2013.

The context for reflection: urban actions in mature tourist destinations

A conscientious reflection on the image of cities in tourist areas must inevitably be based on tourism as a global activity that moves millions of people from all over the world, from urban and industrial settings to places with different appealing resources (those associated with relaxation, culture, nature, or other material or immaterial attractions). Nevertheless, a central characteristic of tourist cities lies in the climate differences with respect to the origin of the traveler. This is seen the world over, from the outbound tourist or source region to the periphery (Gormsen 1997:43). In fact, numerous texts cite similarities between tourist cities, beachfront vacation areas or tourist complexes from one continent to another. This is the interpretive key to understanding that the processes which will be described below, referring to the destinations on the Spanish Costa Blanca, imitate in one way or another other tourist areas which follow a model centered on the product of "sun and beach".

The tourist brand Costa Blanca encompasses the entire region of the province of Alicante, including not only the coastal townships but also those in the interior. This designation, nevertheless, due to its very name and to the efforts undertaken to promote it, is primarily associated with the region situated on the coast and with the development of products focused on the resources of sea and climate. In other words, it is focused almost exclusively on the product of sun and beach. Furthermore, such a static and bare bones image of a region that is really quite diverse focuses tourism activities and their effects on a narrow, coastal strip and mid-range, markedly residential accommodations. We find a predominance of such dwellings for use in tourism dispersed throughout the region, stretching as well into the bordering towns not located on the coast. This fact has marked (and handicapped) the region's external image as an undifferentiated residential space of sun and beach and conditions its competitive capacity and its future economic profitability, making it excessively dependent on the fluctuations of the real estate market and on the building and sales strategies of residential units for tourism.

It seems evident that these dynamic forces of extensive construction growth, conceived from the myopic point of view of mono-production, present clear weaknesses for future viability and represent as well a potential source of conflict from environmental, economic and social perspectives. Nevertheless, until the global economic crisis brought to light threats to the system underlying this model of real estate construction, it was not considered important to define new lines of involvement which would contribute to redesigning the image of the destination, diversifying the business base, and indicating how the destination differed from its competitors (Navalón, Rico 2012: 326).

The restructuring of mature seaside destinations is considered a necessity in view of the profound transformations in the European tourism market and the intense growth in competition at all levels. This situation has severely affected the model of development on the Spanish coast, accelerating the natural process of loss of competitiveness associated with the cycle of tourism destinations after more than 40 years of tourism activity (Perelli 2012).

In the same vein, numerous authors (Antón, Navarro, Perelli, Rullán, Vera, among others) indicate that a large number of the Spanish seaside destinations are gradually incorporating strategies of diversification in their offerings and in the reorientation or change of their promotional images, adding other products and services apart from the primary ones, sun and sand. Logically, however, these actions will essentially signify a reach beyond marketing and will have to be accompanied by a treatment of the urban fabrics generated by tourism and by the preexisting urban spaces.

In our opinion, the recovery of traditional urban centers, those that constituted the initial kernel for tourism in the first phase of development, but which were slowly relegated to an inferior status in the process of developing extensive new accommodations, needs to retake center stage, beginning with deliberate measures, in order to become a potential and unique element within mature destinations.

With this common context and comprehensive inclination as a starting point, we will focus this essay on several arguments referring principally to the Costa Blanca. They may, however, be extrapolated to any region. These arguments stem basically from three main concepts (Lois 2008:24): the changes in motivations and habits of consumption in the demand for tourism; the search for unique features, beginning with the incorporation of local resources and the involvement of the city; and the importance of the attitudes and decisions of the people who make decisions regarding tourism, both public and private, and who consolidate through their decisions and actions the form and function of the region where tourists and residents converge.

Global changes in the demand for tourism that merit response

More than half a century has passed since the birth of democratic tourism affected the middle classes. Since then, tourists have acquired experience and assurance in traveling autonomously and in gathering information. This has permitted them not only to choose destinations based on personal motivations, but has also made them more demanding when it comes to the quality/price relationship. These circumstances, together with the ease of travel due to new airline companies and more extensive use of information technologies in the consumer society of the source markets, contribute to much more unpredictable and autonomous behavior when it comes to demand. And this behavior does not necessarily involve tourism operators, who are gradually being displaced by travel arrangements made by the individual.

In recent years it is the tourist who decides what he wants to do: relax by the seaside, in the countryside or in nature, practice sports, visit cities, or engage in cultural activities. Depending on his preferences, he selects the tourist destination best adapted to his needs. This fact compels the mature sun and beach destinations, anchored in the stereotypical image of a traditional offer centered on climate and proximity to the seashore, to reformulate their marketing strategies if they wish to continue being attractive and competitive in a hugely dynamic global market.

Some authors have analyzed these changes as an evolution in tourism, which they describe as moving from "Fordism" to "post-Fordism". The first phase started in the 1950s, and put simply is seen as the development of the "tourism industry", one that enhances the processes of production and use of tourism in order to offer standardized vacation experiences. This approach of optimizing the organizing system standardizes not only the processes of tourism services in the different sectors but also replicates vacation destinations so they appear to have similar characteristics. The principal characteristic of post-Fordism tourism is the need to show itself as an alternative to Fordist tourism, and the factor that singles this out is the response of tourist demand versus standardization (Donaire 2008). This is a radical change which affects the very heart of the structure of the tourism experience; in spite of the fact that it questions the mass use of traditional destinations, in no way is it inconsistent with the irrepressible increase in the number of tourists worldwide.

At the root of this change we find new types of relationships, which arise due to the growing availability of free time. This is supplemented by the idea referred to by some authors as the *cultural turn*, which synthesizes one of the key characteristics of the post-modern era: the commercialization of time, culture and life experiences (Rifkin 2000). Within this social context, it is not odd that the use of cultural production by a social majority captures the attention of public strategies in economically favorable circumstances. This in turn is translated into the multiplication of cultural possibilities for a society in search of new knowledge and experiences. Thus, citizens in general have more free time, possess a higher level of education and cultural foundation with respect to past generations, which allows them to enjoy in large measure the new possibilities of cultural consumption.

In addition, this experienced and educated tourist also reveals changes in his preference and modifies his behavior, indicating a greater sensitivity toward services focused on authenticity and respect for the resources of heritage sites, whether they are natural or cultural. All this is in accordance with global societal tendencies that demonstrate a greater sensitivity toward sustainability and toward a better environmental management in natural and/or urban spheres.

The new tourist, like the citizen who makes the most of his free time, seeks to enjoy new sensations and to get to know and understand the resources of the cultural heritage found in his home environment or in the places to which he travels. This is accomplished through an understanding of the characteristics, the role, the essence or history of the place. What happens, then, is that this type of cultural experience, engaged in alone or with others, ends up defining the most essential part of the leisure and tourism experience. It is capable of generating a deep satisfaction, in which the consumer-tourist ultimately encounters practicality in his free time and in what he purchases. It can be said that this type of occurrence becomes the center and the objective of leisure and of the trip, and it culminates in constituting a necessity which one will not readily give up (Navalón 2013).

Worldwide, there is talk about an ever more active and selective demand that, nevertheless, doesn't overlook any of the options regarding tourism services. Also, in the tourism destinations along the coast, demand is unpredictable. People might seek out on the same day sun, beach, leisure activities or cultural tourism. Considering motivation, then, we can talk about a new hybrid tourist-consumer. On any given trip, these motivations can meld into more heterogeneous types of consumption, contributing to a complex, competitive touristic panorama. In turn, this can contribute to decline in areas that are not ready to take on the challenge of diversification and differentiation that the demand entails.

The increase in free time in the tourist's place of origin has contributed to the dissolution between the practices of cultural consumption and daily entertainment. Thus, the greater or lesser capacity of tourism areas to satisfy the demands of visitors who are accustomed to consuming products of leisure in their places of residence determines the ability of the destinations to compete. For that, we consider it important to accept as well the dual nature of the use of cities and tourist destinations, as much from the visitors' point of view as from the residents'.

Measures for diversification and differentiation in the urban centers of tourism destinations

As a response to the above, it is logical to propose strategies to diversify the offerings in the different tourism destinations and cities where regional tourism consumption occurs. For that, new products are generated. They are based on the incorporation of resources and services that are attractive to this new demand, and which furthermore are able to extend the period of consumption beyond the traditional high season, focused on summer, the holidays of Holy Week and Christmas, or long holiday weekends.

This challenge then compels us to reflect upon each and every one of the elements which makes up the value chain of the tourist product, and from that point on, the plan of strategic action that will affect the tourism destination and possibly even the urban structure as a whole. The answer can lead us to propose actions for the restructuring of the configuration of the destination itself, oriented toward the same sector of the market; or to the proposal of operations of diversification that entail the enlargement of the portfolio of products; or to the development of operations that seek differentiation, in which unique attributes of the location are highlighted, or to incorporating actions capable of distinguishing the destination from its competitors, whether it be with temporary operations or with prominent architectural or urban projects.

As mentioned earlier when we referred to the behavior of the tourist consumer and of the resident, many different forms and developments can occur in relation to tourism and the cities where tourism is found. It is apparent that today we cannot talk about urban or cultural tourism by referring solely to the large European capitals of the Grand Tour. Tourism in urban spaces offers a multitude of opportunities based on the characteristics of the cities themselves and on the type of tourists they attract (Antón 2008:54). It can be thought provoking to reflect on the city and on tourism in traditional coastal tourism destinations from a variety of perspectives.

Keeping the changes in demand in mind, we can understand the gradual incorporation of "the touristic" in urban planning actions in public spaces of mid-sized cities and of traditional centers of mature tourist destinations. In some cases elements linked to culture which until now have been for the most part neglected, are transformed or adjusted for specific sectors of demand. These might include useful images that adopt a secondary role in order to develop other purposes, in an attempt to better the image of the urban scene and be more attractive to the visitor.

In this way, we can find different types of *actions in the traditional offerings linked to local heritage*, without entailing direct action on cultural heritage sites (even though indirect action may contribute to its conservation). Some such cases could be:

- Heritage sites, which in the destinations of the Costa Blanca do not have enough individual importance to justify tourists traveling to them, are superficially renovated as attractions to generate services that satisfy the motivation of seeking "genuine experiences" tied to the local culture, starting with different strategies of promotion of the heritage sites.
- The stereotype of tourism, identifiable with the local

attributes of the Mediterranean coast, is transformed into the possibility of getting to know the unique and thriving "true local lifestyles".
- Beyond the possible relevance of the unique resources of heritage sites, which are not especially outstanding in this area, one looks for the historic essence of the place, often starting with cultural expressions of the local atmosphere, festivities or local events. Again, these do not include direct involvement with architectural or urban elements.

The urban and architectural heritage and local culture can be stimulated as complementary attractions to the principal product of the coast, starting with the recovery and stimulation of their functional, cultural and urban essence and with various means of architectural and urban involvement. This would also include, nevertheless, the incorporation of adequate descriptive planning, for which one could propose a project of effective communication with the objective of conveying the true meaning of the elements for the visitor, beginning with different means and techniques of tangible or intangible interpretation of the heritage sites.

Unfortunately, in many cases this action of restoration of architectural and urban planning heritage sites involves only the surface of the sites. We see this with projects dedicated to cleaning and reinforcing structures, or in the worst case with a reinterpretation of their original function and an alteration of their identity. That would not achieve a recovery of the local identity, the "why" of the elements, which could restore in an effective fashion a unique and distinguishing resource, one interwoven with culture and history, even if recent. Reality is different, and on many occasions in tourism centers and around heritage sites the incorporation of services and cultural products linked to leisure and recreation (including shopping, night life, street life or gastronomy) is limited, and what is promoted is the cultural consumption itself as a diversifying attraction in the tourism experience in that destination. This does not necessarily imply a reflection regarding the viability and durability of the proposals, but on many occasions it does not even regard an assessment of the suitability of such proposals.

To the best of our understanding, before taking any action, a study of the recognition of the history and function of the site should take place, out of respect for the local identity and the resources in which the essence of these places is found. If we do not follow this procedure, we run the risk of trivializing the heritage site and the urban scenario with the incorporation of repetitive themes and formulas. These may function in other places and may respond a priori to pre-established expectations, but they shortly prove to be false and end up generating a negative experience, and thus negative spontaneous advertising. According to Donaire (2008), one of the paradoxes of new tourism proposals that hope to respond to the need for diversification which demand seeks is the rapidity with which the elements of differentiation can become standardized actions. One needs simply to recall the duplicate presence in nearby destinations of some of the actions "which foster local and cultural heritage", such as medieval markets, festivals, concerts, or contests, all which quickly stop being unique and notable due to repetition and proximity.

Another option for involvement, which proposes to diversify and differentiate tourism, something able to increase the appeal of the destination and to attract tourists visiting the cities, is referred to as the *development of actions ex novo*, according to the ETC Research Group (2005), cited by Antón (2008). In this report, we point out that a part of the milestones, which justify the attractiveness of better-positioned European cities refers to recent aspects of urban, urban development and functional processes not necessarily linked to the pre-existing fabric. The most highly valued are:

- The existence of a creative relationship between traditional cultural products and services, including means of communication, performances, design, architecture or fashion
- The esthetic of the urban landscape and the creating of unique settings
- The option to experience in the city the sense of design (art, architecture, night life, music fashion) associated on occasion with unique elements of architecture and urban planning
- The identification of the city with gastronomy, starting with unique initiatives linked to haute cuisine or local cuisine, to slow food, and niche categories such as wine tourism, among others

It seems clear, then, that the competitiveness of tourism in cities is also closely related to aspects such as the capacity for innovation and communication, the creativity of human capital, cultural and commercial vitality, and to the attitude of the local population vis-à-vis the visitor. The presence of a rich cultural heritage or investing in new sites of a different nature (museums, auditoriums, congress halls, cultural and leisure spaces) could be an important attraction to the tourism destination and to the city, yet they do not guarantee success in the tourism market.

In a similar light, as indicated in the report UrbanTUR 2012 (Exceltur 2013), it seems evident that the capacity to incorporate a differential value in the destination depends basically on the work carried out in orienting these resources toward enjoyment or business, in such a way that it transforms it into a true tourism attraction. Thus, the management of a resource through proactive actions involving different social agents should be the key objective for distinguishing the resource. This means moving beyond the traditional focus of resource management based almost exclusively on the preservation of the cultural heritage site (often with actions focused solely on

fig. 2: This beach-facing image of the town of Teulada-Moraira shows the combining of leisure space. The outdoor terraces, the heritage site information boards and the bicycle racks are brought together in one single space without any particular order or care given to the layout of the elements. Photograph: R. Navalón, 2013.

fig. 3: One of the iconic images of the Costa Blanca is the blue tile domes of Altea, repeatedly pictured in tourism brochures. Nevertheless, this church is not included in tourism itineraries that explain the local culture. Photograph: R. Navalón, 2012.

architectural procedures) and on facilitating accessibility by establishing schedules that streamline the visit (these are generally restricted in the Costa Blanca area, and they do not take into account actions which favor universal accessibility for people with disabilities).

In order to reinforce their competitive capacity, it is necessary to take a chance on establishing initiatives, which incorporate added value in a way that reflects the international patterns. Some of these actions could be:

- The incorporation of the ludic facet of heritage sites (with the programming of performed, guided visits, and the development of multimedia applications to make the information more accessible and satisfactory to the visitor)
- The restructuring and modification of public spaces to boost the perception of a friendly, sustainable and innovative city
- The inclusion of cities in specialized, thematic circuits starting with the incorporation of services added to creative, cultural or heritage site networks
- The support to the development of events
- The strengthening of actions conducive to generating the brand image of the city, starting with effective communication with traditional tour operators, with social networks which favor commercialization and public image, as well as with the residential population, social agents and business associates who work within them

Thus, we can affirm that the tourist image of tourism destinations is conditioned by the comprehensive reputation of the city and its general attributes, with which national and international markets are associated, in environments that are not exclusively based on tourism, but are directly affected by tourism.

With the objective of offering data regarding the behavior of a good part of tourism destinations on the Costa Blanca and more concretely in the urban areas, as a clear comparable example of the actions and management of urban attributes, we offer below evaluative data that affect the city of Alicante, administrative capital of the province and of the tourism area. To that end, the previously cited UrbanTUR 2012 report reflects the relative position of the 20 most successful Spanish tourist cities, based on the volume of travelers, and assessed through 57 indicators that condition the evolution of their competitive capacity in the tourism market.

Among the six core ideas of analysis in the report, we will focus on the column referred to as the *Determinants of urban environment and lifestyle*. According to UbanTUR 2012, these make up an essential part of the experience that tourists perceive and for that reason are decisive in their ultimate satisfaction, contributing additional value to tourism products. Among the competitive determinants of the urban environment, the report includes various aspects, two of which we highlight for their relevance regarding the presentation of this essay:

- *Amenities in public spaces*: assesses the number of existing green spaces in the city as elements that

COMPETITIVE DETERMINANTS OF URBAN SURROUNDINGS AND OF LOCAL LIFE		19	84,5
1. Competitive determinants of the urban surroundings		18	87,4
a	Qualification of public spaces for tourism	3	115,5
a-1	Number of green spaces	4	99,7
a-2	Number of free Wifi zones	2	131,4
b	Attractiveness of public spaces	20	33,5
c	Quality of urban environment	6	113,1
c-1	Air quality	13	87,7
c-2	Efficiency of waste treatment	2	138,5
2. Competitive determinants of local life style		19	81,7
a	Internal reputation of the city	17	77,2
b	Attractiveness of life style as perceived by tourists	14	73,5
c	Promotion of educational excellence	12	89,2
d	Citizen safety	17	86,6

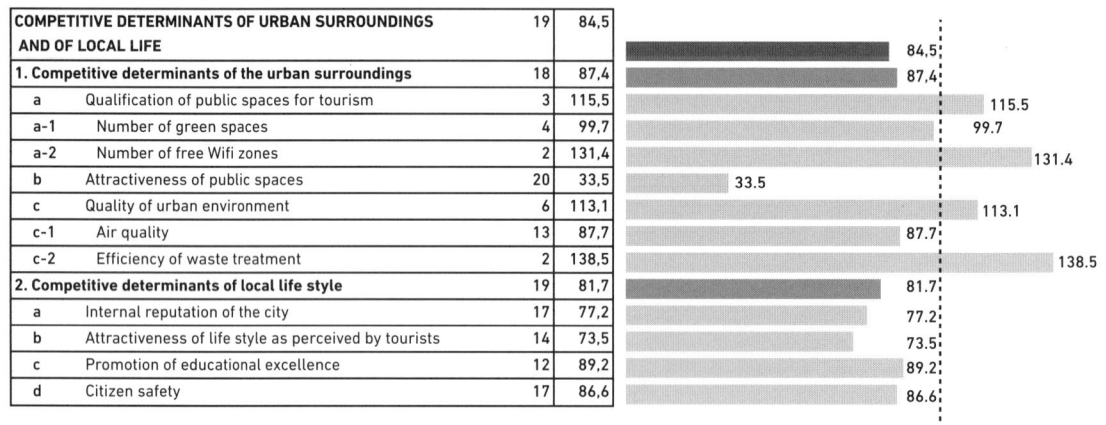

Table 1: Graphic representation of competitiveness from 1 to 20 for the competitive core ideas cited earlier (mean of all urban destinations = 100). Source: UrbanTUR, 2012. Exceltur 2013.

enrich recreation areas for the enjoyment of the citizen, which the tourist appreciates and from which the tourist also benefits. In the same fashion, public areas in the city where tourists can enjoy free WiFi access are included, with the objective of responding to the growing demand for being connected, for personal use and also for searching for information "in situ", which will facilitate enjoyment of the destination as a progressive "smart city".

- *Appeal of public spaces*: incorporates an assessment from local businesses regarding various elements that give form to the quality and enjoyment of the environment (the care taken with facades, the width of sidewalks, the distinction of urban furnishings, adequate lighting, sanitary conditions, etc.) in the areas of major tourism influx in the city where their businesses are located.

For the analysis of competitive determinants concerning lifestyle, other elements that present clear impacts regarding the appeal to the visitor are incorporated, from which we highlight two:

- *Internal urban reputation*: reflects through a wide variety of public opinion indicators, including those that integrate interviews with experts and a citizen survey implemented by Merco, the reputation of different Spanish cities regarding their level of development and provision of services.
- *Attractiveness of lifestyle as perceived by tourists*: incorporates the perception tourists have of the combination of offerings in the city collected by Tripadvisor in their ranking of Spanish cities. In UrbanTUR this is included as an indicator that reflects the image, which the tourist has of the city and its limited ability through the assessment and opinions offered by tourists who have traveled to these cities.

According to these parameters, the evaluation of the city of Alicante is clearly negative in this element of analysis, which we consider key in the image projected by the city and how this image is perceived by social and tourism agents, by the citizens themselves, and by visitors. As the graph from this report shows (table 1), the results for Alicante under *Competitive determinants of the urban environment and lifestyle* situate the city in 19th place out of 20, very far indeed from the optimal place in the comprehensive ranking. As the data show, this position is due in great measure to the poor quality of public spaces in the opinion of local businessmen, in addition to the poor perception of quality of life for tourists according to Tripadvisor.

The positive part of this analysis highlights green spaces, situating Alicante in the 4th position of the total ranking. This element refers to the number of green spaces within the city limits that the tourist can enjoy, starting from the number of square meters of green space per resident and non-resident (tourist).[1] Another positive aspect of the city was the referenced *number of free public Wi-Fi zones* available, which truly bring value to the pleasure-seeking tourist and to businesses. In this regard, Alicante occupies second place.

Unfortunately the rating of the assessment of the quality of public spaces has overall been negative. We understand this parameter as the combination of elements in the urban environment that condition the perception that tourists have and that can affect their level of satisfaction. The indicator gathers the mean assessment of public spaces (architectural attractiveness, beauty and care of facades, the layout of roads, the condition of the pavement, the cutting edge status of urban furnishings and other equipment, level of sanitary conditions, etc.). The majority of these factors have a direct repercussion on subjective perceptions of the city and of the attractiveness of public spaces. For this reason and for this study, we considered that the best indicator of assessment should be the opinions of the business owners themselves who have establishments in the cities and who know the impact these elements have on the sale of their products.[2]

To conclude this distressing panorama, which again situates the city in the worst position, it becomes relevant to pay attention to the parameter of *Internal reputation of the city*, taken from the perception of the level of quality of life the city transmits based on the assessment of citizens and a panel of local management experts.[3] And finally, we must add the clearly improvable element of the *Attraction of lifestyle perceived by tourists*, which refers to the comprehensive perception of the overall tourism offering of the destination, as a means to approximating the ability to welcome, the quality of lifestyle and taking chances on the distinction of the local offering.[4]

By means of concrete examples, which will permit extrapolation, this study proposes an integrated methodology that offers key data regarding ways to analyze the quality of the urban scenario, the perceived quality of life and the tourism image that is projected and received, in order to impact the argument that together these elements condition the competitiveness of an urban tourism destination. We consider it essential to think about these factors, especially if we recognize that all of them depend on planning, scheduling and management carried out by the municipal administration.

Planning and management of the public space – could it be the answer?

In our understanding, the municipal administration can influence the urban and tourism future of the region (Rullán 2008). Involvement of the administration should consider a three-point perspective:

- In the first place, concerning the making of decisions regarding regional urban planning on different scales, and of course on the level of decision making vis-à-vis the form and function of that urban scale as well;
- It is decisive to prioritize the actions which will be the objective for the financing of infrastructures and equipment, as well as the definition, execution and later management of the actions developed in the public space;
- And finally, it is the responsibility of the municipal administration to define in a precise and fair fashion the economic activities that businesses and individuals develop in these areas. The last facet, while not as recognized, is key to the definition of the functions of public space, and as a result, of the use made of public space. All of this has an effect on the atmosphere that is created and on the quality of the public space, beginning with the approval, scheduling, promotion and development of commercial activities, of services and of leisure activities, and thus, also of the perceived image.

In general terms, it is true that in recent decades administrations have made the effort to initiate plans and projects orientated toward restructuring tourism activity, starting with the "modernization" or re-modification of the urban scenario. The plans of Tourism Excellence and Vitality are clearly visible, as they are included in the plans of Vitality of the Tourism Product, propelled by an effort to coordinate the three levels of public administration: national, regional and local. Along these lines and among other objectives, the suggestion was made to correct the deficiencies in infrastructure, equipment and resources of tourism destinations excessively centered during the first stages of Fordism on the development of hotel rooms. This was a neoliberal context, oriented mainly toward the production of spaces for residential tourism, which in many cases had eliminated the need to define and develop central spaces where leisure, recreation, culture and meeting places were favored, as hubs of attraction to generate a true structure of the tourism city. Nevertheless, many of these plans were reduced to superficial urban touch-ups, a simple surface fix to the urban fabric, without managing to resolve other key problems to better the tourism city. Among such problems were a variety of accessibility and/or pedestrian difficulties, traffic jams, and the prioritization of a functional strategy for better use of free, public spaces among other actions.

Beyond the re-urbanization of streets, squares, promenades and parks, in practice these actions have not taken into consideration a reflection regarding a more adequate role for them. Neither have they reflected on how to face the maintenance and management of the use that is made of these spaces. In this way, the complexity of managing each sector and the progressive reduction of the municipal technical and financial structures associated with fiscal consolidation that affects the greater public administration, ends up favoring a delegation of management, and even of decision making, to private business initiatives. This delegation starts with actions that guarantee the viability of the operations in economic terms, something which should also be reflected in the municipal balance sheets.

Within this context of searching for competitive destinations, when an agreement with the investor was possible, the administration contributed to the fact that

fig.4: New buildings along the "paseo de Levante" esplanade contrast with the 19th century constructions along Alicante's seaport, increasing the appeal of the area. Photograph: R. Navalón, 2010.

the business results were the ones they hoped for. They became involved only from the perspective of executing the plans, and of assuming the cost of a large part of these actions to modify infrastructure and urban areas, in the search for the "restructuring" of destinations. But once the public investment of remodeling the street, the square or the esplanade is carried out, without a basic, concrete objective, on many occasions the management of these public works is put in the hands of private companies, which little by little begin to take over the common space, resulting in de facto privatization of their use for the local community and visitors.

Some conclusions

It seems evident that the restructuring of mature tourist destinations such as the Costa Blanca entails a challenge of enormous complexity, and that in order to carry it out a multitude of internal as well as external factors must be taken into consideration. These include changes in motivations and habits in the demand for consumption, expanded use of information technologies and all the processes of the value chain of the tourism product, and changes in global financing and economy. To all that we must add the complexity of the very process of transformation and invigoration of a consolidated urban reality, without taking up more space, which leads to carrying out efforts in those strategies in order to make this all possible.

It has been shown how competitiveness in traditional destinations, in the coastal areas or in cities does not reside only in the value of heritage sites, beaches or climate, but is also linked to perceived urban quality, the ability to innovate, to comprehend and the ability to react to the new needs of ever more demanding and unpredictable residents and visitors.

Therefore, it is important to understand that a strategy for restructuring, diversifying or distinguishing a tourism destination should base itself not only on investment strategies that can seem opportune and ensure short term-effects. On the contrary, it is best to reflect on the image of the destination that one hopes to create and project, starting with the characteristics of local identity. The improvement of the urban environment, from the definition of the form and function most suitable to the use of this space required by society, should be one of the keys to actions capable of generating the urban, business and social atmosphere that respond to this call for renewal.

Notes

1. In order for Exceltur to produce this indicator, information from the Local Sustainability Report (Informe Sostenibilidad Local) was used, by the Spanish Sustainability Observatory (Observatorio de la Sostenibilidad de España).
2. These opinions of local businessmen were collected by the Survey on Tourism Business Confidence by Exceltur (Encuesta de Confianza Turística Empresarial de Exceltur).
3. In the descriptive column *Quality of Life*, from the UrbanTUR 2012 report, the MERCO index regarding the reputation of the city was added, and put together based on surveys (N=9,100) conducted by MERCO with residents of the major Spanish cities. The work was evaluated by a panel of 95 experts in urban management, where the assessment of friendliness, civility, open-mindedness of the locals, appeal, entertainment, and commercial and cultural offerings, among others, were incorporated.
4. The value of this indicator is the position of the city in a ranking of the 25 best Spanish destinations prepared by Tripadvisor (Travellers Choice 2011), based on a large sampling of assessments and opinions of national and international travelers. Alicante does not occupy any of the first 25 places of the Tripadvisor ranking, which accorded it the 26th place.

References

Antón Clavé, S. 2008. Turismo y ciudades: De la oportunidad del turismo urbano a los usos turísticos de las ciudades. In *Destinos turístico: viejos problemas ¿nuevas soluciones?* X Coloquio de geografía del turismo, ocio y recreación. AGE. 53–77, Col. 212. Ed. Universidad de Castilla La Mancha.

Donaire, J.A. 2008. *Turisme cultural: Entre l'experiència i el ritual*. Bellcaire d'Empordà, Girona: Ed. Vitel.la.

Exceltur. 2013. *UrbanTUR 2012, monitor de competitividad turística de los destinos urbanos españoles*.

Gormsen, E. 1997. The impact of tourism on coastal areas, *GeoJournal*, vol. 1, nº 42, p. 39-54.

Lois, R. 2008. Turismo y territorio a principios del siglo XXI: Una reflexión geográfica desde el ámbito de la gestión pública. In *Destinos turístico: viejos problemas ¿nuevas soluciones?* X Coloquio de geografía del turismo, ocio y recreación. AGE. 23–47. Col. 212. Ed. Universidad de Castilla La Mancha.

Navalón, R. and E. Rico. 2011. Estrategias de futuro para el destino tradicional de la Costa Blanca: el Plan de Valorización turística del patrimonio Cultural de la provincia de Alicante. In *XII Coloquio de Geografía del Turismo, Ocio y Recreación*. 365–381. Madrid: Universidad Carlos III.

Navalón, R. and E. Rico. 2012. Renovación de destinos litorales maduros a partir del patrimonio cultural: Plan Costa Blanca Cultura. In *Renovación y reestructuración de destinos turísticos en áreas costeras: marco de análisis, procesos, instrumentos y realidades*, edited by F. Vera and I. Rodriguez. 323–346. Universidad de Valencia.

Navalón, R. 2013. Planificación y gestión turística del patrimonio: conversión del patrimonio cultural en producto turístico. In *Gestión del patrimonio arquitectónico, cultural y medioambiental. Enfoques y casos prácticos*, edited by L. Rubio and G. Ponce. 123–146. Ed. Publicaciones Universidad de Alicante, Univ. Autónoma Metropolitana. México.

Perelli, O. 2012. La reconversión de los destinos maduros del litoral en el actual contexto del cambio global: una reflexión sobre nuevos instrumentos para su impulso. In *Renovación y reestructuración de destinos turísticos en áreas costeras: marco de análisis, procesos, instrumentos y realidades*, edited by F. Vera and I. Rodriguez. 37–54. Universidad de Valencia.

Rifkin, J. 2000. *La era del acceso: La revolución de la nueva economía*. Barcelona: Paidós.

Rullán, O. 2008. Reconversión y crecimiento de las zonas turísticas: Del fordismo al posfordismo. In *Destinos turístico: viejos problemas ¿nuevas soluciones?* X Coloquio de geografía del turismo, ocio y recreación. AGE. 587–626. Col. 212. Ed. Universidad de Castilla La Mancha.

fig. 5 (above): The typical image of Alicante is the "Explanada de España," one of the most emblematic green zones along the city's coast. Photograph: R. Navalón, 2012.

fig. 6 (below): The granting of permits for various handicraft stalls, along with setting up of outdoor bars and restaurants, ends up privatizing public spaces, thus altering the iconic image of the city. Photograph: R. Navalón, 2013.

Benidorm. Esplanades And Ordinary Urbanities

Benidorm. Paseos marítimos y urbanidades ordinarias

ベニドルム海浜遊歩道と平凡な都市性

Miguel Mesa del Castillo | ミゲル・メサ・デル・カスティジョ

La ciudad de Benidorm, situada tan solo a 40 Km al norte de Alicante, es para algunos autores, uno de los laboratorios de urbanismo experimental asociado al turismo más importantes del mundo. A pesar de las reiteradas críticas que se vierten sobre la ciudad y su modelo urbanístico, Benidorm es una de las pocas ciudades de la costa Mediterránea en las que el modelo de explotación industrial de sus principales recursos naturales (el sol y las playas) está asistido por un preciso proyecto de urbanización. Este encuentro entre economía y planificación urbana es lo que ha permitido que la ciudad haya alcanzado altas cifras de rentabilidad.

En Benidorm se dan cita algunos de los argumentos más actuales en los estudios urbanos como el descentramiento de la ciudad como objeto de estudio, su ontología inestable, la atención hacia lo ordinario, el cuestionamiento de ciertos ecocentrismos que conciben la naturaleza y lo urbano como dos esferas separadas e incluso enfrentadas, o la renovación de los instrumentos de observación del fenómeno urbano para ensayar perspectivas relacionales y superar las visiones estructurales que han permanecido casi sin variaciones desde las aportaciones de la teoría urbana de los años 70.

La relevancia y actualidad de estas cuestiones puede observarse en Benidorm siguiendo las estrategias de diseño que han sido practicadas en los proyectos de los dos paseos marítimos que recorren la mayor parte de su franja costera. Este escrito se propone desvelar cuales son los enfoques que están representados en cada uno de los dos proyectos y cómo han interpretado la ciudad y lo urbano en un caso tan particular como el de Benidorm.

アリカンテ県の県都アリカンテ市から北へわずか40kmに位置するベニドルム。このリゾート都市において、ツーリズムと密接な関連をもって進められた都市計画的実験は、複数の研究者が指摘するように、世界でもとりわけ注目すべき重要な事例のひとつである。ベニドルムという都市やその都市計画モデルについては、これまでに度重なる批判がなされてきた。しかし、数ある地中海沿岸都市のうち、その主たる天然資源（太陽と砂浜）の産業的利用が、そうした産業モデルに正確に呼応した都市開発プロジェクトによって裏付けられているのは、ベニドルムを含めわずかしかない。この経済と都市計画の蜜月関係こそ、ベニドルムが実現した高い採算性を支える立役者なのである。

ベニドルムでは、都市研究における最先端の議論のいくつかがなされている。例えば、研究対象としての都市の脱求心化、その不確定な存在論、平凡さへの着目、そして自然と都市的なものを2つの相容れない、あるいは対立する領域だとみなす「環境中心主義」に対する疑念の呈示。あるいは70年代の都市理論が貢献して以降何ら変化を見せなかった構造論的ヴィジョンを超えて、関係論的な展望を検討するための、都市現象の観察手段の更新、といったものである。ベニドルムにおいて、上記の命題がもつ重要性と現代性を明瞭に見出すことが出来るのは、海岸線の大部分に沿って走る2つの海浜遊歩道のプロジェクトにおいてであり、そこでどのようなデザイン戦略が実行されたのかを分析することによってである。本論文は、この2つの海浜遊歩道プロジェクト各々が、いかなる観点に立脚して計画され、どのようにベニドルムという非常に特異な事例の上にあって、その都市および都市性を解釈したのかについて、明らかにするものである。

Introduction: Some numbers

Present day Benidorm is the result of the growth of a small fishing village, which until 1960 had 6,000 inhabitants, a number which reached 73,000 in 2012. The latter figure excludes the fluctuations in temporary residents associated with the tourism industry, especially in the summer, when the total population of the city can reach up to 400,000. This is a very important figure, considering that the population of Alicante, the capital of the province, barely reaches 335,000.

The first bungalows were built on the Levante beach, in 1925, but it was not until the 1950s that the great transformation of the municipal space was begun, first with the cessation of the *almadraba mayor*[1] due to its low economic yield, and four years later with the passing of local tourism legislation under mayor Pedro Zaragoza Orts. Zaragoza, then only 28 years old, proposed an urban future for Benidorm directed at favoring the establishment of the tourism industry as the principal economic engine.

From that point on, the city has been described in a variety of ways, most of which have not been complimentary. It has been stigmatized as the low-cost tourism[2] city plan par excellence, or the urban paradigm of mass tourism in the same way that the European working classes (the major clientele in Benidorm) have been stigmatized. Tourists in Benidorm have been called irresponsible consumers, coarsened by their own anxiety or by cultural conditions associated with tyrannical consumption habits, bad manners and contempt for the most elemental forms of coexistence. As a result of this prejudice, some have voiced opinions in favor of reviewing the business objectives of Benidorm, in order to have them reflect more closely the questionable and discriminatory "quality" tourism model, which would look at orienting the Benidorm offering to consumers with more purchasing power. These proposals are presented as much from a conservative position as from a supposedly intellectually progressive one, and as has been explained in depth by some observers of British society, these groups have really not reflected much on their own class trajectory. Owen Jones, for example (Jones 2012), has revealed the true programs of social stratification and segregation hidden in the more or less consciously classist elaboration of this type of discourse.

In any event, beyond revealing the ideological motivations which these stories embody, we have to begin by tearing down some of the commonplaces which connect mass tourism to low industrial productivity, consumption of resources, limited environmental responsibility, and a great impact on the region. To that end it is important to document a brief quantitative record of what is happening and what has happened in Benidorm with respect to its efficacy as a model of exploitation of resources. Because, as we shall see, the truth is, Benidorm is a very profitable business.[3] Without going into too much detail, a series of figures confirmed by various statistical studies[4] can be useful in understanding the scope that Benidorm represents in quantitative terms. The city receives 75 million visits (number of visitors times number of nights they stay) on an annual basis, the highest figure in Europe after London and Paris. Roughly 43% of the hotel activity in the Community of Valencia and 60% of that in Alicante is concentrated in Benidorm. The average yearly hotel occupancy in 2011 was 79.96% (HOSBEC n.d.). After Madrid and Barcelona, Benidorm is the third most popular tourism destination on the peninsula, as well as being the principal tourism destination on the Mediterranean coast.[5]

Almost 100 million tourists have visited Benidorm since the 1960s, many of them repeat visitors. Benidorm has accumulated global earnings close to 135,000 million euros in the last 40 years, and as such it is one of the most productive businesses in Spain. It enjoys as well an excellent distribution of benefits, since the business activity associated with tourism is very evenly allocated and does not belong solely to large hotelier industries, as is common in many other destinations.

The city offers 150 hotels with 40,000 beds; 383 restaurants; more than 1,000 bars; 60 function rooms; 170 pubs; 63 travel agencies; 1 water-ski cableway; 11 campgrounds (which provide 12,000 spaces); 2,000 businesses; 6 consulates; 69 banking establishments; 4,600 beach chairs; 1,400 beach umbrellas; 1 water park; and 3 theme-parks.

The inhabitants of Benidorm come from 121 different countries. The population oscillates between 150,000 and 600,00 people throughout the year, but the number of permanent residents is 73,000 (according to the 2012 census). More than 85% of the population surveyed in the census was not born in Benidorm (Instituto Nacional de Estadística 2013), a situation which supports an extraordinarily cosmopolitan society.

Additionally, from a strictly architectural and urban planning perspective, Benidorm is the city with the largest number of skyscrapers per capita in the world (SkyscraperPage.com 2013), which allows it to place high on indices of compactness, one of the most telling indicators of urban sustainability. Furthermore, and contrary to general opinion, it is one of the least dense cities in the region, at least until recent times, when a number of disastrous urban projects have consumed part of the municipal lands protected by the 1963 General Plan.

Scantily-clad girls, the bikini plan

The urban model of Benidorm has been widely discussed and defended by many authors not always inclined to favoring a speculative focus on regional resources. These writers include J.G. Ballard (Ballard 2013), town planners and sociologists such as Henri Lefebvre,[6] Mario Gaviria and José Miguel Iribas (Gaviria and Iribas 1977), or more

fig.1: View of the Poniente Esplanade. Photograph by the author

recently the Dutch architectural studio MVRDV (MVRDV 2001), which dedicated an entire study to explaining the urban uniqueness of the city of Benidorm. Such uniqueness can be summed up in the four principles observed by the urban sociologist José Miguel Iribas, one of the great defenders of the model: a balanced distribution of benefits; rejection of sprawl; the exceptional nature of culture; and – even though a priori it may unbelievable – environmental thoughtfulness.

The idea of driving economic development via tourism was a program that had become the obsession of several municipalities on the Spanish Mediterranean coast. Numerous development models were designed to exploit the available resources, essentially the hours of sunlight and beaches, although they were not always equally successful. Such is the case, for example, of tourism cities like Marbella, Torremolinos or areas of great natural beauty such as La Manga del Mar Menor.

The success of Benidorm, explains Iribas (Iribas 2007), is owed principally to the fact that three decisive decisions were made for the future city. These are expressly different from the other models of development:

- Urban planning would provide special support to propel, develop and stipulate the established industrial model, which would be tourism.
- The market will emerge mainly from mass tourism.
- No distinction (referring either to nationality or social background) will be made between the different origins of the tourists.

Although they required a great amount of determination when faced with multiple offers and pressures, the first two were not difficult to carry out. The third, however, was more problematic, as it would involve more agents as well as local inhabitants.

During the decades of the 1950s and 60s, Spain was a country fundamentally dominated by the moral guidelines imposed by the national Catholic ideology, a fact that greatly complicated the acceptance of certain behaviors that were considered immoral. Franco's legislation prohibited the use of the bikini on the beach, rejecting a trend that was already very common in the rest of Europe, especially in the United Kingdom and the Scandinavian countries, two of the principal markets that the tourism project of Benidorm hoped to conquer. The battle to authorize free use of the "two-piece" bathing suit invented by Louis Reard in 1946 became at that time, for the Benidorm of the Catholic dictatorship, a steppingstone to assure the establishment of the programmed tourism model. The bikini was at that moment (clearly in spite of its sexist and sensual symbolic charge), an emblem of

fig.2: View of the Levante Esplanade. Photograph by the author

modernization, and in brief a material device involving public participation in the effort to relax strict socio-religious precepts.

Whether due to its symbolic impact or to its effective economic returns, the truth is that the "exceptional legal nature" granted to Pedro Zaragoza by the chief of state forms part of the mythological history of Benidorm. It could be said that the authorization to wear a bikini is the foundational myth[7] of Benidorm, today an entire urban program based on the ordinary. Upon the death of Pedro Zarazoga, the conservative British newspaper *The Telegraph* presented an almost mythical story in his obituary published in April 2008:

> Having arranged for water to be pumped to Benidorm from 10 miles distant to service the village, Zaragoza set about encouraging package tour operators who could fly plane loads of tourists to Spain. Initially he contacted airlines in Germany and Scandinavia, and came up with the less than snappy slogan "sun and beach" to attract visitors from northern Europe.
> It was primarily the British who responded, and the women brought with them the bikini, leading to the most celebrated episode in Zaragoza's career as mayor. He had seen the two-piece swimming costumes in magazines, and knew that – in northern Europe – they were considered unremarkable. In Spain, however, they were banned by General Franco's regime.
> In 1953 – on the principle that "you couldn't stop it" – Zaragoza authorised the wearing of bikinis at Benidorm. No one in the country had attempted this, and there was uproar. As members of the Civil Guard scuffled with scantily-clad girls on Benidorm's beaches, the local archbishop threatened to excommunicate Zaragoza, who decided to appeal directly to Franco.
> At 6am one morning he set off for Madrid on his Vespa motor scooter, arriving in the Spanish capital eight hours later. "I changed my shirt but I went in to the General with my trousers spattered with motor oil", he later claimed. "He backed me, and the bikini stayed." (Telegraph 2013)

This story has seminal importance when understanding the urban exceptionality of the Benidorm project. One could affirm that the socio-spatial result of the actual city is historically linked to a very un-architectural event, one that is more related to exotic behaviors or the tolerance of the regime toward customs hailing from Northern Europe. Thus, Benidorm became one of the spaces of tolerance of social behaviors that arrived from abroad. It was a place where the rigid moral laws of Franco's dictatorship could be regionally suspended. It was a conquest that triggered for its mayor three threats of ex-communication from the

Catholic Church, which, as one can imagine, was quite a grievous threat within the system of Spanish values of the 1950s.

In large measure, though, thanks to something so banal and superficial as the defense of the bikini, Benidorm is today one of the most important European tourist cities, visited throughout the year primarily by the English and the Scandinavians. Here, we can observe phenomena of great importance for contemporary urban studies, such as informalities, on-the-spot urban planning, architectures of leisure, vertical urban planning, densities, everyday architecture, and the overlapping of public and private spheres.

The urban model of Benidorm was a trailblazer in Europe. The opening of large avenues, the unrestrained height of the buildings, the regulations regarding the views, the incorporation of the beaches into the urban environment, the low occupancy rate of buildings per lot, the risks taken with the urban density of green spaces in the semi-private sector (which belong to the owners of the dwellings but add to the public green space), and at the same time the tolerance towards a certain illegal nature in the occupancy of the ground floors and their provisional extension into the streets, all contribute to the fact that the urban planning of Benidorm is a case study of extraordinary interest. This is true above all, if we take into consideration the exceptional modernity of the proposals included in the General Plan, which favored the unregulated emergence of certain spontaneous urban plans.

The plan

The General Plan of Benidorm was the first of those written in Spain[8] to take into consideration the entire extent of municipal lands. This decision allowed the process to take on regional planning in a global fashion, protecting from speculation the most valuable ecological lands, such as the Sierra Helada and the Isle of Benidorm. This act demonstrated an environmental concern rarely seen in other coastal areas less frequently scorned by the most popularized critical discourses. In addition, after its redaction in 1956, the Plan was modified and rewritten in 1963 in order to adjust the proposals and facilitate their implementation, a display of the flexibility of the process of writing the document.

The basic principle of the Plan was to simultaneously establish urban regulations and the tourism product. In other words, the new Plan meant to transfer the spatial dimension, which the industrial project required in order to make it viable, to the design of the city. The coordination between the tourism focus linked to the model of the development of municipal resources and the urban design is one of the most unique characteristics of the project of the new city of Benidorm as an urban plan intended to stimulate and attract tourism of the masses.

Furthermore, the construction of the airport in Alicante contributed to driving the exponential growth of the stable population of Benidorm in the 1960s and mid 1970s, until it reached more than 25,000 inhabitants in the census of 1981, a figure which has continued to grow to 75,000 in the 2010 census.

Iribas identifies the four central principles that characterize the uniqueness of the urban plan of Benidorm (Iribas 2007):

- A balanced distribution of the benefits of tourism amongst all sectors and a strong push for participation of local parties (86% of the population works in the tourism sector), a not-so-common situation in the panorama of the international tourism industry, which has become more interested in the elite or "quality" models such as those developed in the Caribbean, the Middle East, Brazil or Southeast Asia, seeking a client with greater purchasing power and concentrating the business initiative in the large holdings of the tourism industry which have promoted the advent or intensification of phenomena of social stratification and exclusion.
- Compactness. Rejection of the suburban model of low density. This allowed the city to maintain important land reserves (until recently, with the squandering of disastrous initiatives such as Terra Mítica). In many analyses this value has been confused with density. Benidorm is not, in reality, a dense city because it has maintained large tracts of undeveloped municipal lands.
- It is a model in conflict with the dominant trends in the discipline. The value of the model has only recently been recognized in the academic sphere as a valuable contribution to contemporary urban planning in Spain. In general, the tourism industry has called for much more conventional urban models, especially in

recent times as the Mediterranean coast has suffered a ravenous consumption of its regional resources due to the awful (and frequently corrupt) public administration and the limited innovative profile of the urban planning initiatives that have been carried out, most of which have clung to the idea of tourism of "quality" which has imposed the pursuit of a tapestry made up of the sprawl of single-family dwellings.
- Environmental thoughtfulness with concrete decisions as to the protection of lands with a high ecological value, such as the Sierra Helada and the Isle of Benidorm.

The beach at Benidorm, a new city

One of the documents that has contributed most notably to disseminating the importance of Benidorm as an urban laboratory is the one written between the summer of 1972 and the winter of 1975 by the team The Seminary of Urban, Rural and Leisure Sociology (*Seminario de Sociología Urbana, Rural y del Ocio*), which until that point had been located in Madrid. In order to carry out the investigation, a large group of interdisciplinary experts took up residence in Benidorm for almost three years, becoming part of the public life of the city, of its routines and of its seasonal rhythms.

The result of the investigation was the publication of various studies regarding ecology, tourism and urban planning as well as an extensive piece on Benidorm published in two volumes. City Hall had commissioned the winning team of a competition to write up the Study on Socio-Urban Planning, Socio-Tourism and the Future, which preceded the General Plan of Urban Planning in Benidorm (Gaviria and Iribas 1977). The contract stated that the team writing the report would reside in Benidorm for the duration of the study. The experience was a huge success and today it is still one of the central landmarks in the literature on urban sociology and tourism.

The analysis, directed by Mario Gaviria, José Miguel Iribas, Françoise Sabbah and Juan Ramón Sanz Arranz, was written over different stages by more than 70 investigators and included Henri Lefebvre as a consultant. It is comprised of almost 800 pages, and presents in great detail the evolution of the city from 1965 until the date of the study.

In the long chapter dedicated to the beach, the study concludes that the beach at Benidorm brings together the requirements that qualify it as urban, due to its high degree of integration into the structure of the city, a condition that can also be verified at the beaches in Gijón, Barcelona, San Sebastián and Cannes, in France. As in the other chapters, the one centering on the beaches includes a series of recommendations, some very ambitious, which anticipate several of the proposals incorporated later on, to a greater or lesser degree, regarding the beaches and the future esplanades. Nevertheless, many of the recommendations were never followed, for example, the construction of swimming pools along the esplanade, the installation of artificial beaches on 20 floating rafts anchored slightly off shore, the perfuming of the sand (something that had been experimented with in Cannes), the elimination of vehicular traffic, the promotion of nighttime sea bathing by illuminating the water from the shore to a distance of 100 meters, and even the heating of the beach during the off season.

All of these measures encourage the idea of beach conceived as yet one more urban space, one that requires substantial investment and very careful attention to municipal services. In this way the idea of a beach understood as a natural space, separated from urban life and offering an encounter with the natural environment, no longer has any meaning in Benidorm. Nevertheless, recognizing the importance the beach plays in the chain of production of entertainment that the city should be means it should be designed in great detail.

In order to be efficient, however, the design should above all be inspired by the conditions that an attentive observation of daily life presents in these spaces. The beach, as yet another urban space, is the foundation of multiple relations and forms of sociability, and as such its design should contribute to the articulation, strengthening or softening of this sociability. For this reason, the team of investigators of the Seminary of Urban, Rural and Leisure Sociology dedicated a very important part of their efforts to carrying out ethnographic investigations in situ that collected the different uses, cycles, transitoriness and simultaneities, in addition to more technical aspects, such as water quality and the color of the sand or its temperature. All this provided an enormous battery of data that permitted the elaboration of a series of proposals that were offered as intensifiers or condensers of the most ordinary social activities, such as sun bathing, swimming or the large-scale use of beach chairs and pools.

fig.3: The Poniente Esplanade from different angles. Photographs by the author

The *chavvy* urban planning of Benidorm

The interest that the theory of architecture has in incorporating into its analysis categories and instruments provided by the study of the ordinary is nothing new. Referring to architectural criticism, the scientific literature on Benidorm has a clear antecedent, which can contribute to the explanation of the model, in cities such as Las Vegas or some of the historic cities along the North American coast. The first of such studies was conducted by Venturi Scott-Brown and Izenour in the essential work *Learning from Las Vegas* (Venturi, Scott Brown and Izenour 1972), one of the most influential texts on architectural theory of the 20th century. In addition we find the writings of Yoshiharu Tsukamoto (Tsukamoto 2010) or of Andrés Jaque (Jaque 2011) addressing the reach of the ordinary in architecture. More recently, Enrique Walker has taken up this topic in a series of decisive articles that have had a strong impact on the field in Spain (Walker 2010).

In the same fashion, the case of Benidorm would contribute to broadening the theoretical field in two ways. On the one hand, it would orient the gaze toward the culture of the ordinary, the apparently secondary or even the frivolous. The academic viewpoint might consider this inconsistent and not very worthy of study. On the other hand, it would recreate the descriptions of a city, incorporating relational factors and contributions from the social sciences, deeming the practices in the city to be on the same level as the stages that support them.

One of the principal characteristics of Benidorm is that it has been instituted as the city of leisure for an important part of the European subaltern classes, especially those from the United Kingdom, who thanks to offerings like Benidorm have had access to consumption that otherwise would be unattainable:

Precisely 61% of the foreign visitors are from Great Britain, almost 30% of the total annual tourists (Benidorm City Hall 2013). The majority of these vacationers are from working class societies, with little purchasing power, who come to Benidorm looking for exactly what it offers: sun, beach, alcohol and sex at affordable prices. This category of visitors presents us with a now well-established description of the clientele of Benidorm, reinforced by dozens of newspaper articles, television programs[9] and an identical depiction in all of the condescending tourist guidebooks that have belittled Benidorm as a place where bad taste, ignorance and vulgarity prevail.

This vision of the ordinary as a part of reality that should be displaced from academic discussions, due to the limited quality of its offerings and its intellectual irrelevance, is something that occurs particularly in architecture. It is, however, a constant in many aspects of

fig.4: The Levante Esplanade from different angles. Photographs by the author

recent criticism. Nevertheless, for many authors of other disciplines such as sociology, anthropology, urban studies, or literary or film studies, the ordinary is an important source of information and inspiration.[10] In order to understand the current role of Benidorm in contemporary mass culture, it is absolutely necessary to consider the transformation that European society has undergone in the last 30 years and how it has produced its own social tales to reinforce the politics of stratification, disintegration, and discrimination against the poorest sectors of society. As a city, Benidorm has been denigrated by a tale as prejudicial and offensive as the one which European working classes have had to withstand, victims of a class-oriented demonization, using the words of Owen Jones (Jones 2012), for putting into operation a political program and a new design of extremely reactionary social stratification.

A critical reflection on the two esplanades in Benidorm could represent an excellent opportunity to address some recurring issues in architectural criticism and in the theoretical renovation of the discipline by offering perspectives that consider the ordinary as alternate and deregulated forms of the reconstruction of societies. What policies and societies are embodied in Benidorm's esplanades? This is the question we have to ask ourselves.

Esplanades

The Levante (East) Beach and the Poniente (West) Beach make up the majority of the coastline in Benidorm. They have been the object of two of the most important maritime esplanade projects, which bring together the relationship between the coast and the city. Nevertheless, there are great differences between these two spaces, which transfer to the architectural and urban planning designs many of the controversies concerning the city that have been debated. In this sense, both projects embody ideologies of urban planning materialized technologically as political presences.

Poniente Esplanade (2009)

The more recent of the two esplanades is an excellent design, which received the FAD city and landscape award in 2010 for *"separating and joining two very different worlds with a sophisticated topography"* (emphasis added) according to the presentation by the jury.

Carlos Ferrater and Xavier Martí's project makes skilled use of many of the themes typical of the architecture found at the seaside: the rhetoric of the waves, the stone breakwaters, and the foam. These elements suggest as with the plastic arts ways with which to explore the formal proposal. The continuous curves satisfy functional demands such as accessibility, the separation of vehicular traffic, spaces for rest and relaxation, benches and steps, access to parking lots, sanitation, etc. The entire project is built with white concrete as the principal material, which could be interpreted as a universal model of the cliff, presented as a geological syncretism of the rocky edges of the Mediterranean coast, reinterpreting the plasticity of the natural modeling produced by the pounding of storms and the wind.[11]

In spite of the fact that with this project, the authors defend a radically innovative planning with respect to "what different esplanades we know have been" (OAB 2013), the truth is that the proposal gathers certain themes that have already been explored in other places, such as the articulation between the space of the city and the esplanade as a main function, and not just something that protects the residential zones.[12]

From a relational focus, the motivation of the jury that granted the prestigious award is shocking, because it expresses a vision of "the natural" and its relationship to "the artificial" as separate spheres, which other disciplines, such as political ecology, have been challenging for decades. And perhaps this is the most important objection that one must make regarding this project.

On the Poniente Esplanade, the reconstruction of a maritime landscape aims to recover natural values and separate nature and culture, urban space and natural space. A beach program is favored, then, that distances the beach from the city and establishes a limit that allows one to distinguish one part from the other. The esplanade, with its white presence in the city landscape, with its tautological outline and its marked itineraries in architecture of folds. Thus, Ferrater's project proposes once again metalinguistic, formal, functional or programmatic problems, leaving behind the importance of relational values proposed by the originality of the urban planning of Benidor.

Levante Esplanade (2002)
We could say, then, that the more recent construction, the Poniente Esplanade, centers on the symbolic recuperation of the "natural" values of the beach, while the Levante Esplanade is the result of the emergence of the ecosystemic dimension of the urban condition.

Both works correspond, therefore, to very different tourism projects. The first appears to offer a renewed stake on the beach as a natural space, separated from the city and protected from the hubbub, from dark corners and the tendency towards disarray, while the second proceeds to intensify precisely that which the other seemed to want to weaken: urban activity. That is to say, the Poniente Esplanade, in my opinion, proposes itself as a filter for that which is not normal in order to facilitate a "naturalized" use of the beach.

Nevertheless, it is precisely this risky stake on the urban that makes the Levante Esplanade extraordinary. The project of Martorell, Bohigas and Mackay (MBM) uses very little "construction" material, employing instead a great deal of urban intensity. In this case we move from the regime of objects to that of the relationships which these activate, in such a way that the services of the beach – including rental of beach chairs, pedal boats, beach umbrellas, showers, foot showers, children's games, segways, electronic strollers and amphibian wheel chairs for the persons with disabilities, among many other objects and beach installations – are not disconnected from bars, pubs, restaurants, souvenir and "vacation" clothing shops which are situated on the walkways facing the esplanade. In addition, the terraces of the high residential buildings, which line the length of the beach, become privileged box seats to the extraordinary spectacle of the beach and esplanade. Everything forms part of the same choreography in which the urban, pleasure tourism, unprejudiced human relationships, having fun for a reasonable price, the sun, the sand and dance music all mix together with large groups of "senior" tourists traveling in electric chairs in both directions, joggers, stag and hen parties, small rides for children, and an impressive array of tattoos and piercings on sunburnt skin. And this takes place with relatively little seasonal variation, an achievement that is also in part due to the superb architectural design of the esplanade.

Finished in 1996, the plan for the Levante Esplanade was begun in 1993 by the architects Josep Martorell, David Mackay and Oriol Bohigas. The esplanade was meant to enhance access to one of the most famous urban beaches in Europe, and at the same time provide a new public space that would intensify seaside activities. The project decisions were relatively simple: to maintain the current street level, allowing the elevation of the esplanade to be just a few centimeters higher than the level of the sand; to use wood as the paving material to transition between the sand and the street (reminiscent of important precedents such as Atlantic City, Ocean City, or Coney Island); to use native plantings of palms that flow onto the beach; to solve the lighting concern with a series of lamp posts that also flow onto the beach and from which cables with lights are strung, reminiscent of the festival lights that were temporarily hung in the streets during festivities.

Through these four strategies, MBM facilitated the *urbanization* of the beach, the definitive incorporation of the urban, offering it at almost no cost. The festive lighting, as the most notable design element of the proposal, is an invitation to celebrate urban life and a joyful, do not "return to normal" use of the city. In fact, the success of the proposal confirms it as such.

The Levante Esplanade articulates the relationship between two spheres, which are equally recognized as urban spaces: the beach and the city streets, discrediting the childish idea that the beach at Benidorm, where the most varied of human activities unfold, such as cable water-skiing, swimming, *goffmanian*[13] conversation or discrete underwater sex, practiced as much during the day as at night, is something more "natural" than what happens in the streets.

Conclusions

The two esplanades in Benidorm, constructed ten years apart, not only represent a materialization of two very different models of industrial development of tourism resources, but also offer two radically different positions regarding the possibilities of architectural interventions in the technological articulation of socio-cultural contexts. The more recent (the Poniente Esplanade) recovers and exploits the "romantic" idea of nature separated from the sphere of the human or the cultural, and maintains the ancient notion of the esplanade as a defense against the pounding of the sea, arranging the architectural transaction toward a modulating function of the two spheres, that of nature and that of city.

The Levante Esplanade, on the contrary, is not presented as a connective element between two spheres in conflict, but one that accepts (and exploits) the ecosystemic condition of the urban, assuming a vision of nature which also includes the human, the material and the technological, participating in the constitution of a complex assembly formed, as Bruno Latour suggests (Latour 2008), according to hybrid dialogues in which humans and non-humans relate to each other horizontally in non-hierarchical networks.

The Levante project, however, also assumes the ordinary as not only a commercial strategy but also one that incorporates design itself as a factor. The garlands of the fairs, the lighting up of the sand, the wooden boardwalk areas from which you can contemplate the daily spectacle of the beach, and the scarce "authorial" ambition reveal a sensitivity toward the banal, the superficial and the irrelevant as a form of reclaiming more horizontal and less prejudicial social reorganizations.

fig.5: The Poniente beach. Photographs by the author

Notes

1. The *almadraba mayor* is a tuna fishing technique dating back to pre-roman times, employed along the southern and southeastern coast of Spain (Atlantic and Mediterranean), in the north of Morocco and in Italy. It involves a labyrinth of nets attached to boats positioned along the migratory tuna routes, from the Atlantic to the Mediterranean and back, from the Straits of Gibraltar to Sicily. The almadraba in Benidorm was one of the most important and the fishermen considered themselves to be great experts in this technique.
2. We have to point out that the so-called low-cost industry, as we will see, does not imply more modest benefits, but just the opposite, at least in the case before us.
3. The idea of the city as a hub of competitiveness has been widely discussed and discredited by authors such as Amin and Thrift. This essay does not expect to defend the idea that the city has a special dimension that could in and of itself generate economic returns, nor does it present Benidorm as a model city of global economy (rather the contrary, viewing it as an example of a fluctuating urban economy and not one of connected centralities). Instead, it simply tells a story about the city that is different from the one commonly seen, beginning with the results of its economic plan, with a marginal focus adopted to explain the general running of the economy of cities. For more documentation about this subject see Amin and Thrift (2002).
4. The majority of this data is taken from municipal statistics and from the National Institute for Statistics, although there are still investigations being carried out to collect data based on other indicators, such as water and energy consumption or urban solid waste, which perhaps could produce more precise figures for such a unique case as Benidorm, given the oscillations in population.
5. This is a value that cannot be compared with the tourism centers on the Canary Islands due to the diversity of climate conditions and the prolongation of the high seasons on the islands.
6. Between 1972 and 1974, Henri Lefebvre was invited by town planner and sociologist Mario Gaviria, who had been his student, to participate in an investigation that Gaviria was carrying out in Spain regarding new tourism cities. The study focused above all on Benidorm.
7. A foundational myth is one that explains the origin of a city. In the case of Rome, for example, it is that of Romulus and Remus, raised by a she-wolf. In the case of Athens it is the competition between Poseidon and Athena. The bikini is the foundational myth of ordinary urban planning that Benidorm represents.
8. The General Plan of Urban Planning of Benidorm is today the object of study in multiple academic areas. It was drawn up by prestigious architects and urban planners of that time, such as Manuel Muñoz Monasterio, Luis Rodríguez Hernández and Francisco Muñoz Llorens, who had taken on the task of projecting the new arrangement of the Playa de Levante (the East Beach), which already presented in a nascent form the principal ideas of the future Plan.
9. In 2008, for example, the television series *I Love Benidorm*, broadcast on ITV, registered astronomically high audience numbers, up to 28% of the viewing figures.
10. This idea has been recently discussed by many authors who, after the recent death of two of the great Spanish film directors linked to the ordinary, Jess Franco and Bigas Luna, have defended their respective film making and the example that both made of the categories of the banal, the superficial and the grotesque. For more on this, see Ferré (2013). In the field of sociology see "Sociología ordinaria" (2013)
11. In regards to this, see the statement of the project published on the website of the OAB study ("Proyectos OAB" 2013)
12. There have been some esplanades constructed recently in Spain that represent very similar interests and concerns, such as the one in Vinarós (Vicente Guallart, 2009), or the one in Torrevieja (Carme Pinós, 2000)
13. The importance for urban studies of symbolic interactionism and ethnomethodology have not yet been sufficiently recognized in the disciplinary frameworks of architecture.

fig.6: The Levante beach. Photographs by the author

References

Amin, Ash, and Nigel Thrift. 2002. *Cities: Reimagining the Urban*. Cambridge: Polity.

Ballard, James Graham. 2013. What I Believe. Retrieved August 26 from http://www.jgballard.ca/uncollected_work/what_i_believe.html

Benidorm City Hall. 2013. Benidorm en cifras 2012 (Benidorm in figures 2012). Retrieved from http://portal.benidorm.org/nuevociudadano/sites/default/files/secciones-concejalias/benidorm_en_cifras_2012.pdf

Ferré, Juan Francisco. 2013. La vuelta al mundo: Homenaje a Jess Franco. Retrieved May 19 from http://juanfranciscoferre.blogspot.com.es/2013/04/homenaje-jess-franco_12.html

Gaviria, Mario, and José Miguel Iribas. 1977. *Benidorm, ciudad nueva*. Madrid: Editora Nacional.

HOSBEC (Asociación Empresarial Hostelera de Benidorm y la Costa Blanca). n.d. Retrieved from http://www.hosbec.com/

Instituto Nacional de Estadística. (Spanish Statistical Office). 2013. Retrieved August 26 from http://www.ine.es/

Iribas, José Miguel. 2007 Aprendiendo de Benidorm: Pedro Zaragoza, 1922-2008. *Arquitectura Viva* 117 (November):128.

Jaque, Andrés. 2011. Eco-ordinary. Etiquetas para la práctica cotidiana de la arquitectura. Madrid: Universidad Europea de Madrid.

Jones, Owen. 2012. *Chavs: The Demonization of the Working Class*. 2d ed. London:Verso.

Latour, Bruno. 2008. *Reensamblar lo social : una introducción a la teoría del actor-red*. Buenos Aires: Manantial.

MVRDV. 2001. *Costa Ibérica*. Barcelona: ACTAR.

OAB. 2013.Proyectos OAB. Retrieved May 26 from http://www.ferrater.com/_proyectos/proyectosFrags/fragProyectosDatos.php?id=11&idioma=1

SkyscraperPage.com. 2013. Benidorm Skyscraper Diagram. Retrieved May 22 from http://skyscraperpage.com/diagrams/?cityID=602

Sociología ordinaria.2013. Aprendiendo de lo banal, lo frívolo y lo superficial. 2013. Retrieved May 26 from http://sociologiaordinaria.com/

Telegraph. 2013. Pedro Zaragoza. 03 April 2008. Retrieved May 26 from http://www.telegraph.co.uk/news/obituaries/1583716/Pedro-Zaragoza.html

Tsukamoto, Yoshiharu. 2010. *Behaviorology*. New York: Rizzoli.

Venturi, Robert, Denise Scott Brown and Robert Izenour. 1972. *Learning from Las Vegas*. Cambridge: MIT Press.

Walker, Enrique. 2010. *Lo ordinario*. Barcelona: Gustavo Gili.

Commons-based Urbanism: Can Alicante Be a Case Study?

Urbanismo de los comunes: ¿puede ser Alicante un caso de estudio?

「コモンズ」型都市計画：アリカンテはケーススタディの対象となり得るか？

Enrique Nieto | エンリケ・ニエト

La ciudad de Alicante constituye un buen ejemplo de la llamada ciudad mediterránea, resultado de una gran cantidad de entrecruzamientos, pactos y controversias que impiden una aproximación simplificada a su realidad. Además, un clima benigno y una gran disponibilidad de costa configuran unos rasgos identitarios especialmente deseables para industrias de masas como el turismo. Frente a las dinámicas locales, estas industrias responden a tendencias globales, y se aproximan a los hechos urbanos con herramientas generalistas poco atentas a los fenómenos emergentes locales. Paradójicamente, tanto el turista como los distintos activismos emergentes de la ciudad son abordados por las instituciones como elementos pasivos ajenos a las verdaderas dinámicas productoras de ciudad. Sin embargo, las nuevas herramientas de análisis derivadas de las ciencias sociales, así como las nuevas tecnologías de gestión de la información apuntan a la ciudad como un objeto descentrado, a la vez que iluminan la capacidad creativa de cualquiera de las especies sociales que habitan la ciudad. Paralelamente, una nueva sensibilidad social demanda formas de gobernanza más frágiles y participadas. En este contexto se propone la ciudad de Alicante como un caso de estudio óptimo para testear nuevas aproximaciones al turismo más sensibles y atentas a las controversias locales, capaces de integrar la capacidad creativa de cualquiera de los agentes que informan los hechos urbanos.

アリカンテは、絶え間ない交錯、協定、議論の蓄積の上に形成されたいわゆる地中海都市の好例であり、その複雑な実情を解明するのは決して容易ではない。一方、この地域の特徴となっている温暖な気候と沿岸部へのアクセスの良さは、ツーリズムに代表される大衆産業の進出にとって、きわめて望ましい条件を提示している。こうしたマス産業はグローバル指向が強く、都市事象に普遍的な手法をもってアプローチする傾向があるため、勃興しつつあるローカルな現象とほとんど関係を持たず、地域的原理と対立することがしばしばある。他方、奇妙なことに行政その他の機関は、観光客の存在も、都市内で勃興しつつあるさまざまな社会活動も、都市生産活動の真の原動力となるにはほど遠い、受動的な要素と見なしてきた。しかしながら、社会科学が生んだ新たな分析ツールや新しい情報管理技術により、都市が脱求心的な対象と捉えられるだけでなく、都市に居住する社会的種族のいずれもが持ち合わせている創造的能力に脚光が当たるようになった。また同時に、近年、よりフラジャイルな参加型の行政のあり方を求める、新しい社会的感性が育ってきてもいる。こうした状況を踏まえ、本論では、地域的な議論により敏感に反応し、都市の事象を形づくっていく因子それぞれの創造的能力を統合することができる新たなツーリズムへのアプローチを試みるために、アリカンテをその試みの格好の研究対象として提案する。

Controversial planning of the Mediterranean city

The city of Alicante could be considered a paradigmatic case of the so-called *Mediterranean city*. Its historical evolution appears linked to powerful networks of cultural and commercial exchange, favored by the bounty of the sea and a climate particularly favorable to human settlements. At the same time, this predisposition toward exchanges has multiplied the number and disparity of conflicts, which took place during times past, and which in many cases have been reconfigured as instruments of growth for the city itself. Within this framework of great instabilities, some key aspects of contemporary urban investigations, such as the processes of stabilization of identities starting from the confluence of local and global dynamics, allow us to re-describe many Mediterranean cities as true sociotechnical laboratories. Examples of this growing interest in the specificity of the Mediterranean city would be the numerous investigations centered on understanding them, as for example the investigative program *Ciudades mediterráneas* [Mediterranean cities] developed by the Mies Van der Rohe Foundation (n.d.), or the master's program "Intelligent Coast" developed by the Universidad Politécnica in Cataluña (UPC 2007).

In addition, however, Alicante is also an example of a type of urban planning that emerged in Europe throughout the second half of the 20th century, informed by a simplifying model of urban planning concerned with adapting existing urban settings to the modes of industrial production, for which the city would be one more product. Its ways of doing feed off the paradigm of functional specialization; while in industry they adopted the form of Taylorism, in urban planning it was zoning carried to the limit by Le Corbusier and the Athens Charter that played a decisive role. These patterns still govern a large part of urban production today. We find, thus, strongly regulating tools of action such as monofunctional zoning, hierarchical structures, formal clarity, confidence in the experts, etc., tools directed at the precise manufacturing of a final image of the city in which the form of the different parts can be explained in their smooth relation to the rest of the elements. From this point of view, the city clearly exemplifies the ability of reason to control and govern a great heterogeneity and multiplicity by starting from the organization of its simple elements (fig. 1).

We must add that since the 1960s the city of Alicante has thought about its economy in relation to the promise of beneficial migration from Northern Europe by populations eager to enjoy the sun, the beach and a certain attractive local identity, resources seemingly free and renewable which the cities of the *Mediterranean Arch* have in abundance (Pérez García 2010). This comprehensive objective is not foreign to traditional local dynamics. But, as we presently understand it, it deals with a design that was established from the perspective of a myth of constant and unlimited progress, which introduced for Alicante the horizon of tourism as a common objective upon which the city would stake a great part of its expectations. With time, this objective has been supported by the efficiency of tools derived from marketing or information management, which have displaced the simple image of urban planning toward the more complex goal of strategic urban management. The *smart city* is one of the most successful products of this displacement. We must point out, however, that the limitless confidence in centralized planning and management, as well as tourism as a propelling force depend on a mechanistic conception of human production, whose anomalies are seen as pathologies to be excluded through an intensification of regulations and through their exclusion from studies and investigations centering on the city.

Alicante, thus, like other sister cities, can be imagined from a distance as a city that opens onto a maritime front destined for easy leisure activity and relaxation, a historic center that represents the essential origin of the city, a port zone that updates the economy and enables connectivity through the sea, local traditions that establish identitary patterns, 19th-century city expansions that accommodate the bourgeois lifestyles associated with glamorous commercial urban fabrics, working class suburbs that are grouped in urban units clearly organized according to specific designs, the scaled appearance of other compact functions such as the University, industrial areas, green spaces, etc. (fig. 2).

From the multiple critical questions derived from simplifying models of behavior toward the city, two are of central interest to this essay, originating from several unique features that the city of Alicante presents. The first contributes to modes of thinking about urban facts. For some authors, any approach to the understanding of a city requires the assumption of a temporal change that is thought to have installed us in a third modernity characterized by such disparate phenomena as greater reflexivity, new types of social relationships, the structure and impact of networks, cognitive capitalism, and the role of information technologies. These profound changes would make a unified project of the city unfeasible, pointing instead to the study of the city as a laboratory, where a heterogeneous multiplicity of information – capable of forming urban consistencies not very open to being controlled and regulated either by public institutions or private forces – happens in a radically relational manner. In fact, some of the recent methodological advances in analyses coming out of the social sciences appear to question the assessment of the city considered as an isolated fact reduced to basic units, providing contemporary diagnostic tools which explore the urban fact from more open perspectives. In general they point to the ontological impossibility of thinking about urban facts disconnected from the multiple sociotechnical networks through which they pass, networks that are permanently

fig.1: View of Alicante from the harbour. Photograph by the author.

involved in the formation of collective hybrids. From this point of view, a detailed study of the mapping of the bars of the city, one of the key elements that shape the identity of Alicante, would allow us to detect their infiltration into economies of scale, their role as spaces of alternative socialization, their configuration as hubs for the formation of dissident identities, etc. At the same time, this access to the visible aspect of the complexity that the product "bar" is experiencing would permit us to move away from the naïve view that relegates them to elements of the tourist attraction.

If the first critical question deals with modes of thinking about the city, the second addresses modes of producing it. At present, still influenced by the legacy of a modernity that would assign a visual value to the different functional units that make it up, it seems that to make a city refers to questions of formal organization and growth management. Nevertheless, important questions have arisen lately regarding new forms of governance, introducing doubts regarding the forms of justice inherent to determined modes of making a city in a centralized fashion, proposing alternatives, which contemplate a horizon of the urban facts more open to heterogeneous participation in which citizens can contribute more actively to the material definition of their surroundings. We find, however, that although the *smart city* cited earlier seems to maintain the models of autonomous and centralized management, the participant models seem to ignore the role of experts. What is clear is that affirming the common condition of the city would demand greater reflexiveness and risk in order to position the new systems of analysis and information management at the service of the city, not to affirm what is already known, but as a condition to maintain and preserve, as a system to guarantee true democratization of the city.

We are aware that urban identity and the attachment of communities to their own places can be essential for sustainability as a whole. We know as well that cities today are driven to specialize and compete with one another in order to be more attractive to tourists and to fluctuations in wealth. While this competition implies the recovery of eroded historic centers, the revitalization of obsolete industrial zones, or a push for areas involving cultural practices, it often leads as well to the objectivizing and standardizing of cities, with a subsequent loss of identity and a decline in the overall quality of life for the inhabitants. What is, in this framework, the opportunity for Alicante? What is the role of uniqueness, where does it reside? In this essay we will study some of the controversies surrounding these questions, oriented toward the consideration of Alicante as a crisscrossing of intercultural experiences. This questions the static regimes of analysis of the urban fact starting with its unfinished laboratory state.

Beach spa resorts and urban anomalies

Since the end of the 1950s, and until the outbreak of the economic crisis in 1973, the so-called *tourism boom* took place in Spain. This consisted of an accelerated growth of infrastructures – urban or otherwise – placed at the service of new products associated with the tourism of sun and beach. Starting with an intense state-run plan in Fordism style and motivated by the technocratic government of the dictator Franco, the first urban developments were oriented toward offering the potential tourist an enhanced consumption of sun and beach, and were connected by the emerging network of highways or by the international vibrancy of some of the airports – the Canary Islands and the Balearic Islands. When this developmental impetus

fig.2: View of Alicante from Santa Bárbara Castle. Photograph by the author.

reached Alicante in the 1960s, it encountered at least two peculiarities. On the one hand. we are dealing with a city overlooking the sea, which presents unique features and an established constructed cultural heritage with several complexities that greatly exceeded the simplifications found in other constructions situated on virgin coastlines. It serves as an example that the General Plan effective at that time did not bring together any special limitations with respect to the possibilities of tourism for the city. On the other hand, however, emerging tourism infrastructures had already existed in Alicante for many years – beach spa resorts, small urban hotels, train routes programmed from the state capital – all linked to economies grouped in distributed networks, which had successfully updated the urban landscape to the new demands of tourism from the local socioeconomic ability to welcome them (fig. 3, fig. 4).

As occurred in other coastal cities, these beach spa resorts operated during the hundred years between 1860 and 1960. There were a number of infrastructures oriented toward intensifying and making the experience of sea bathing for pleasure at urban beaches more practical; small artifacts of enormous constructive complexity, some permanent and others removable, were positioned somewhere between architecture, urban planning, and mechanical artifacts that exemplified the relational constitution of the objects. In this case they signified as well the introduction of the latest technologies with stone, steel, or style, in a city far removed from the production centers of innovation through such an apparently depoliticized activity as tourism. Their origin needs to be connected to the culture of hygiene, as well as to the incipient phenomenon of mass tourism, which at those initial moments still focused on the existing urban areas. Without a doubt, the beach spa resorts helped to construct the identity of coastal cities like Alicante, starting with technological implantation oriented at bettering the services the city could offer, where a great difference between tangible and intangible cultural heritage could not be noticed.

In this context of intense economic development, the Hotel Gran Sol and the Hotel Meliá appear at the beginning of the 1960s as advanced substitutes for the old style beach spa resorts, establishing significant episodes of the complexities inherent to the clashes between local and global dynamics about which we are speaking. In both cases we find urban planning operations developed from the ground up, or public initiatives that move away from the hygienic goal of academic urban planning oriented toward the design of a formally recognized urban product, in order to embrace the anxieties of the expansionist formation of a less and less regulated market. The first instance, the Hotel Gran Sol, gives rise to a building that multiplied by four the heights anticipated in the General Plan, making the most of the strategic opportunity so that a bourgeois city could have an urban plan inspired by New York, although in this case with the goal of tourism as the economic motor. In the case of the Hotel Meliá, it is noteworthy that it originally appears as a spa-hotel, trying to appropriate the modest connotations of the name "spa" in order to hide the constructive reach of a building until then without precedent in Spain. Far from strengthening the sea bathing experience, in reality it excludes it from all programming, concentrating instead on the production of maximum economic benefit (fig. 5, fig. 6).

As of today, we still lack a relational study from an eco-systemic perspective of the economic, cultural and social crisscrossing that mobilized around these beach spa resorts, and a comparison with those produced by hotels such as the Gran Sol or Meliá, or by other products equally supported through monofunctional strategies. One

fig.3: View of the old bathing facilities placed in Postiguet beach. Author unknown.

fig.4: View of the last bathing facilities with the Meliá Hotel initial construction, 1967. Author unknown.

must keep in mind that the beach spa resorts represented a flexible establishment, seasonal in many cases, easy to adapt and to renovate, while the hotels asserted a strong visual presence, which intended to legitimize the development premises through the consistency of materials and the form of their products. Since then, there have been difficulties in adapting to the new sensitivities of the city, demonstrated over the years by this type of infrastructure. The management of the beach spa resorts occurred through administrative transfers, which permitted diversification and control of the results, and which could at any moment be revoked by the authorities. The hotels and small-scale vacation homes that appeared close to the port were on the same scale as the city, and the buildings became absorbed by a city which was gradually experimenting with new economic forms without producing prominent ruptures with its recent collective imagination. By contrast, the large hotels or touristic establishments, as has recently occurred during the first decade of the 21st century with golf resorts, suggest establishments having very little to do with the preexisting ones. They believe in a logical efficacy never sufficiently proven, but one which in any case excludes controversies such as sustainability or identity that could interrupt their expansionist desires.

Dissidence and urban assemblages

The move from the seasonal beach spa resort to the grand hotels highlighted the difficulty of approaching the tourist phenomenon as an isolated event subject to one-time programing, transferable from the drawing board to the urban scene without attending to the symmetric character of the phenomena nor of the hybridizations with other types of realities. For some authors, one of the difficulties in understanding the repercussions of tourism as an urban reality is precisely its virtual performative potential. Meanwhile, urban studies insist on working exclusively with the scale of the modern, of the already produced (Farías 2011). From this perspective and as with any other type of urban practice, tourism practices coexist in a non-peaceful manner with other layers of the city, from transit regulations and pedestrian traffic to commercial activities or environments of political repression. Only in this fashion can we understand how today, in a public space like the Postiguet Beach, nighttime access is prohibited, since it is considered a place dedicated exclusively to swimming, an activity that only occurs in a standardized fashion during the day. This type of anomaly, as well as those cited earlier, should not be seen solely as catastrophes derived from corrupt political systems that interfere with "natural" ways of producing a city in favor of the production of a unique image. They should as well be addressed as symbols of resistance vis-à-vis unilateral systems of designing the future of the city, since paradoxically they question aspects such as the role of the experts in decision making, or the difficulty that citizen anxieties encounter in operating in expert produced surroundings such as those that have adopted the design of the city.

From this somewhat more symmetrical perspective, is interesting to observe how Alicante's historic city center, one of the constituting elements of the identity of any Mediterranean city, also accommodates episodes of urban disagreement such as the sale and distribution of drugs, with the particularity in this case in that it is carried out in a "traditional" manner by the "grandmothers" of local families very central to the local identitary landscape. Spanish laws do not allow imprisonment of people over

70 years old, and therefore they are protected under the legal systems that control public wellbeing. In this fashion, the same people who contribute to the production of an idyllic identitary landscape with their flower pots and other domestic possessions are the very ones who produce a dissenting counterproposal with respect to the normative joint efforts which operate in the city, making it apparent that one cannot think about the space without the joint practices which continually re-describe it (fig. 7).

This off-center vision of the city contributes to an object of study whose fragility originates in its multiple and elusive contemplation: a city – the urban fact – that only perceives itself in its instantaneous activation, in its singular results as heterogeneous associations. An idea that leaves behind concepts such as limit, densities or morphologies to concentrate on its evolving character, one whose emerging condition also exceeds a view of the city as a mere meeting place or the sum of multiple elements. In this regard the idea of *urban assemblage* could be useful. This designates the way in which a city can become a tourism product in which public buildings, marketing campaigns, political decisions, landscapes, morphologies, etc., come together (Farías, Bender 2010). For this to happen, however, it is necessary to exclude the idea of unity or completeness in favor of the possibility of this "assemblage", as well as to accept that the urban is a function emerging from the processes of multiple connections, while nothing alters the vulgar or basic condition of its single elements. "(T)he city therefore is not a reality that is out there, but one which is made literally from urban assemblages, through which it can become in multiple ways" (Farías 2011). The city is therefore a contingent, located, partial and heterogeneous achievement that in any other form implies the representation of a nonexistent object.

Do we want to be *smart*?

The above referenced examples illustrate some of the controversies that enliven the debate about the city of Alicante, and about the urban reality in general. As a whole, it brings to light the difficulties of continuing to think about the city as a single object able to be tamed. We have seen as well that new methods of analysis derived from the social sciences insist on the appropriateness of a simultaneous and intertwined reading of information, supported by a widespread development of information technologies that allow us to question general theories in favor of specific cases. Numerous experts have called this period the third modernity, characterized by a growth in uncertainty and risk, but also by the availability of tools to navigate in a new context dominated by forms of production derived from cognitive capitalism (Ascher 2007; Bauman 2000; Castell and Borja 1998; Augé 1999).

Nevertheless, confidence in the centralized management of the city appears to have been reconfigured in new paradigms of the production of the city, such as those known as the *smart city*, which appear to be sensitive to the appropriateness of new forms of urban management in the context of new technologies, thus indicating the importance of social and intellectual capital. They offer the new city an entire repertoire of business strategies for its holistic management, interested especially in networks of infrastructures, including intangible networks belonging to contemporary flows of information. The basic objective is to convert the product of the city into a competitive, sustainable environment, within the context of a global market in which the city would be inserted as one more product. IBM, for example, modernizes the philosophy of the *smart city* in the commercial product *Intelligent Planet*. To this end they have established a very successful platform, which is at the service of all types of organizations – large corporations, city halls, etc. – where management tools and administrative resources are indexed. The product is oriented toward achieving a more intelligent world, which in essence means a more interconnected and organized one. From this viewpoint, according to IBM, "The most intelligent cities drive sustainable economic growth and prosperity for their citizens. Their leaders have the necessary tools available to analyze the data that will permit them to make the best decisions, anticipating problems in order to resolve them in a proactive fashion, and coordinate resources to act in an efficient manner" (IBM n.d.).

A development closer to the city of Alicante is the project *Intelligent Cities*, which proposes two strategic plans to concretely advance toward the new technological society and toward an understanding of the specific aspects of telecommunications and information technologies (Tissat S.A. 2006). This model seeks to reduce the importance of public administrations in the processes of the creation of the city. In this context, they are re-described as suppliers of contents and digital services of added value. Also in a future context, the *Fundación Metrópolis* operates with the same confidence in new technologies to stimulate the intelligence of regions (Vegara 2009; Fundación Metrópolis 2010). Its work for Alicante and other similar cities relies on the virtues of professional management, as well as on a progressive relocation of the role of public institutions in the processes of the creation of the city. Its success would be based on the creation of the environmental conditions that would be necessary to permit complete autonomy of the project, on an economic as well as on a management level, defining new economic models and developing an offering of services oriented toward the citizen.

Without a doubt, two of the most relevant aspects of the concept of the *smart city* are the work with specific information regarding each environment and the application of new technologies for its treatment. Nevertheless, these models insist on working from a single, hierarchical management system with a strong corporate root. They begin with a confused reflection of identity, understood in its double condition as clearly determined historical inheritance and as a closed and unquestionable horizon, and for whose existence a great number of resources are designated. This use of identity production as a skilled synthesis of the city maintains some of the problems derived from the modern vision of urban facts. For example, it doesn't solve the problem of the origin of identitary productions, nor does it appear to question the legitimacy of the appropriation by institutions of the cultural heritage, which without a doubt belongs to everyone that participates in urban practices, which give them their origin. In fact, for some contemporary authors, identity would be no more than a mystification of the modern paradigm of power, assigning to the state – modern urban planning – or to delegated corporations – IBM's *Smarter Cities* or similar products – the difficult job of managing the riches, with which we would be better off not bothering ourselves. Thus, "For almost three centuries, we have thought about democracy as administration of the public sphere, in other words, as the institutionalization of the state appropriation of the ordinary" (Revel 2011), which in the case of cities like Alicante, is achieved through the establishment of a collective identity which would see, through the success of the tourism industry, the legitimization of intrinsic abilities and of well-conducted political labor.

In our judgment, this appropriation of identity for the development of urban products does not seem to be sensitive to the political and shared scope of the city. In addition, a problem is revealed when we think that it is no longer possible to forget the pedagogic dimension of the city as a battlefield where we face a plurality of negotiated situations and opportunities, even when this occurs at the cost of some efficiency. For us, the city is also the place where bodies, objects and spaces are able to take up other arrangements, and it is precisely there that a political dimension lies, one that takes on a much more fragile assessment of concepts such as identity (Ranciere 2009).

A tourist in your own city

We observe, therefore, that despite their virtues it is difficult to find in the *cities-as-product* models thoughts regarding the status that urban realities acquire in their different practices, or regarding the long-term responsibility that they project on the city. As a whole, these models appear to protect the static character of the urban identity through supposedly necessary expert assessments, as well as through exclusive control of management systems, recapitulating a hierarchical vision of learning and of decision making regarding the city, which assumes the inability of the citizens to participate in an active fashion in the configuration of their surroundings. These models of the creation of the city, like those inherited from the modern movement, study the city as one more tourist, ready to consume the city-product that others have thought up and designed.

So as not to fall into these mistakes, we need to advance the idea that the city is a common good that emerges from a multiplicity of singularities that neither the public nor the state construct, but one that is constructed on the margin of both, and whose common belonging should remain guaranteed in the tools that manage and produce it. In our judgment, behind the need to decentralize decision-making regarding the city lies the previously described new political perspective on the city and on the public. This reconsideration would be useful for the reformulation of urban realities as well as of the identities which emerge from them, and would allow for a rethinking of the tourist as a qualified active agent who participates in his/her own way in the debates and controversies of the city and whose interactions are also creative, especially if they are integrated into local networks. If it no longer seems so opportune to think about the city in terms of active producer and passive consumer, neither does it seem appropriate to think about the tourist and the local citizen as irreconcilable and opposing species, seeing that both would be participating in a common production of the city.

For this new approach to urban realities, technologies are contributing sophisticated tools that allow for an understanding of the city as groups of distributed networks, where the systems of decision making do not require unified solutions. For some time now, these changes have been revealing a dismemberment of the creative potential of architecture as a discipline and of architects as producing agents, contemplating as well an active role for a greater number of agents who intervene in the production of the city. It is also from this perspective that the spontaneous character of the domestic acquires a relevance which until recently has gone unobserved. This vital emerging condition of the city is constructed starting with dispersed information originating "at the bottom" that is found in numerous urban practices, compelling institutions to re-describe their roles in the processes of production of reality. Architectural schools, for example, should remodel their methodological catalogues to adapt to new situations, and in reference to that we want to identify the work developed over these last years by several professional groups at the University of Alicante.

In fact we already have numerous examples, which have appeared in the area of the influence of the city of Alicante, which incorporate new information technologies as well as a consideration of the political layout of the city. These examples use the city as a laboratory of experiences where learning and production are woven together, and where stages and participation are inseparable. The *plataforma creativa Arrsa*, for example, proposes to bring to life the utilization of architecture as a catalyzer for the self-construction of society. As they themselves explain, "we use different means and we

fig.5: View of Gran Sol Hotel from inner Alicante. Photograph by the author.
fig.6: View of Gran Sol and Meliá Hotels from the marina esplanade. Photograph by the author.
fig.7: Street of Santa Cruz neighbourhood. Photograph by Ainhoa Martínez Jover.

experiment anew with each project, but ... they all have a commonality: to put in place conversations involving the agents of the process promotor-user-citizen-builder-architect-regulations-systems-infrastructures-materials-institutions-companies blurring the limits which define them" (Arrsa 2010). It is obvious that this change in perspective requires remodeling ways of thinking about the city and of knowing, which explains the appearance of centers for collaborative learning. The *Master DIWO* is one such center, arising due to the need of a group of people to continue training themselves to develop new professional profiles on the margin of official institutions, which appear to have excessively and in an exclusive fashion regulated a common cultural heritage such as the city and learning (Master DIWO 2011). In the same vein, *Espacio Gruyere* offers itself as a transversal confluence where sharing investigations are supported by "environments and processes of work removed from a socioeconomic system in crisis, that permit professionals to move in a friendlier and more fertile environment, open to many more possibilities of professional and personal development" (Espacio Gruyere 2012). Other elements with a strong projection in digital networks like *Alicante Vivo* (Alicante alive), establish effusive relationships between the history of the city and the transformations of the present, explaining the complexity of survival and the need to construct the conflict with participation and negotiation (Alicante Vivo 2007).

In the case of Alicante we are dealing with initiatives that aspire to pay attention to consistent yet open products, alternative ways of reprogramming the use of the city in its attribute as a heterogeneous assemblage, whose long-term objectives are explicit but whose means and instruments are re-described based on the obtained results. Only in this way can the configuring role of the urban reality of cultural initiatives like *Ciudad de la Sombra* or *Donyet Ardid* be understood, something which could very well establish complex relations with the city from audiovisual communication in the first place or from the circus arts or jugglers in the second. In this way, social activism, professional innovation, transgression in the use of the city, etc. show the creative possibilities of urban dissent and of the potential which encloses its anomalous position in the mapping of episodes that take place in the city (Donyet Ardid 2008; Ciudad de la Sombra 2009).

As Manuel Borja-Villel explains, the increase in the benefits of the status of the citizen points to a new institutionalism that recognizes that "the dichotomy between public and private on which social organization has sustained itself for the last century and a half no longer works" (Borja-Villel 2011), since the creative dimension that defines our society is found in both spheres, and institutions are able neither to represent society with exactitude nor adapt to it. Nevertheless, we maintain our confidence that "institutions are the principle structures of the invention of all things social, in an affirmative and not limiting creation. This is more important in our time because in modern western society the art of government does not consist of applying repressive measures, but in keeping them internal" (Ibid. 2011). For that, public administration should advance in the development of new governance that increases the possibilities of interaction with this type of emergence, proposing itself as a type of moderator between different interests, more than aspiring to setting itself up as the sole producer of the city.

Therefore, if what we want is to give continuity to the laboratory character that the Mediterranean condition allocated to the city of Alicante, the challenge for public institutions in charge of the administration of the city, as well as the educational institutions of architects and of different social agents, consists of being capable of rethinking institutions from the perspective of what they have in common. In this way, the citizen will recognize his unconditional status as producer of the city, and in a similar fashion, a new space of opportunity will open for classic tourists to be integrated into the dynamic networks in which their modes of being and of living the city will be recognized as activities charged with meaning, and defining in their full right the urban fact.

Alicante as a case study

This essay brings together such disparate phenomena as spontaneous domestic activism and several global tendencies-turned-industries, such as tourism. In a paradoxical fashion, we have attempted to recognize the *invasive character* that this activism has on the city, as well as the *subversive character* that tourism provides to the planned construction of the city. The main objective was to make a bit more symmetrical the approach to both urban species, and thus recognize their essential creative role, and in passing make apparent the need to contemplate their identifying contributions and their ability to produce the city in a lateral fashion. It is true that the city of Alicante has already been addressed as a case study in numerous investigations involving the Mediterranean city. From its radical present, however, it appears as well to offer itself as a case study favorable enough so that risk finds a technical and politically qualified ally in its public institutions, and in private institutions a producer of heterogeneities open to debate and to producing controversies regarding topics for which we are all responsible. We must recognize these emergences, study them and give them a letter of necessity. It's all about something like that.

Without a doubt the experiential and provocative capability of both realities eludes centralized strategies and requires a mediating role to which we are not very accustomed. Can Alicante become a case study of this type of emergence in such a way as to fully construct a different mapping of citizenship? What type of changes in the management of the city do these models of involvement in our reality anticipate? How do they participate in the production of the identity as a whole of a Mediterranean city like Alicante? Can advanced forms of tourism capable of interacting with the citizenship in a more creative way exist? Is this necessary or at least desirable? What does being a tourist mean in the new social network?

References

Alicante Vivo. 2007. Asociación Cultural Alicante Vivo. Retrieved 15 March 2013. From: http://www.alicantevivo.org/

aRRsa!. 2010. aRRsa! Plataforma Creativa para la reconfiguración de los procesos de construcción del entorno. Retrieved 20 April 2013. From: http://arrsa.org/

Ascher, Francois. 2007. *Examen clinique: Journal d'un hypermoderne*. L'aube: La Tour d'Aigues.

Augé, Marc. 1999. *An anthropology for contemporaneous worlds*. Stanford, California: Stanford University Press.

Bauman, Zygmunt. 2000. *Liquid modernity*. Cambridge: Polity Press.

Borja, Jordi & Castells, Manuel. 1998. *Local y global: la gestión de las ciudades en la era de la información*. Madrid: Taurus.

Borja-Villel, Manuel. 2011. Hacia una nueva institucionalidad. *Revista Carta*. Primavera-Verano. Vol. 2:1–2.

Ciudad de la Sombra. 2009. Ciudad de la Sombra. Retrieved 8 March 2013. From: http://ciudaddelasombra.blogspot.com.es/

Donyet Ardid. 2008. Donyet Ardid. Asociación de malabaristas y Artes Circenses de Alicante. Retrieved 08 July 2013. From: donyetardit.blogspot.com.es

Espacio Gruyere. 2012. eGruyere: Otra forma de trabajar. Retrieved 10 August 2013. From: http://egruyere.net/blog/

Farías, Ignacio. 2011. Urban asssemblages: ANT and the examination of the city. *Athenea Digital - Revista de pensamiento e investigación social*. 11(1):15-40.

Farias, Ignacio & Bender, Thomas. 2010. *Urban assemblages: how actor-network theory changes urban studies*. London; New York: Routledge.

Fundación Metrópoli. 2010. *Fundación Metrópoli. Landscape intelligence: Visions and projects of the Fundación Metrópoli*. Fundación Metrópoli para la Innovación y Diseño del Territorio.

IBM. n.d. IBM-Smarter Planet. Retrieved 30 August 2013. From: http://www.ibm.com/smarterplanet/us/en/overview/ideas/index.html?re=sph.

Master DIWO. 2011. Master DIWO. Retrieved 02 July 2013. From: http://masterdiwo.wikispaces.com/

Mies Van der Rohe Foundation. n.d. Mediterranean Cities Program. Retrieved 14 April 2013. From: http://www.miesbcn.com/en/chair.html

Pérez García, Francisco. 2010. El desarrollo del Arco Mediterráneo español. Trayectorias y Perspectivas. Retrieved 10 March 2013. From: http://www.ivie.es/downloads/2010/10/PP_premio_AME_Ivie_241110.pdf

Ranciére, Jaques. 2009. *El espectador emancipado*. London: Verso.

Revel, Judith. 2011. El dominio de las sombras. *Revista Carta*. Primavera-Verano 2011 Vol. 2:3–5.

Tissat, S.A. 2006. Ciudades Inteligentes. Retrieved 20 July 2013. From: http://www.ciudadesinteligentes.es/ilive/Main

UPC. 2007. Intelligent Coast. Retrieved 18 April 2013. From: http://www.intelligentcoast.org/index.html

Vegara, Alfonso. 2009. *Provincia de Alicante Programa Innovación+Territorio*. Alcobendas, Madrid: Fundación Metrópoli.

The Street:
A Celebration of Transformative Architectural Installations

La calle: una fiesta de instalaciones arquitectónicas transformativas

街路：変移的建築装置の祝賀

Mio Suzuki | 鈴木美央

A menudo parece que en la ciudad actual, puesta a merced de una élite política y empresarial, los ciudadanos han olvidado sus derechos. Quedan sin embargo lugares donde las actividades ciudadanas siguen transformando la forma y el sentido del espacio urbano: las calles, plazas u otros espacios públicos de cualquier ciudad. En este artículo se reflexiona sobre cómo las actividades transforman la ciudad a través de un ejemplo concreto: el grafiti. Esta práctica considerada arte por unos, o un acto antisocial por otros, no deja de generar polémica. Los municipios en general lo rechazan pero los museos y galerías de arte lo tratan como obras de arte y lo exponen en sus salas. Por las diferencias de calidad y las circunstancias particulares, es difícil evaluar unívocamente el impacto urbano del grafiti. En todo caso, cabría destacar el caso del este de Londres donde el grafiti como elemento de identidad local ha logrado un amplio reconocimiento tanto por residentes como por turistas. Otros casos similares de actividades que dejan huellas en espacios urbanos incluyen eventos gestionados municipalmente como mercadillos o festivales, u otras actividades, ilegales o alegales, como la ocupación no autorizada del espacio público para terrazas de bar, o la cultura del patinaje. Cualquiera de estas actividades pueden considerarse acciones arquitectónicas efímeras, pero de un gran dinamismo y poder transformativo. Renovar la ciudad a través de la acumulación de pequeños elementos manipulables y editables por cada individuo permite su transformación continua. Depender únicamente de grandes proyectos de renovación urbana tiene limitaciones en estos tiempos de cambio político-económico cada vez más acelerado. En la medida en que los ciudadanos puedan transformar sus propios espacios urbanos, la ciudad mantendrá su animación, transformándose constantemente y creando lugares atractivos.

現代、都市は一部の政治家や資本家の欲望のままに形成され、都市の住民たちは彼らが本来所有しているはずの権利を忘れてしまっている。しかし、都市の中でも人びとの活動が積極的に都市空間の形態と意味を変容させている場所がある。それはどこにでもある公共空間、街路空間である。街路空間は都市の重要な要素として多くの研究者や設計者が関心を示してきた。ここでは街路空間での人びとの活動が都市を変容させる例としてグラフィティを考察する。街路上の壁面に絵や文字を描くグラフィティは芸術か反社会的行為かという議論を常に生んできた。自治体はグラフィティを地域に悪影響を及ぼすとし排除しようとする一方、美術館やギャラリーは芸術作品として展示を行っている。グラフィティの質や地域の状況が異なるため、グラフィティが都市に与える影響を普遍的に位置づけることは不可能だが、ロンドンでは地域のアイデンティティとして住民、観光客双方に対して一役担っていると考えられる。街路上でのアクティヴィティが集積することにより街路空間に影響を与える同様の例として、合法的に管理されたストリートマーケットや祭り、公共空間の非公式利用として飲食店における席の利用やスケートボーディングなどがあり、これらは可変的な建築行為といえる。このような個人が編集できる小さなエレメントの集積によって都市を更新することは都市の継続的な変化を可能とする。経済、政治など変化が加速する現代において大規模開発のみに依存することには限界があるのではないだろうか。都市の住民自身が個々に都市空間を編集することによって自分たちを満足させる行為が成立すれば、都市は状況に応じて継続的に変化をしながら賑わいが保たれ、魅力的な都市空間が形成されるのではないだろうか。

fig.1: Shutter lettering spread in East London by graffiti artist Ben Eine (London, May 2009). Photographs by Guillermo Álvarez.

Who owns the city? It is neither governments nor developers; it should be you, the citizen. However, we easily forget our rights and responsibility to the city we live in, amongst urban situations shaped by a small political and economic elite after their own desires. David Harvey argues that the "right to the city", first proposed by Henri Lefebvre, is a right to change ourselves by changing the city, and calls it one of the most precious yet most neglected of the human rights (Harvey 2003). Although at present it seems that many of our rights are being dismissed, there is a place where we can find people actively intervening in the city environment and transforming its shape and meaning: the street.

The street

The street has long been recognized as a key element of the city by researchers and urban designers. In the modernist period, when the growing ubiquity of the automobile was becoming evident, Le Corbusier described the old and the new ways of moving through the city as "man's way" and the "pack-donkey's way":

> MAN walks in a straight line because he has a goal and knows where he is going; he has made up his mind to reach some particular place and he goes straight to it. The pack-donkey meanders along, meditates a little in his scatter-brained and distracted fashion, he zigzags in order to avoid the larger stones, or to ease the climb, or to gain a little shade; he takes the line of least resistance. (Le Corbusier 1924)

In his plans for a "Contemporary City of Three Million People", Le Corbusier proposed a grid highway system regulated by straight lines amongst high-rise buildings. Similarly, Ebenezer Howard (1903) designed the Garden city, which included a transportation hub and the densest parts of the city in the center with an outer street network to connect the Garden city to the rest of the nation.

On the building scale, some architects intended streets for people to be elevated within buildings, while keeping streets on the ground for the exclusive use of vehicles. Moisei Ginzburg (1932) designed the Narkomfin Apartment Building in Moscow using interlocking apartment units to allow hallways to be placed at every third level. He named them "street decks", as he saw them as providing a means of social communication. His concept influenced Le Corbusier's utopian city living design as represented by the first Unité d'Habitation built in Marseille in 1945, which was designed to house approximately 1,600 persons with an internal shopping street on the middle level. In the post–World War II era in the UK, Alison and Peter Smithson proposed "streets in the air" in their designs for Robinhood garden, a social housing project in the city of London, and they rigorously separated the pedestrian streets from the ground, a design practice that became popular at the time.

Modern architects abolished the traditional street, but acknowledged its importance by proposing "streets in the air" within buildings. Other researchers and architects, like

Jacobs or Gehl, tried to tackle the topic of the street from a completely different perspective: the importance of the psychological and social aspect of street.

> The functionalists made no mention of the psychological and social aspects of the design of buildings or public spaces. This lack of interest is also evident regarding the public spaces.... Functionalism was a distinctly physically and materially oriented planning ideology. One of the most noticeable effects of this ideology was that streets and squares disappeared from the new building projects and the new cities. (Gehl 1980).

Jane Jacobs emphasized the significance of streets in relation to the safeness of an entire city:

> Think of a city and what comes to mind? Its streets. If a city's streets look interesting, the city looks interesting; if they look dull, the city looks dull. More than that, and here we get down to the first problem, if a city's streets are safe from barbarism and fear, the city is thereby tolerably safe from barbarism and fear. When people say that a city, or a part of it, is dangerous or is a jungle what they mean primarily is that they do not feel safe on the sidewalks. (Jacobs 1961)

The street is also understood as a crucial element in the formation of the identity of city. Kevin Lynch (1960) distilled the physical form of cities into five elements – paths, edges, districts, nodes, and landmarks – and concluded that paths (the streets, sidewalks, trails, and other channels in which people travel) are the most important element in the built environment, arguing that a major street identity is what determines the image of a city. In recent years, with the further globalization of economic activities, the homogenization of shopping streets has become an issue of concern. Major shopping streets are becoming dominated to a significant extent by chainstores, and are losing their distinctive character. The New Economics Foundation, a British think tank, named it "Clone Town" describing it as "The loss of local identity on the nation's high streets" (New Economics Foundation 2005).

The street has also an important role as an interface between the public and private realms, since it is usually a public domain while the space adjacent to it is a private domain. When an interface blurs by someone's behavior or activity, a street starts to be a more dynamic entity which embraces multiple meanings. Robert Venturi (1972), in his famous examination of Las Vegas strip, extended the interface from simple public-private matter into wider discussions: continuity and discontinuity, going and stopping, clarity and ambiguity, cooperation and competition, the community and rugged individualism.

Graffiti

The following reflections were triggered by the research workshop held in Alicante (Spain) in 2012. The results, discussed in detail in Part II of this book, showed a significant difference on the perception of graffiti between local Spaniards and Japanese visitors. Locals considered graffiti to be a form of art, whereas visitors associated them with comments such as "dirty" and "unsafe". These comments reflect feelings of risk and uncertainty, which, as Jan Gehl writes, play a decisive role in a given situation (Gehl 1987).

Here I would like to take the example of graffiti to explore the controversial character of street activities. Graffiti have always provoked arguments over whether they are art or vandalism. Most local authorities argue that graffiti have a major impact on people's perception of crime levels in a community and diminish the local environment, while many established museums and galleries, including Tate Modern, the most visited modern art gallery in the world, welcome graffiti and exhibit them on their walls.

In East London, once one of the city's poorest areas and now at the heart of London regeneration schemes, graffiti seem to be acknowledged by both tourists and locals. Tourists armed with cameras come to see graffiti and locals celebrate them as part of the district's identity. When a new graffiti is put on a wall on a street, people can be seen passing by and enjoying discussions about it. Also, the emergence of celebrity graffiti artists, such as Banksy and ROA, was a major factor accounting for the popularization of graffiti in the area.

Street graffiti possess values that are often neglected. Firstly, they confirm the social importance of the streets, as discussed by the researchers cited earlier. Secondly, graffiti are accessible for everyone. Unlike an art work in a museum, there is no need to go to a designated place and pay an entrance fee. Graffiti can be experienced in daily life just by walking down a street, or may be seen from one's window. Lastly, they spread gradually by stimulating others on a street and evolve through natural selection. It is not necessary to promote this through curators or art institutions, as it happens by itself on the street.

Although graffiti show positive possibilities in many

ways, Hackney Council, a local government in the northwest part of East London, proclaimed zero tolerance for graffiti and "cleaned" many graffiti which have been untouched for years prior to the 2012 Olympics. That triggered another discussion over graffiti in the area, and in BBC interviews a spokesman for Hackney Council stated that "it took time to decide whether something was graffiti or street art which should be preserved" (Cafe 2012). The issue here is who decides, and what criteria should be used to draw that ambiguous line. Controversies that surround graffiti will continue and the implications of graffiti for a city are not easily determined due to their own varying quality and the diversity of the city context. However, one could argue that graffiti contributed to establishing East London's image, together with factors such as the area's lower rents, which attracted young artists and musicians. In the case of East London, the area has now become recognized for fostering leading-edge fashion, arts and design. It is a good example of urban requalification by the emergence of a cluster of street activities and not by planning by developers or architects.

Clusters of street activities

When a certain number of people engage in the same activities repeatedly on a street, it transforms the streetscape and makes it more than a circulation route. It gives a new identity to a street, in other words, an identity is created by the collection of individual activities, small but fundamental elements of a city.

Liberally interpreted, these activities may be classified into two types. One is the organized/controlled cluster of street activity, such as street markets, street parties, and traditional festivals, which are usually organized by governmental bodies or nonprofit organizations. Although they are controlled to some extent by their organizers, and rules are written in regulations, in a practical sense they actually consist of small creative actions by individuals. For instance, street markets in London, popular among both locals and tourists, are administered by local authorities who provide only guidelines and market pitches to the stallers and make sure they follow the rules. However, the actual streetscape, the way commodities are displayed, is created by the stallers. Some stallers bring shelves and tables to put their goods on, while others use the existing built environment, hooking their clothes on a building wall adjacent to their pitch, hanging their necklaces on the spikes of a gate, or placing their records directly on the ground.

From the range of available possibilities, they chose what suits their commodities and the surrounding environment and all together they bring a significant change to streetscape. Therefore this type of street activity is a combination of top-down (administrators providing a framework) and bottom-up (individuals forming the actual streetscape).

The other type is the spontaneous cluster of street activities that includes graffiti, skate boarding, and illegal street catering. This type is less definitive and obvious than the previous type as it tends to be an unofficial use of public space and it appears spontaneously. Although it may involve illegal actions, it may also take on an exceptional role, as can be seen from the example of graffiti in East London. Also in this type, micro-negotiations to avoid conflicts with neighbors can be found. For example, our research in catering establishments setting seats illegally on a public street in Tokyo (Inoue, Suzuki, Almazán 2013), a city where street use is restricted exclusively to circulation use due to legal regulations, shows that shop owners provide elaborate designs of terrace seating to suit local situations. The street is occupied while keeping the width for cars to go through, tables and seats are easily removed if necessary, and seats are set only at night when a street is less busy. This type is a simple bottom-up phenomenon but displays numerous tacitly agreed orders when examined closely.

A key here is that both types, organized or spontaneous, are based on architectural installations located in the street space. These installations include physical forms while having a close relationship with individual activities that change those physical forms. In this sense, we can consider them as architectural installations with a transformative potential.

Transformative architectural installations: smallness, editing, creativity

In cities in developed countries, due to the scarcity of available land and its extremely high prices, new urban development relies on high-density projects, which often means high-rise buildings. In my experience as an architect working for Foreign Office Architects, I have engaged in the design of various large-scale projects, including high-rise buildings and master-planning in the UK, Malaysia, South Korea and Czech Republic. It is obvious that large-scale projects have the potential to transform the city in every aspect. However designing them becomes tricky in practice, as they involve too many factors which

fig.2: Graffiti tour conducted in German on Brick lane, East London (London, September 2013). Photograph by Mio Suzuki

fig.3: Graffiti artist at work (London, May 2009). Photograph by Guillermo Álvarez

keep changing for their own reasons. Even if architects work in good faith to meet the initial requirements, changes come one after another and the proposal can start to lose its meaning and contain discrepancies. This may be considered the nature of architecture. However, the issue becomes more critical in large projects due to their scale, the speed with which those projects appear in the city, and the social responsibilities which they entail.

Rapid change in economic and social structures has been the norm since the start of the modern era, and the common practice of architecture too often relies on aspects which are vulnerable to change. In my opinion, editing city fragments that are small enough for individuals to work on has great potential as a way to modify city environments and keep cities viable. By editing I mean the daily actions taken by a great number of individual in response to social, political, economic and cultural consequences. The edited spaces grow and decay organically and enable the city's metabolism to keep running continuously without subjecting the city to large "shocks". Since this process is a direct reflection of people's creativity, creative people, such as designers and artists, have a significant impact on this process.

Unfortunately at the present time the way most governments deal with urban planning tends to interfere with people's active commitment to city environments. Some urbanists have tried to get citizens involved in urban design, as in the participatory design process, but the results have been far from empowering individuals. If urban policies make full use of citizens' potential and actions, they can become one of the most effective ways to create a better city. This could be a key factor to answer the many issues that urban planning is facing, such as shrinking and aging populations, increasing crime rates, and loss of the sense of community. The day such policies are implemented, there may be a breakthrough and we all may be able to say out loud "we own the city".

References

Cafe, Rebecca. 2012. London 2012: Banksy and street artists' Olympic graffiti. BBC, 24 July. http://www.bbc.co.uk/news/uk-england-london-18946654

Environmental Enforcement, London Borough Of Hackney. 2012. Graffiti. http://www.hackney.gov.uk/ew-graffiti-584.htm#.UhyjcRvJSLU

Gehl, Jan. 1987. *Life Between Buildings*. Translated by Jo Koch. New York: Van Nostrand Reinhold.

Harvey, David. 2003. *The Right to the City*. International Journal of Urban and Regional Research. Vol. 27.4:939-41.

Howard, Ebenezer. 1903. *Garden Cities of To-morrow*. Gloucester: Dodo Press. 1898.

Inoue, Gaku, Mio Suzuki and Jorge Almazán. 2013. A Study on the Spatial Characteristics and the Actual Usage of Street Terrace Seating (in Japanese). AIJ Journal of Technology and Design, Vol. 19, No. 42:699–704.

Jacobs, Jane. 1961. *The Death and Life of Great American Cities*. New York: Random House.

Le Corbusier. 1924. *The City of To-morrow and Its Planning*. New York: Dover Publications.

Lynch, Kevin. 1960. *The Image of the City*. Cambridge: MIT Press.

New Economics Foundation. 2005. *Clone Town Britain: The loss of local identity on the nation's high streets*. London.

Venturi, Robert, Denise Scott Brown and Robert Izenour. 1972. *Learning from Las Vegas*. Cambridge: MIT Press.

fig. 4: Street transformation: Columbia road flower market (London, September 2013)
fig. 5: Fresh vegetable from just outside London: Battersea market (London, September 2013). Photographs by Mio Suzuki and Gaku Inoue

Toward Building A "Healthy" and Sustainable Urban Identity

Hacia una identidad urbana "saludable" y sostenible
"健全"で持続可能なアイデンティティの構築に向けて

Yukino Tairako | 平子雪乃

Como concepto de la psicología el término identidad no se refiere a la individualidad personal determinada por una serie de características objetivas, sino a la conciencia individual que surge como resultado de la acción conjunta de los puntos de vista subjetivo – la autopercepción – y objetivo – las expectativas y la aprobación sociales. Desde la perspectiva de la psicología una identidad saludable emergería por tanto de un proceso de integración tanto de la autopercepción como de la realidad social. El mismo principio sería aplicable a la identidad de una ciudad, que deberá determinarse adecuadamente en relación con su contexto, Es decir, no debe haber demasiada discrepancia entre las evaluaciones internas y externas sobre esa ciudad.

En principio, la identidad de la ciudad se desarrolla con naturalidad a lo largo de su historia. Sin embargo, los grandes cambios sociales de las últimas décadas han transformado drásticamente su fisonomía y han provocado rupturas y confusiones en la identidad urbana existente. Este proceso no debe entenderse solamente como una "crisis de identidad", sino también como una oportunidad para obtener una nueva identidad y un incentivo para su desarrollo. ¿Qué proceso debe seguir una ciudad para reconstruir una identidad sostenible y "saludable"? Para explorar posibles respuestas, llevamos a cabo un taller con residentes y visitantes en la ciudad de Alicante. A través de una serie de cuestionarios comparamos los puntos de vista subjetivo-interno (la percepción de los residentes) y el objetivo-externo (la evaluación por parte de visitantes). El resultado se llevó más tarde a una serie de debates donde confluyeron e interactuaron ambos puntos de vista. Este entrecruzamiento de miradas ha mostrado una nueva imagen urbana y con posibilidades de contribuir a reinventar una identidad para la ciudad de Alicante.

心理学の領域におけるアイデンティティという概念は、客観的な特徴によって規定されるひとりの人間の個性ではなく、本人の自己認識という主観的視点と社会からの期待や是認という客観的視点の両方が作用して成立するその人らしさの認識である。健全なアイデンティティを構築するためには、個人の主観的視点と社会的現実とを統合していく過程が必要とされる。同様に、都市におけるアイデンティティについても、その都市アイデンティティが周辺地域との関係性の中に適切に位置づけられ、内部評価と外部評価の間に大きな齟齬がないことが重要であろう。本来、都市アイデンティティは長い歴史の中で自然に醸成されていくものである。しかし近年では急激な社会変化が都市の姿を大きく変え、既存の都市アイデンティティの崩壊や混乱が容易に生じ得るようになった。それは都市にとって危機であると同時に、新しい都市アイデンティティを獲得し、発展を促すための好機でもある。アイデンティティの危機に陥った都市が健全で持続可能なアイデンティティを再構築するためには、どのような過程を経ることが望ましいのだろうか。それを模索する試みとして、アリカンテ市において内部の主観的視点（住民の認識）と外部の客観的視点（訪問者の評価）を調査し、その上で双方の視点の相互作用が生じる場を設け、都市の価値を再発見することを目的としたワークショップを行った。この住民側と訪問者側の視点の相互作用を通して得られた知見は、これまでにない新しい都市の姿を反映するものであり、今後、アリカンテ市の都市アイデンティティの再構築に貢献できる可能性があるだろう。

Identity in psychology

*Identit*y is a concept that arose from theories on the life cycle of individuals. Originally it was a term referring to the developmental tasks of individuals in their youth when they are asking such questions as "Who am I?", "Where am I going in life?", and "What are the meanings of my life?", and ultimately finding ways to answer the above-mentioned questions with affirmation and conviction. It later came to be applied more widely to explain various psychosocial situations, and used with reference to groups such as states, nationalities, and professions. In such cases, to simplify, it is often used to denote a recognition of what makes the person (or the group) distinctive.

In defining a person's identity, there are three criteria of the self: *sameness*, *continuity*, and *belongingness* (Nakanishi 1985). *Sameness* refers to the sense that "this person existing here has certain invariable qualities, when seen from both the viewpoint of that person and of others." Although various aspects of that person may emerge at various times, depending on the situation, it is desirable to be able to sustain an unwavering image of what is essential about oneself. *Continuity* is the sense that "who I have been, who I am and who I will be continue to constitute the same person". While growing up and getting older, a person may experience changes in physical condition and social status, but it is important to feel that one is essentially the same person. *Belongingness* is the sense that "I belong in some way to a social group, and I feel concord with that group". This sense is supported when the individual takes up an expected role in the society, and that role is recognized positively by others. A well-established identity, according to the definition described above, can be expressed in plain terms as follows. The person in question believes that "this is the kind of person that I am, and this is what makes me different from other people"; as for the present self which continues from the past, and for the person he or she will become in the future, the person thinks "I am comfortable being me" and is confident that "I will be able to get by as myself" and has a sense of self-efficacy, thinking that "I am accepted as who I am by others" and "my life in society is meaningful". Furthermore, others accept and value the individual with the kind of self-awareness described above as a member of the social group.

While terms like "individuality" and "characteristic" are used to speak objectively about the qualities of a person, as they can be used to describe a certain person as "that kind of person", the concept of identity includes both subjective and objective views of a person, i.e. how one feels about oneself subjectively and how those around a person objectively perceive that person. For example, an objective evaluation of a person as competent by someone else does not suffice to constitute an identity. It is not until it gets combined with the self-perception that "I am competent", the will that "I want to be competent", and the value judgment that "competence is an important and desirable characteristic" that it finds a place in the person's identity. In other words, what is most notable about the concept of identity is that it is formed in an intersubjective domain that includes both the person in question and society, through interactions between objective and subjective evaluations of the individual.

Erik Erikson, who proposed the concept of identity, describes the state of having acquired a sense of identity as follows: a sense of being "all right", and a sense of being oneself, a sense of becoming what other people trust one will become (Erikson 1959). Erikson stressed that the foundation for acquiring this sense is acquisition of the basic trust that develops in the infantile years and the experience of mutuality with a caregiver. Basic trust means that the infant feels confident that his or her bodily organs are functioning well and that he or she will continue to exist, making various adjustments. This confidence is acquired through the experience of a caregiver who is alert to the infant's needs and provides appropriate care and comfort. During this period, the question of whether or not this experience is supported by the confidence that the caregiver is trusted within a social framework has a great influence. Basic trust is supported and nurtured by manifold social relations surrounding the infant. On this foundation of basic trust, which is acquired in the earliest stages of development, the child acquires a sense of *autonomy*, *initiative*, and *industry*, and, in the last stage before becoming an adult, takes up the challenge of establishing an identity. During this period, adolescents are placed in a situation called a "psychosocial moratorium", in which they are temporarily free from real social obligations and find niches in some sections of their society through free role experimentation. They gradually establish their identities while repeating this process, in which they try out a role in their actual social lives, adjust the role according to feedback from others, and then try it again. Finally this sense of identity is confirmed when an individual discovers a point where one's real-life self and one's future self are in concord with the expectations of society. Erikson emphasizes that identity is closely related to social reality. For the establishment of a healthy identity, the real-life conditions and social expectations that surround the individual and the process of mutual interaction to integrate the two should be considered significant, instead of focusing only on the subjective feelings and hopes of the individual.

Urban identity

How can we apply this concept of identity to cities? Let us imagine a city with a "healthy" identity, based on the three criteria of *sameness*, *continuity*, and *belongingness*. Then we can say the following.

First, with respect to *sameness*, it can be imagined that people recognize the distinctive character of the city in

fig.1: Reading the questionnaires.

fig.2: Making cards.

comparison with other cities, and share one image which integrates various aspects of the city. For example, it may be a situation in which most of the residents believe that "We live in a city by the sea that has a vibrant, open atmosphere." Next, with respect to *continuity*, the city as it exists today should be an extension of the city's history and traditions. Though the city's appearance might change over time, it is desirable to retain elements that remind one of its history and traditions throughout the cityscape, and desirable for the process of how the newer elements have accumulated and layered over the then-existing city and have eventually led to the current city to be observable. In contrast, cities that have experienced widespread destruction of the cityscape by war, disasters or large-scale redevelopment may lose touch with their history and traditions and may be expected to face difficulties in maintaining continuity. Finally, with respect to *belongingness*, we can imagine an urban identity in harmony with the context of the surrounding region. It is preferable that both residents of the city and outsiders have an affirmative view of the urban identity, and, as a precondition for that, for there to be no be major discrepancies between how the urban identity is seen by residents and how it is evaluated and what is further expected of it by outsiders. For example, residents might think that "We live in a city by the sea that has a vibrant, open atmosphere" and take pride in it, while outsiders agree with this favorable view. On the other hand, if visitors from the outside find the city cold and unwelcoming, then that gap must be resolved. Otherwise, fewer and fewer people might visit the city and the tourism industry might decline, without people on the inside knowing why.

The point to emphasize here is that the healthy urban identity described above does not have a simple diagram in which the subjective viewpoint from inside the city (the image of the residents) develops separately from the objective viewpoint from outside the city (the evaluation and expectations of outsiders), with no problems arising when they happen to agree and problems arising when they do not agree. During the process of the identity of a city being established, or the process of it being modified over time, it is important for the process to be mutual, with the urban identity being formed under the influence of both inside and outside viewpoints. The gap described above does not arise when an identity develops naturally over the years through interactions between inside and outside. However, an identity that is formed arbitrarily on the basis of a limited viewpoint will often lead to friction with various elements around it. The degree to which interactions between inside and outside contribute to identity formation is an important factor in establishing a healthy identity.

Identity crisis

Erikson discussed several problems that represent crises in the development stages where individuals acquire identities (Erikson 1968). They include *identity diffusion*, when a clear identity cannot be established; *identity confusion*, when a person's ideas about the self are fragmentary and cannot be integrated into a consistent identity; and the *choice of the negative identity*, when an individual adopts values that expose the individual to danger or chooses a role that is unacceptable to society. When an individual falls into a state of *identity diffusion* or *identity confusion*, the individual experiences feelings of uncertainty, such as "I no longer know what kind of person I really am" or "I don't know what to aim for from now on", falling into a state of ambivalence and disorientation without any guidance for deciding what to say or do in daily life. In that state, social activities such as selecting an occupation and engaging with others become

fig.3: Categorizing and titling.

fig.4: Formulating and connecting.

provisional and fall short of their potential productivity. For the individual to enjoy a stable and productive life in society, it is necessary to establish a consistent identity, whatever that may be. Conversely, the *choice of the negative identity* manifests itself in various forms, such as alcoholism, delinquency, and membership in anti-social groups, and the individual may engage in self-harmful behavior or experience a wavering identity due to the lack of recognition from society. This choice of the negative identity is a somewhat extreme example. However, given that the concept of identity includes the elements of recognition from others and agreement with social reality, problems of some sort are likely to arise when there are significant discrepancies between an identity embraced by an individual and the objective evaluations of others. Erikson says that the sense of identity is strengthened by the recognition of real accomplishments that have meaning in their culture (Erikson 1959). In other words, a prerequisite for the establishment of a stable identity is a certain degree of agreement between subjective perception and objective evaluation, and furthermore the recognition given by others has great significance.

These crises are especially commonly observed among adolescents, who undergo substantial bodily changes and mental maturation. They come to notice that they are no longer the same persons they were in their childhood, and search for answers to questions such as "Who am I really like?" and "How should I live from now on?" Finding answers to those questions while creating a new self-image is a life cycle challenge that they must face. It can be experienced as a crisis or uncertainty, but it also can be a creative process that embraces possibilities for growth and development. This is applicable not only to adolescence but also the entire life span: people continue to grow throughout their lives, responding to changes in their social position or the surrounding environment by rebuilding their identities. Indeed, a crisis can arise in the opposite case, when an identity is too rigid and inflexible. A certain degree of stability can be maintained by solidly defending an established identity, but friction with others is likely to increase because it cannot respond to changes in the environment. Holding fast to this kind of inflexible identity means to shut out all possibility for growth and development.

Because identity is a concept that includes mutuality between the self and society, it is continually under the influence of the surrounding environment. It is natural for conditions in the real world to change from moment to moment, which means that the identity of an individual must also make fine adjustments according to changes in the outer world. To use the metaphor of building materials, hard materials like stone and steel are strong but lack flexibility. For that reason, they collapse suddenly when subjected to a force that they cannot withstand. But flexible materials like wood and bamboo can change their shape when subjected to a force and thus relieve the pressure. The shape may change, but it is rarely lost completely, and it can return to the original shape when the pressure is removed. In the same way, the solider and more inflexible an identity is, the more vulnerable it is to change and the greater the danger of falling into identity diffusion due to some unforeseen event. When a change occurs in the surroundings, the gap between a solidly defended identity and the evaluation and expectations of others may gradually increase, leading to maladjustment.

In biology there is a concept called "dynamic equilibrium". At the microscopic physical level, organisms are always in a dynamic state, continually engaged in a process of breaking down and regeneration, altering components. But since the changes are very small compared to the size of the human body, the organism as a whole appears to maintain the same shape and functions

(Fukuoka, 2007). As no person lives completely alone, and no city is completely isolated from its surroundings, they cannot passively continue to have fixed identities with no changes at all. Rather, to maintain stability in a world where everything is changing, it is better to continually make small changes amid countless interactions with the surroundings. In other words, if a stable identity is desired, it must be flexible and premised on the ability to keep changing.

Identity crisis in the city

Until fairly recently, the identity of a city was fostered naturally on the basis of the history and traditions of a region, and passed down as such. However, advances in architectural technology and easy access to standard materials have led to uniform cityscapes, while increasing diversity in the lifestyles of residents has widened the range of activities in a city. There is a wider range of choices in urban design, so that cities can develop in any direction that is desired. To put it another way, cities must re-select their identities autonomously. Also, the ebb and flow of people and things in contemporary society has accelerated, raising the possibility of sudden major changes. When a major change occurs in a city, it may be difficult for the city to maintain its traditionally established identity, and rebuilding of the identity of the city will be required. But if the change is too large and too sudden, the process of forming a new identity may not be able to keep up, raising the danger of identity confusion. Similar to an individual suffering from identity confusion, the city falls into a state of confusion without a clear sense of self or vision for the future, and the city's sense of cohesion may collapse. On the other hand, if the city stubbornly holds fast to its former identity while the surrounding society keeps on changing, it is likely to result in friction between that inflexible identity and the surroundings. The city may well lose its chance to develop and be left behind by contemporary society. In this way, changes in a city and its surroundings can lead to an identity crisis for that city.

While identity confusion is a crisis, it is also an opportunity to gain a new identity and to develop. If it is possible to reevaluate and rebuild the city's identity in a way that agrees with current circumstances, it may be possible to create a new way of being, one that would not have been available only as an extension of simply maintaining the traditional identity.

As Alicante, the city focused on, has developed as a tourist destination, architecture and a lifestyle attuned to the needs of tourists have become controversial, with a gap emerging between the evaluation and expectations of outsiders and the image of the city held by its residents. If Alicante embraced the viewpoint from within and affirmed an identity solely in line with the wishes of the residents, it would become an exclusionary city and suffer friction with the tourism industry. Tourism is a vital industry, and losing it would be an immeasurable setback. This problematic situation could be precipitated by an attempt to maintain an inflexible identify. On the other hand, if an attempt is made to encourage the tourism industry by adopting policies that cater only to the needs of visitors, the traditions of the city and the dissatisfaction of the residents will be omitted, leaving only a superficial identity that lacks a foundation. Like a floating flower with no roots to the ground, this kind of identity is liable to be swept away with the slightest change in the wind. Reliance on this kind of superficial identity raises the risk of falling into identity confusion when conditions change again. What Alicante needs now is an identity that will be sustainable over the long term even in the face of change, one that is rooted in existing foundations – the traditions of the city and its residents – while at the same time responding to the needs of tourists from the outside.

Rebuilding an identity

To approach the question of rebuilding an identity, let's start by considering the process of identity formation. As an identity is built up over many years of life experiences, the entire process cannot be considered here. Instead, the focus will be on a recurring theme, namely mutual engagement between the self (interior) and society (exterior).

As described earlier, the process of identity formation requires an interior subjective viewpoint, an exterior objective viewpoint, and engagement between the two. The objective aspect of the identity is determined by assessing oneself objectively and comparing oneself to others. That comparison reveals a certain individuality, something that is clear to all, and makes up part of the identity. It is close to what is expressed by the concepts of "individuality" or "characteristic." However, an identity is not complete only with this kind of objectively obtained information. It requires another half, namely information acquired subjectively: in the form of questions such as what I think of myself, how I want to present myself to others, and what kind of person I want to become. Introspective reflection on our inner lives proves meaningful in acquiring this type of information. Ultimately, when integrating the objective viewpoint from outside with the subjective viewpoint from inside, work needs to be done in the intersubjective domain between the two. A healthy and sustainable identity is established only through relatedness with entities such as society and culture, and also with mutual engagement with others.

More specifically, a person searching for his or her identity goes through the following process. First, he or she gathers objective information about his or herself, compares the self to others, and looks for something original and noticeable about the self. Then, while referring to feedback from others about his or her words or actions, he or she explores how he or she is perceived by others. Alternatively, sometimes direct feedback and opinions from others help him or her come to see aspects that had not been noticed before. At the same time, he or she also needs to spend time exploring internal subjective senses, thinking about the future: "What kind of person do I want to become?", and "What do I want others to think of me?" After gathering all this information, it is time to compare notes and ask once more, "What kind of person am I?" For example, he or she may say, "Personally, I don't think I am good at talking with others", but "A friend of mine says I am easy to talk to." Looking back, perhaps he or she realizes that there were actually not many occasions when a conversation stalled and became awkward. On the basis of that information, he or she might adjust his or her self-image to think "I am not good at talking with others, but I am not bad at it either", or perhaps, even more precisely, "I am not a good talker, but I am a good listener." In this way, one forms an identity by gathering various kinds of information from the inside and outside viewpoints and considering how to fit it all together, in a process that is repeated unconsciously over and over. The process of rebuilding an identity is the same.

A similar process is necessary when rebuilding the identity of a city as well. The subjective viewpoint from the inside is the image of the city held by its residents, and the objective viewpoint from outside is the evaluation and expectations of visitors. It is advisable to gather information from both viewpoints, compare notes, and finally, amid mutual interactions, put them all together in a single image of the city. The purpose of the workshop that we conducted in Alicante was precisely to actualize one aspect of this process of reconstructing an identity. It was structured in two stages, with individual fieldwork followed by group discussions: an attempt to pick up the different viewpoints of residents and visitors and, through direct interactions, to integrate them.

Construction of an urban identity and methods used in the workshop

The methodology and the results of this workshop will be described in detail in will be described in detail in Part II of this book. Here I would like to discuss the methodology and the contribution it can make to Alicante's identity.

As described earlier, two viewpoints are required in the process of forming an identity: the subjective viewpoint from the inside and the objective viewpoint from the outside. In other words, to establish the identity of Alicante, two approaches are needed: an approach oriented toward gathering information from the inside, by clarifying the image of the city held by residents; and an approach oriented toward gathering information from the outside, by investigating the image of the city held by non-resident visitors.

In the first stage of the method used in this workshop, participants were asked to walk around the city individually and to report on places that, in their judgments, were "good places" or "bad places". Information was recorded by filling out questionnaires on the spot that were distributed in advance, and also attaching photos. The main purpose of this stage was to record explicit data for the inside and outside viewpoints, including data which up to then had not been consciously recognized. Residents were represented by Spanish students, whose data reflected the subjective viewpoint from inside. Visitors were represented by Japanese students, whose data reflected the objective viewpoint from outside. The survey framework and question items were designed to extract the subjective evaluations and impressions of the participants in a form that was as pure as possible. Photographs were used as supplementary objective information. The use of a common framework such as questionnaires was one technique that facilitated the collection and comparison of individual evaluations and impressions. In particular, the semantic differential method (SD method) is an effective way to convert vague impressions, intuitions, and moods into objective data, as the overall quantitative evaluation of multiple adjectives. At the same time, the answers to this questionnaire served as a preparation for the discussions of the second stage, because while answering the questions the participants needed to verbalize their vague feelings, comparing and making connections between their inner feelings and intuitive impressions and information about the outer world and features of the place. This is important because knowledge becomes available for use in discussions and the process of thinking and judgment only when verbalized and stored in the form of verbal data.

At the point when the first stage ended, inner and outer viewpoints still existed separately, and simply gathering their data together will not result in the rebuilding of a healthy identity. What is more important in the formation of identity is in the next stage. In this second stage, the Spanish and the Japanese students conducted group discussions on several themes, using material from the evaluations and impressions gathered by individuals in the first stage. The reason why discussions were incorporated here is that they represent the interaction between inner and outer that occurs during the formation of an identity. During this process of comparing the inside and outside viewpoints and achieving a mutual understanding of judgment criteria and the reasoning behind the evaluations, new viewpoints and judgment standards were born, none of which had been discovered in the first stage by either the Spanish or the Japanese students. They were discoveries that could be made only through mutual interaction.

The first discussion was about "good places" and "bad places". The participants were instructed to create affinity diagrams based on the KJ method (Kawakita 1996) to sort their features into logical groups. This work revealed correlations between elements that could become criteria of judgment for "good" or "bad", and helped to visualize the differences in viewpoint between the Spanish and the Japanese students. At the same time, it helped to organize ideas and think about the final issues. One characteristic of the KJ method is that it is a bottom-up approach that can organize knowledge based on the actual information gathered in the first stage of on-site research. This method makes it possible to obtain knowledge rooted in actual data that reflects real conditions in the city. Another characteristic of this method is that the data is organized cooperatively, so that knowledge is produced only when all participants reach a consensus. In the case of this workshop, it was important to avoid bias toward the viewpoint of either the resident Spanish students or the visiting Japanese students. In that respect, it was an appropriate method for the purpose.

The task posed to each group was to examine the places selected by individuals in the first stage, to identify places selected as "good places" and "bad places" by the Spanish students, to identify places selected as "good places" and "bad places" by the Japanese students, and finally to discover places that would be "good places" for both. By sharing their viewpoints, they were able to recognize differences in the places selected as "good" and "bad", and to recognize the differences in their standards for judgment. On that basis, they were able to look for things that both sides could agree upon. This process could be said to correspond precisely to the mutual interaction that is so important in the process of identity formation. Those places that were finally selected as "good places" by both sides should serve as clues for establishing an identity for Alicante that will include both inside and outside viewpoints.

Toward building a "healthy" and sustainable urban identity

As described up to this point, an identity is based on both a subjective viewpoint and social reality, and whether it is that of an individual or a city, an identity is formed through mutual interaction with the surrounding society. When a city is facing an identity crisis and striving to rebuild its identity, two things need to happen. First, it should conduct research into the subjective and objective viewpoints from inside and outside, such as the image of the city held by its residents and the evaluation and expectations of visitors. Second, it should create a forum to integrate those two viewpoints. When this is done, it is important that inside and outside viewpoints are grounded on reality. In other words, they should reflect the actual state of the city and real-life opinions to the best extent possible. When integrating the viewpoints identified in the research, it is desirable that a forum should be provided for mutual interaction between the viewpoints, instead of simply juxtaposing the data. It is knowledge obtained through repetitions of this kind of organic process that will provide the foundation for rebuilding a healthy and sustainable urban identity.

The various types of information obtained by the methods used in this workshop – including the features of the city of Alicante, differences in the viewpoints of the Spanish and the Japanese students, and places selected by both as "good places" with their reasons for selecting them – are insights obtained from a small sample, and they on their own merits alone cannot be regarded as conclusive for a new identity for the city of Alicante. Nevertheless, insofar as they consider not only the viewpoint of residents of Alicante but also that of visitors from outside, the insights obtained here have something new to offer. The fact that they were obtained through a process that satisfies the necessary conditions for the formation of a healthy and sustainable identity – gathering

fig. 5: Completed diagram.

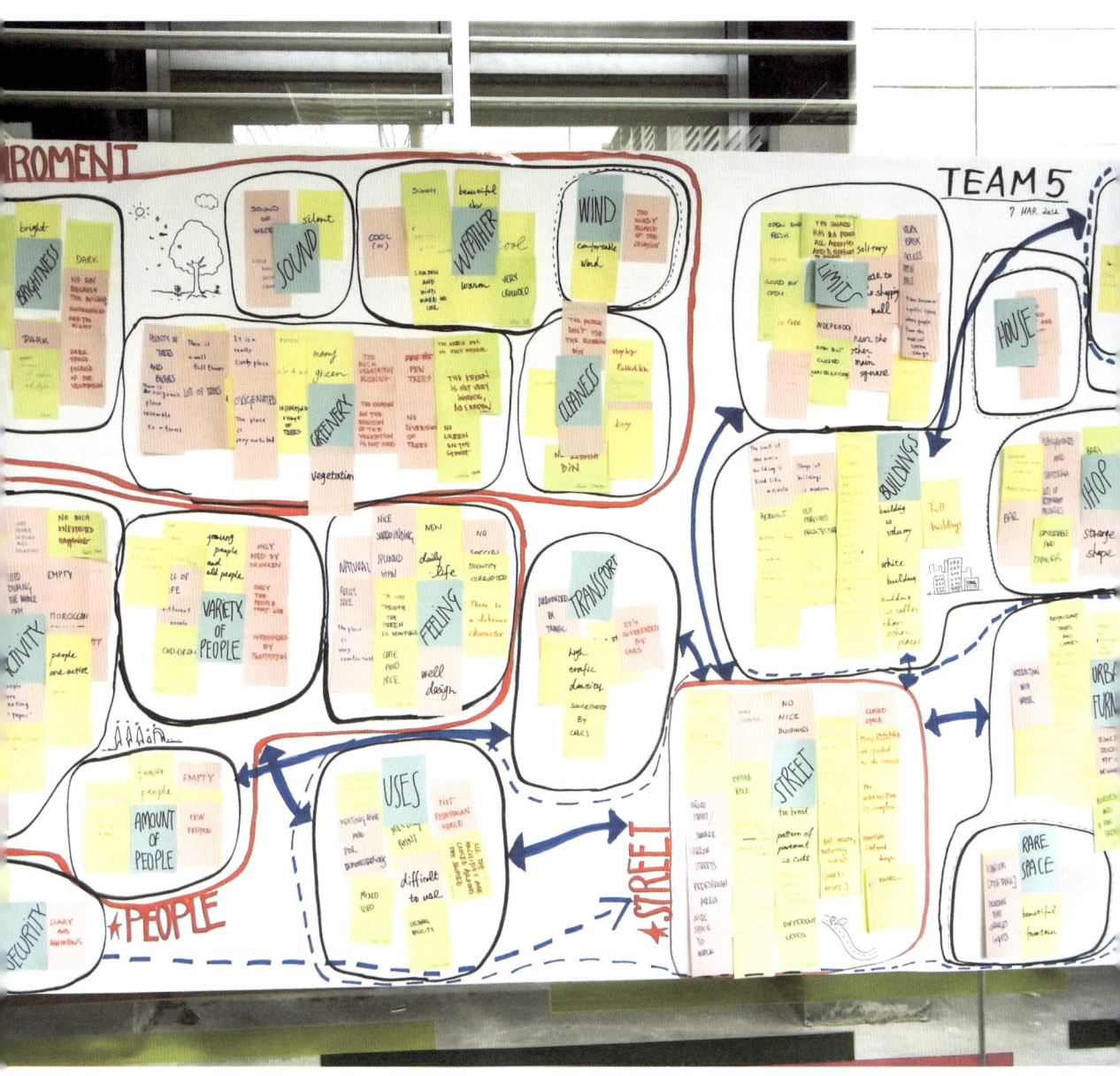

information rooted in reality, clarification of inside and outside viewpoints, and searching for new ideas through interactions between these viewpoints – is what gives these insights their greatest significance. Rather than a simple collection of facts or armchair theorizing, the results of this workshop are living knowledge obtained by walking the streets and engaging in face-to-face discussions. We hope that they can contribute something to the future development of the city of Alicante.

References

Erikson, E. H. 1959. *Identity and the Life Cycle*. International Universities Press.

Erikson, E. H. 1968. *Identity Youth and Crisis*. W. W. Norton & Company.

Fukuoka, Shin-Ichi. 2007. *Seibutsu to museibutsu no aida* [Between the inanimate and biological]. Kodansha Gendaishinsho.

Kawakita, Jiro. 1996. *KJ hou: Konton wo shite katarashimeru* [KJ method: creating ideas from chaos]. Vol.5 of Kawakita Jiro Collected Works. Chuokoronsha.

Nakanishi, Nobuo; Masanori Mizuno; Koichi Furuichi; Akihiko Sakata. 1985. *Identity no shinri* [The psychology of identity]. Yuhikakusensho.

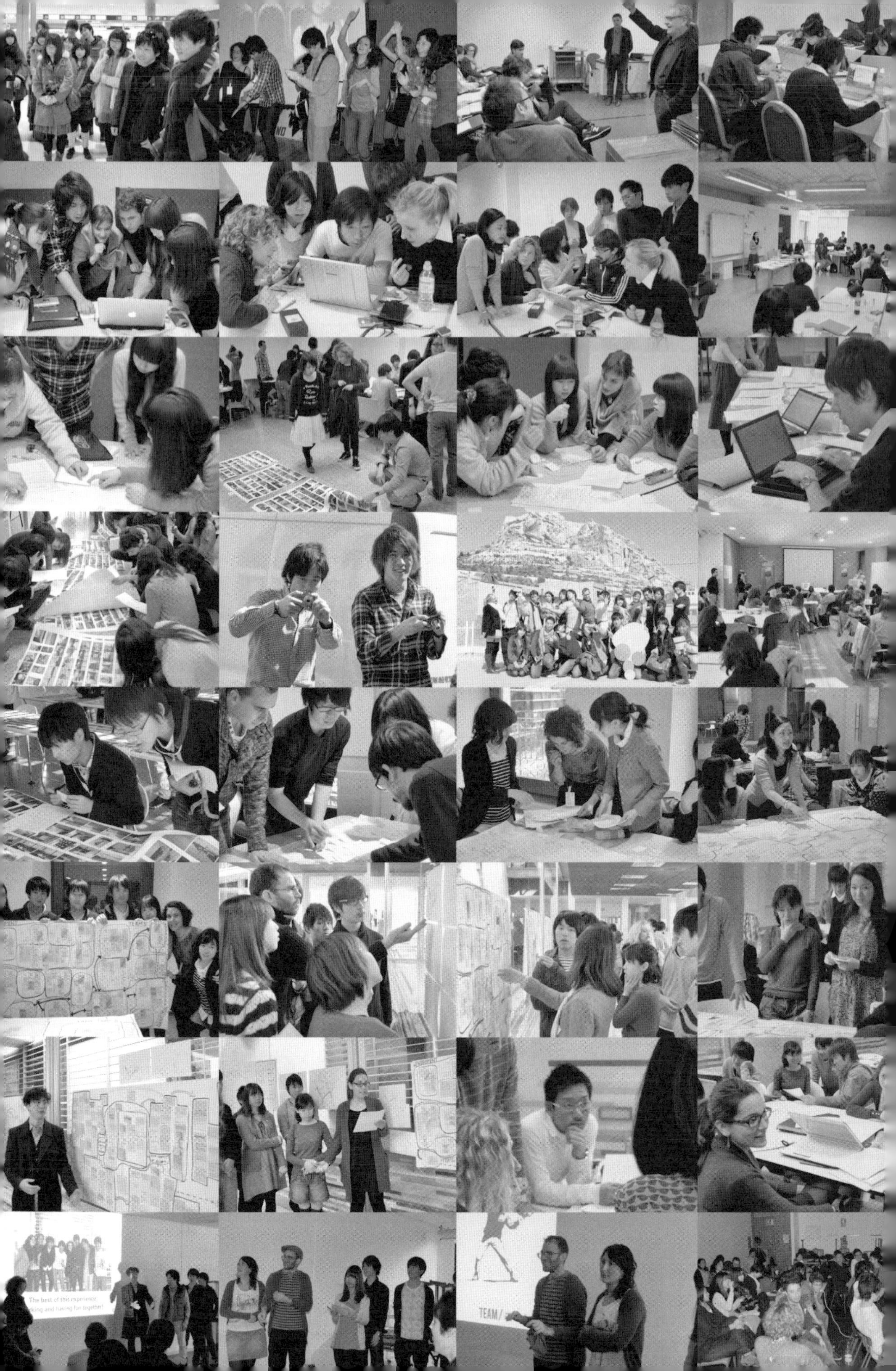
The best of this experience:
and having fun together!
TEAM /

PART II
URBAN EXPERIMENT
EXPERIMENTO URBANO
都市的実験

Collective Urban Drift

Deriva urbana colectiva
集団的都市の漂流

Jorge Almazán, Mio Suzuki, Yukino Tairako, Shun Kawakubo, Gaku Inoue
ホルヘ・アルマザン、鈴木美央、平子雪乃、川久保 俊、井上 岳

La competencia entre ciudades con el fin de atraer visitantes conlleva a menudo una pérdida de la identidad local y un deterioro de la calidad urbana para los residentes. Este estudio explora la identidad urbana de la ciudad de Alicante a través de una investigación intercultural que compara las opiniones de residentes españoles y visitantes japoneses. Los resultados, obtenidos mediante trabajo de campo y encuestas, sugieren una serie de cualidades concretas para evaluar el espacio público. Algunas de ellas relacionadas con el trasfondo cultural (por ejemplo la "limpieza" para los japoneses, o el "colorido" para los residentes), otras relacionadas con el nivel de familiaridad con la ciudad (como la "comodidad" para los residentes), y finalmente cualidades como la "vitalidad" que parecen tener un fuerte atractivo intercultural. La pérdida de identidad urbana es un problema que debe abordarse desde múltiples perspectivas. En el caso de Alicante, la animación y vitalidad en las calles, como cualidad que claramente valoraron tanto los residentes como los visitantes de este estudio, puede ser un factor decisivo para reforzar el atractivo de la ciudad sin deteriorar el entorno cotidiano de los residentes.

観光客にとって魅力的であろうとする都市同士の競争は場所のアイデンティティの損失や現地住民にとっての都市空間の質の低下に繋がることがしばしば見受けられる。本研究は現地住民と観光客の見解の比較を目的にアリカンテ市の都市アイデンティティを日本人とスペイン人による異文化間調査によって探求する。結果、都市空間の一般的な質は文化的背景によるように見られるもの（日本人にとっての清潔感、スペイン人にとってのカラフルさなど）、その場所に対する精通の度合いによるもの（現地住民にとっての利便性など）、そして生き生きとした様といった質では文化を横断して強い魅力があるといったことが示された。フィールドワークでのマッピングやアンケートシートの記入を通じて得られたこれらの結果は、アリカンテ市のアイデンティティを再考する上で示唆に富む有益なものであり、現地住民にとっても旅行者にとっても質の高い満足のいく都空間を形成していく上でも参考になるものと期待される。

1. Outline

This study aims to identify public spaces, their general qualities, and the reasons why those qualities are preferred over others in the study case of Alicante. In particular, we aim to understand differences in preference between locals and visitors, in this case, from Japan. The study follows a circular process of evaluation in two phases. In the first phase – *Collective Urban drift* – Japanese and locals visited the city and registered their impressions individually. In the second phase – *Cross-cultural Debates* – they discussed the commonalities and differences in their impressions through a group discussion method, and they chose spaces based on those discussions, reconnecting the reasoning back to actual urban spaces.

The first phase is a quantitative study based on questionnaires and statistic analysis. It records individual opinions and the focus is on abstract qualities – both negative and positive. The second phase, on the contrary, is a qualitative study, based on group discussions. It records opinions of Spanish-Japanese mixed groups and the focus is on specific places – with an emphasis on positive or good characteristics.

2. Purpose

The aim of the first phase is for local Spaniards and Japanese visitors to respond to three questions: 1) *which places are good and bad*, 2) *which external tangible elements make those spaces good or bad*, and 3) *which internal feelings make that space good or bad*. Finally, the aim is to compare the results between both groups of respondents (local and visitors). This investigation does not claim to clarify cultural differences, nor to extract definitive conclusions on Alicante. Rather, cultural difference is used as a tool for reflection, a way to make partially explicit some trends in our perception of the city which might not be entirely subjective, but collectively and culturally driven.

3. Methodology

The two groups, local Spaniards and visiting Japanese, completed a questionnaire survey on 5 March 2012 while walking freely in the central areas of Alicante for half a day (Table 1). Participants were asked to choose and register their impressions about urban public spaces, as defined in next section. This method combines several methodological references. The most important is the situationists' drift and their psycho-geographies. In a more scientific way, the method was also inspired by the quantitative investigations applied to cases in Japan in which participants freely chose urban spaces and landscapes (Tabata and Nishide 2007, Yamamoto et al. 2005, and Oishi et al. 2007). In a qualitative way, Sepe (2009) also performed similar fieldwork in Barcelona. The methodological originality of the present study lies in its combination of several methods used separately in the above-mentioned studies, and especially, combined with a cross-cultural comparative approach.

Table 1: Survey outline and sample number

Survey period	5 Mar. 2012, 12:30 to 20:00 approximately, cloudless sky		
Respondents	University students (average age for Japanese: 20.4 years old; for Spaniards: 25.1 years old)		
Methodology	Field survey (respondents were encouraged to answer the questionnaire for more than 6 urban spaces)		
Sample number (Num. of students)	Total: 43 students. 24 Japanese students (15 males, 9 females) and 19 Spanish students (6 males, 13 females)		
Samples number	'Bad' places	'Both' Places	'Good' places
Japanese	61	21	82
Spaniards	49	23	56
Total per category	110	44	138
Total	**292** (Average number of responses: 6.7/respondent)		

4. Object of survey: public space

Participants were asked to find *urban public space* within the five central districts of Alicante. The five sectors correspond with the geographical, historical and tertiary centre of Alicante. It is the area most visited by tourists, and where locals gather for entertainment, shopping and administrative services. The rest of the city are mainly neighbourhoods with a more local and residential character. What follows is a description of the five sectors, which are commonly accepted subdivisions of the city (fig. 1).

• *Mercado-San Antón*. This sector consists of two different areas, one is part of the *ensanche* ('widening' in Spanish), the Mercado area, and the other is the San Antón neighbourhood, which was established in the 18th century outside the city walls. Although morphologically the areas are different, they share the characteristic of surrounding the central areas and having a similar socio-economic situation. The use is predominantly residential.

• *Casco Histórico*. This is the oldest sector, which coincides with the existing city until the 17th century. The limits correspond with the city walls built in the 16th century. Morphologically it has two areas. One is the area corresponding to the old Arab city on the outskirts of Mount Benacantil, which has narrow streets adapted to the topography. The other is the area urbanised after the Christian Reconquista in the 13th century, which has a lower and less steep topography and a grid street pattern. This sector contains residences, night entertainment establishments, and some cultural centres promoted by the city government.

• *Seafront*. This sector contains the areas facing the beach, on the south-east side of Mount Benacantil, and the sport marina. Behind this front there are sectors corresponding to all the historical phases of urban evolution. This sector is characterised by a strong presence of touristic activity, due to the attractiveness of the sea, the beach, the marina port and all the related recreational services.

• *Ensanche-Diputación*. The *ensanche* is the area developed after the demolition of the city wall in 1858. Regular street grids with wide boulevards, and larger blocks characterise this area, which was completed by the end of the 19th century. The area combines residences, offices and commerce.

• *Centro*. This sector contains three historical expansions. The city expanded into the southernmost section in the 18th century and the middle section in the first half of the 19th century. The northern section is part of the expansion after the demolition of the city walls in 1858. Geographically the sector is the centre of the survey area. In the southern and middle section streets are narrow, but wider than in the historical centre. The area contains a street grid that becomes more regular to the north, with bigger blocks and wider streets. The area accommodates shopping and recreational facilities, with few residences.

Within those districts, participants were instructed to choose 'public spaces', as the main shared realm of visitors and locals, and evaluate them following a questionnaire. The definition of 'public space' is diffuse, due to the different cultural and personal ambiguous boundaries between the public and private realms, and especially due to the new typologies of urban spaces in contemporary cities. For this survey, participants were instructed to include 'positive spaces', 'negative spaces' and 'ambiguous spaces' according to Carmona's (2010) classification, which

Table 2: Urban space types (adapted from Carmona, 2010)

	Space type	Examples
Positive spaces	Natural urban space	Rivers, natural features, seafronts, canals
	Civic space	Streets, squares, promenades
	Public open space	Parks, gardens, urban forests, cemeteries
Negative space	Movement space	Main roads, motorways, railways, underpasses
	Service space	Car parks, service yards
	Leftover space	SLOAP (space left over after planning), Modernist open space
	Undefined space	Redevelopment space, abandoned space, transient space
Ambiguous space	Interchange space	Metros, bus interchanges, railway stations, bus/tram stops
	Public 'private' space	Privately owned 'civic' space, business parks, church grounds
	Conspicuous spaces	Cul-de-sacs, dummy gated enclaves
	Internalized 'public' space	Shopping/leisure malls, introspective megastructures
	Retail space	Shops, covered markets, petrol stations
	Third place spaces	Cafes, restaurants, libraries, town halls, religious buildings
	Private 'public' space	Institutional grounds, housing states, university campuses
	Visible private space	Front gardens, allotments, gated squares
	Interface spaces	Street cafes, private pavement space
	User-selecting spaces	Skateparks, playgrounds, sport fields/grounds/courses
Private spaces	Private open space	Urban agriculture remnants, private woodlands
	External private space	Gated streets, private gardens, private sport clubs
	Internal private space	Offices, houses, etc

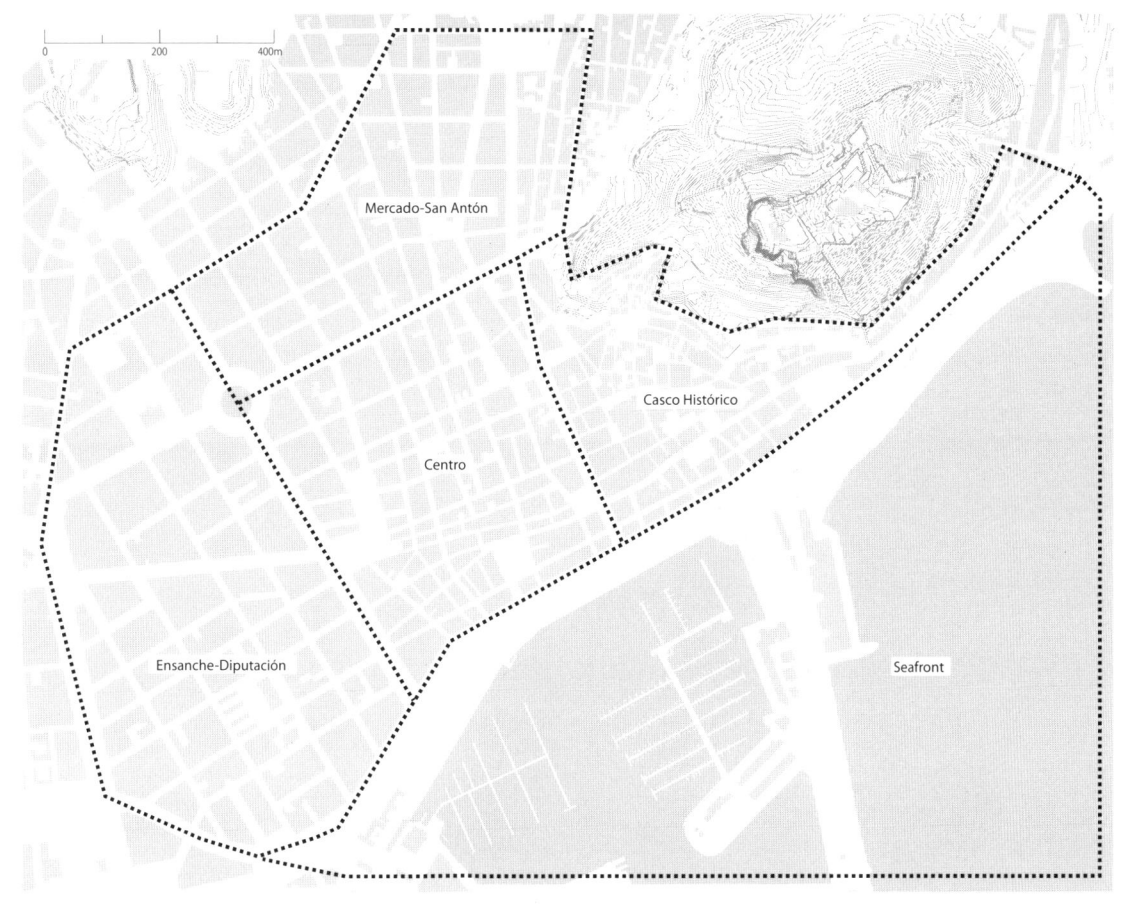

fig.1: Surveyed districts

covers 20 urban spaces in a continuum from clearly public to clearly private (Table 2). His classification at the same time addresses function, perception, and ownership and can be said to cover in a coherent and non-judgemental way most of the spaces that contribute to the public life in a contemporary city. It defies the traditional notion of public space as a non-charged, publicly owned, outdoor space, in order to include all places that play a role in social exchange and interaction. Private spaces were not included, since homes or offices are not a common shared space by locals and visitors. Carmona's classification covers urban spaces at different scales: interior and exterior, private and public ownership, and free or charged entrance.

5. Questionnaire survey

A questionnaire was distributed to all participants, together with a map of the survey area. Participants were asked to walk freely in the above-mentioned five areas, with the condition that they had to pass through each district in order to understand and evaluate the spaces. Participants were also asked to write their impressions on-site (not after the survey finished), in order to record the vividness of their experience of urban space. The questionnaire contained the following steps:

Step 1   Choose an area and circle it on the map. In total, choose at least three good places, three bad places, and optionally any other additional place that has both good and bad aspects.

Step 2   Draw on the map the route taken to arrive at the area.

Step 3   Take at least three photographs of the area.

Step 4   Evaluate the area: Is it good, bad, or does it have both good and bad aspects?

Step 5   Free description of reasons: Why do you think that the area is good/ bad or has both good and bad aspects? Write the reason.

Step 6   Choose outer characteristic elements from a list (see fig.4) and describe its condition if necessary.

Step 7   Rate the selected area (according to the semantic differential (SD) method, in order to show the internal psychological factors affecting evaluation).

Step 8   Write any additional free comments about the area.

Reducing the actual complexity of urban space to only two categories ('good' or 'bad') is an obvious oversimplification. However, as urban designers or architects, decisions are based on enhancing certain values considered as positive and avoiding or reducing features considered negative. Furthermore, first impressions on space, at a very intuitive level, are often expressed in simple terms such as 'good' or 'bad'. In any case, this oversimplification is only a tool to trigger a more refined and analytical study, as discussed in section 7.

fig.2: 'Good' places for Japanese visitors and local Spaniards participating in the survey

fig.3: 'Bad' places for Japanese visitors and local Spaniards participating in the survey

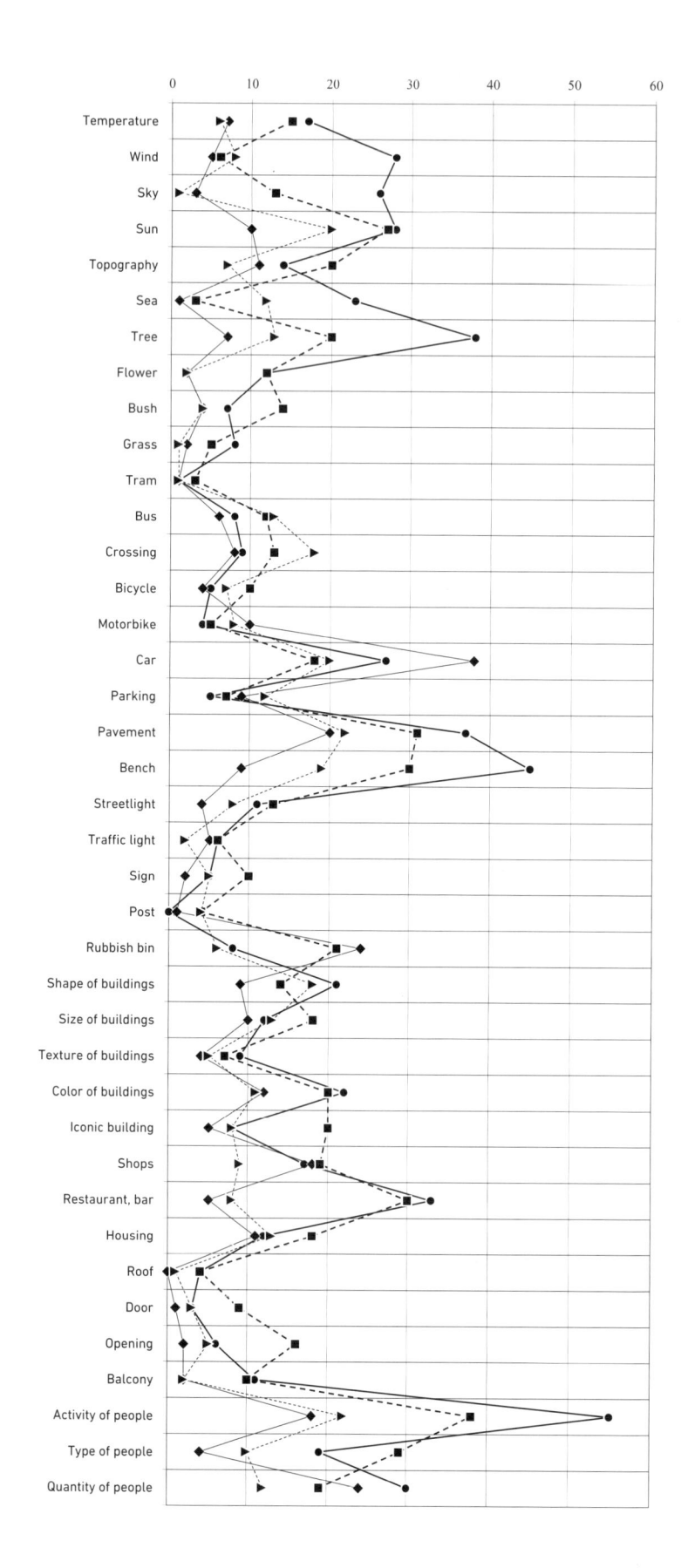

fig.4: Sum of characteristic outer elements
(Step 6 of the questionnaire)

Local Spaniard responses
- - - ■ - - - Elements related to good places
········▲········ Elements related to bad places

Japanese visitor responses
——●—— Elements related to good places
——◆—— Elements related to bad places

Table 3: Japanese visitor responses: Elements selected more times than the average and freely added elements by two or more persons

Elements related to good places		responses
Activity	GJ1	55
Bench	GJ2	45
Tree	GJ3	38
Pavement	GJ4	37
Restaurant	GJ5	33
Quantity of people	GJ6	24
Wind	GJ7a	28
Sun	GJ7b	
Car	GJ8	27
Sky	GJ9	26
Sea	GJ10	23
Color of building	GJ11	22
Shape of building	GJ12	21
Type of people	GJ13	19
Temperature	GJ14a	17
Shops	GJ14b	17
Average		16.8

Other: Fountain (4), Playground (3)

Elements related to bad places		responses
Car	BJ1	38
Rubbish bin	BJ2a	24
Quantity of people	BJ2b	
Pavement	BJ3	20
Shop	BJ4a	18
Activity	BJ4b	
Color of building	BJ5	12
Topography	BJ6a	11
Housing	BJ6b	
Sun	BJ7a	10
Motorbike	BJ7b	
Size of building	BJ7c	
Parking	BJ8a	9
Bench	BJ8b	
Shape of building	BJ8c	
Average		8.1

Other : Graffiti (9)

Table 4: Local Spaniard responses: Elements selected more times than the average and freely added elements by two or more persons

Elements related to good places		responses
Activity	GS1	38
Pavement	GS2	37
Bench	GS3a	30
Restaurant	GS3b	
Type of people	GS4	29
Sun	GS5	27
Rubbish	GS6	21
Topography	GS7a	20
Tree	GS7b	
Color of building	GS7c	
Iconic building	GS7d	
Shop	GS8a	19
Quantity of people	GS8b	
Car	GS9a	18
Size of building	GS9b	
Housing	GS9c	
Opening	GS10	16
Average		15.1

Other : Fountain (3), Chairs (3), Graffiti (2), Castle (2), Stairs (2), Playground (2), Advertisement (2)

Elements related to bad places		responses
Activity	BS1a	22
Pavement	BS1b	
Sun	BS2a	20
Car	BS2b	
Bench	BS3	19
Crossing	BS4	18
Tree	BS5a	13
Bus	BS5b	
Size of building	BS5c	
Housing	BS5d	
Quantity of people	BS6	12
Color of building	BS7	11
Type of building	BS8	10
Average		9.2

Other : Fence (3), Neglected building (3), Casino (2)

Table 5: Summary of the five most selected elements and frequently appearing annotations

		Related to good places	Annotations (number)	responses	Related to bad places	Annotations (number)	responses
Visitors ranking (most voted elements)	1	Activity [GJ1]	Sitting (9), talking (7), eating(5)	55	Car [BJ1]	Parked cars on the street (13), many (10)	38
	2	Bench [GJ2]	Many (16), benches in open space (2)	45	Rubbish bin [BJ2a]	Many (8), large (4), dirty (2)	24
	3	Tree [GJ3]	Many (7), palm trees (6), tree-lined road (4)	38	Quantity of people [BJ2b]	Few (11)	24
	4	Pavement [GJ4]	Wide (11), unique (4)	37	Pavement [BJ3]	Narrow(5), dirty(2)	20
	5	Restaurant [GJ5]	Many (6), terraced cafe (5)	33	Shop [BJ4a]	Closed (5)	18
					Activity [BJ4b]	Not active (2)	18
Locals ranking (most voted elements)	1	Activity [GS1]	Diverse: walking/sitting/playing/etc. (12), staying (3), everyday life activities (2)	38	Activity [BS1a]	No activity (7), marginalized/social outcasts (3), only touristic activities (1), only activities for the rich (1)	22
	2	Pavement [GS2]	No clear relation with judgment of place	37	Pavement [BS1b]	Lack of appropriate pavement for pedestrians (2)	22
	3	Bench [GS3a]	Place to sit (7), outdoor space used as bench (1)	30	Sun [BS2a]	Dark or dirty due to lack of sunlight (9)	20
	4	Restaurant [GS3b]	Presence of restaurants (6)	30	Car [BS2b]	Bad spatial solution of parking (2), heavy traffic (1), unsafe (1), bad access for the cars (1)	20
	5	Type of people [GS4]	Diverse ages and types (17), contact with local people (8), contact with foreign shop owners (4)	29	Bench [BS3]	Lack of benches (3), uncared state (1), no users of benches (1), bad urban situation of benches (1)	19

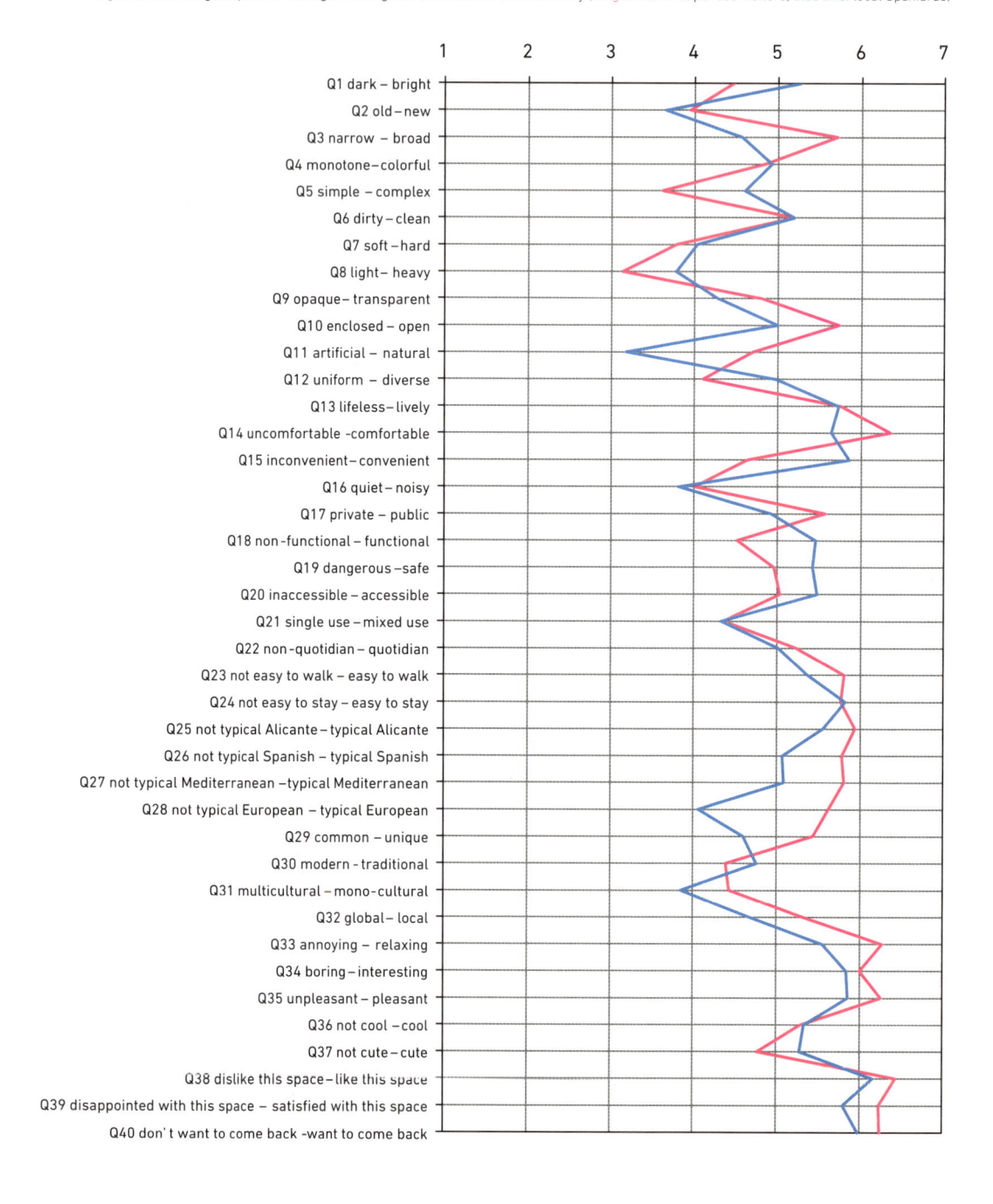

fig.5: Results on 'good places': Average of ratings for each item of the SD survey (magenta line: Japanese visitors; blue line: local Spaniards)

- Q1 dark – bright
- Q2 old – new
- Q3 narrow – broad
- Q4 monotone – colorful
- Q5 simple – complex
- Q6 dirty – clean
- Q7 soft – hard
- Q8 light – heavy
- Q9 opaque – transparent
- Q10 enclosed – open
- Q11 artificial – natural
- Q12 uniform – diverse
- Q13 lifeless – lively
- Q14 uncomfortable – comfortable
- Q15 inconvenient – convenient
- Q16 quiet – noisy
- Q17 private – public
- Q18 non-functional – functional
- Q19 dangerous – safe
- Q20 inaccessible – accessible
- Q21 single use – mixed use
- Q22 non-quotidian – quotidian
- Q23 not easy to walk – easy to walk
- Q24 not easy to stay – easy to stay
- Q25 not typical Alicante – typical Alicante
- Q26 not typical Spanish – typical Spanish
- Q27 not typical Mediterranean – typical Mediterranean
- Q28 not typical European – typical European
- Q29 common – unique
- Q30 modern – traditional
- Q31 multicultural – mono-cultural
- Q32 global – local
- Q33 annoying – relaxing
- Q34 boring – interesting
- Q35 unpleasant – pleasant
- Q36 not cool – cool
- Q37 not cute – cute
- Q38 dislike this space – like this space
- Q39 disappointed with this space – satisfied with this space
- Q40 don't want to come back – want to come back

fig.6: Results on 'bad places': Average of ratings for each item of the SD survey (magenta line: Japanese visitors; blue line: local Spaniards)

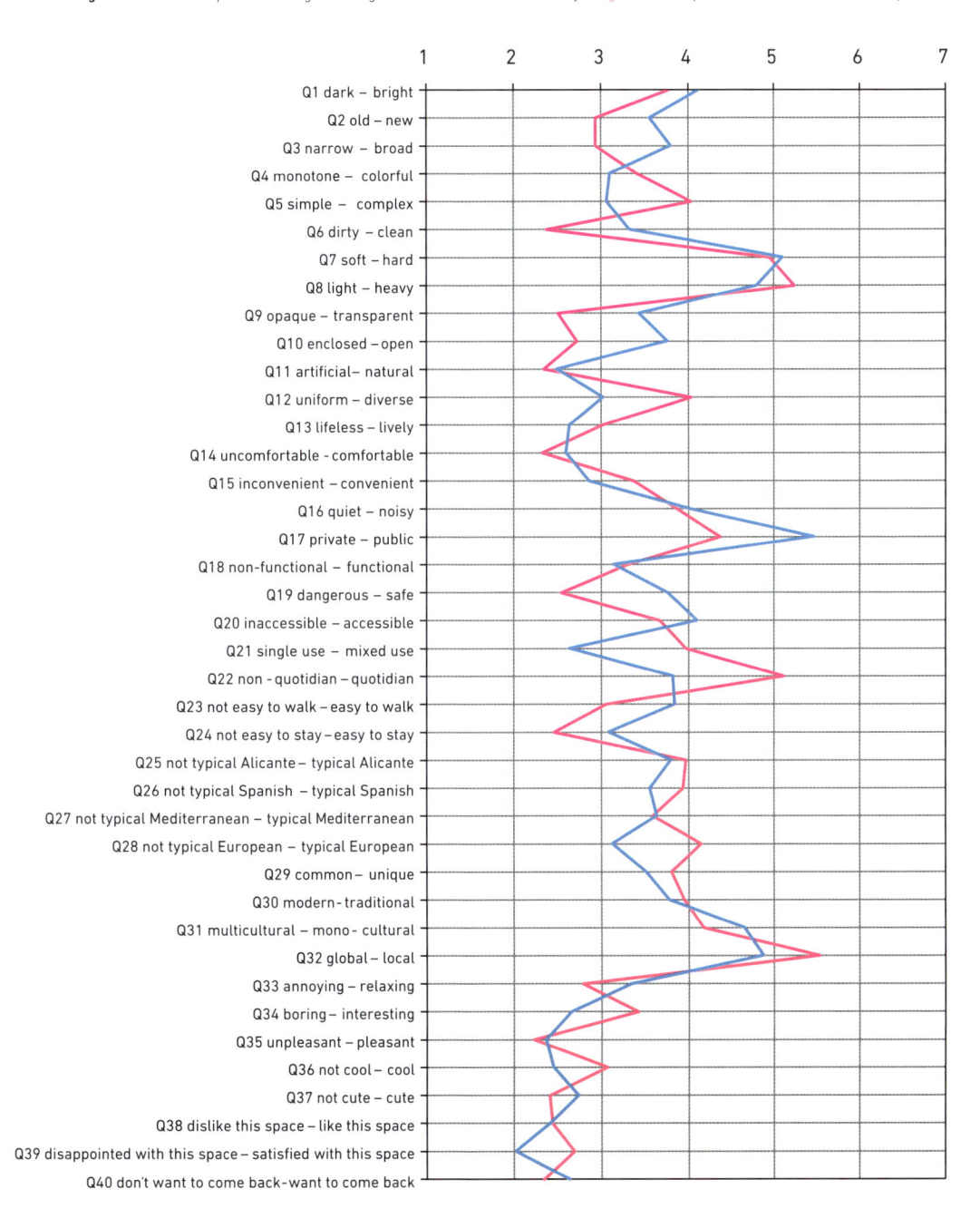

	1	2	3	4	5	6	7

Q1 dark – bright
Q2 old – new
Q3 narrow – broad
Q4 monotone – colorful
Q5 simple – complex
Q6 dirty – clean
Q7 soft – hard
Q8 light – heavy
Q9 opaque – transparent
Q10 enclosed – open
Q11 artificial – natural
Q12 uniform – diverse
Q13 lifeless – lively
Q14 uncomfortable – comfortable
Q15 inconvenient – convenient
Q16 quiet – noisy
Q17 private – public
Q18 non-functional – functional
Q19 dangerous – safe
Q20 inaccessible – accessible
Q21 single use – mixed use
Q22 non-quotidian – quotidian
Q23 not easy to walk – easy to walk
Q24 not easy to stay – easy to stay
Q25 not typical Alicante – typical Alicante
Q26 not typical Spanish – typical Spanish
Q27 not typical Mediterranean – typical Mediterranean
Q28 not typical European – typical European
Q29 common – unique
Q30 modern – traditional
Q31 multicultural – mono-cultural
Q32 global – local
Q33 annoying – relaxing
Q34 boring – interesting
Q35 unpleasant – pleasant
Q36 not cool – cool
Q37 not cute – cute
Q38 dislike this space – like this space
Q39 disappointed with this space – satisfied with this space
Q40 don't want to come back – want to come back

Table 6: Results of multiple regression analysis using Japanese student data ($R^2=0.872$)
(Results for Japanese are indicated with the capital letter J)

Variables	Unstandardized Coefficients B	Std. Error	Standardized Coefficients Beta	t value	Sig. (p value)	95.0% Confidence Interval for B Lower Bound	Upper Bound
(Constant)	-0.261	0.392		-0.664	0.507	-1.035	0.514
Q6-J dirty – clean	0.225	0.044	0.246	5.126	0.000	0.138	0.312
Q8-J light – heavy	-0.102	0.046	-0.092	-2.227	0.027	-0.193	-0.012
Q13-J lifeless – lively	0.113	0.036	0.125	3.097	0.002	0.041	0.185
Q24-J not easy to stay – easy to stay	0.304	0.040	0.350	7.620	0.000	0.225	0.383
Q27-J not typical Mediterranean – typical Med.	0.150	0.041	0.149	3.623	0.000	0.068	0.231
Q28-J not typical European – typical European	0.147	0.046	0.121	3.212	0.002	0.057	0.238
Q29-J common – unique	0.122	0.040	0.105	3.046	0.003	0.043	0.202
Q30-J modern - traditional	0.107	0.034	0.094	3.157	0.002	0.040	0.174

Table 7: Results of multiple regression analysis using Spanish student data ($R^2=0.689$)
(Results for Spaniards are indicated with the capital letter S)

Variables	Unstandardized Coefficients B	Std. Error	Standardized Coefficients Beta	t value	Sig. (p value)	95.0% Confidence Interval for B Lower Bound	Upper Bound
(Constant)	0.564	0.471		1.199	0.233	-0.367	1.496
Q4-S monotone – colorful	0.105	0.051	0.122	2.066	0.041	0.004	0.206
Q5-S simple – complex	0.157	0.052	0.168	3.017	0.003	0.054	0.261
Q8-S light – heavy	-0.233	0.058	-0.216	-3.993	0.000	-0.349	-0.118
Q15-S inconvenient – convenient	0.216	0.063	0.226	3.450	0.001	0.092	0.339
Q24-S not easy to stay – easy to stay	0.197	0.048	0.245	4.099	0.000	0.102	0.292
Q25-S not typical Alicante – typical Alicante	0.141	0.051	0.156	2.749	0.007	0.039	0.242
Q29-S common – unique	0.285	0.057	0.285	4.969	0.000	0.172	0.399

6. Analysis

From the questionnaire three analyses were conducted. The results of each analysis are described in the following sections, followed by a discussion of the results in section 7.

6.1 Analysis 1:
Overlapping of selected places

All 292 places selected by respondents were combined into a single map. To easily visualize the results, each place was represented with a 10% transparency, so that the level of darkness visually shows the number of respondents who chose a place. The resulting maps (fig.2 and 3) confirm clear differences between the two groups: While Japanese visitors considered central boulevards (e.g. Federico Soto Avenue, Doctor Gadea Avenue) and the seafront areas to be 'good', the local Spaniards did not select those places, and as in the case of the seafront, they even considered them to be 'bad'. There was also few similarities when choosing 'bad' spaces. One clear example is the above-mentioned seafront. Another example is the northern districts with a clear concentration of bad spaces for the Japanese visitors, but not considered as such by the Spaniards. A detailed, place-by-place evaluation requires a separate study, but for the purposes of this study, it will suffice to confirm that there are not only similarities but also very clear differences. The goal here will be, by means of the following two analyses, to identify the reasons for this different evaluation.

6.2 Analysis 2:
Characteristic outer elements

After choosing a particular area, participants were asked to select elements characterizing that area, and freely write annotations describing in detail their impressions about those elements (Step 6 of the questionnaire). The sums for all elements selected by respondents are summarized in fig.4. These results give an idea about which tangible external elements are selected by people when observing a place as 'positive' elements contributing to the quality of the place, and also as 'negative' elements. It is possible to identify the connections between specific elements and the judgment of a place as good or bad, by examining the free description of Step 5 or the free annotations of Step 6 of the questionnaire.

By summing all elements and separating them into four categories ('good' and 'bad' for local Spaniards, 'good' and 'bad' for Japanese visitors), it is possible to identify consensus over particular elements that affect the evaluation of space. To help identify elements, these have been codified with two letter and a number. The first letter (G or B) means 'good' or 'bad'. The second (S or J) denotes 'Spaniards' or 'Japanese'. For example, the most voted 'good' element for Spaniards is codified as GS1; the second is GS2, and so on. Table 3 and Table 4 show a list of the elements selected a number of times equal to or greater than the average. From this list, as the elements that most clearly seem to influence judgment, the authors have decided to highlight the top five most selected elements in each category (Table 5), since the purpose of this study is to identify strong tendencies in the evaluation of place. The authors believe that unconventional, subjective, and exceptional points of view should also be considered in urban design. However in this study the focus is rather on consensus and strongly shared inter-subjectivity. Table 5, which shows these top five elements with a summary of the most frequent annotations, can be summarized as follows.

'Good' elements for Japanese visitors. When Japanese visitors judged a place as good, the most selected item was "activity" of people, especially sitting, talking, and eating. The second item was "bench": Japanese highlighted the high number of benches and the fact that they were located in open spaces. The third was "trees", highlighting their number, the presence of palm trees, and the placement of trees along the streets. In fourth place is an the appreciation of pavement, often considered "wide" and "unique". Finally, the presence of restaurants, especially their high number and the terrace cafes, seemed to have an influence toward a positive appreciation of space. In the category 'other', where respondents freely added other elements not included in the questionnaire, "fountains" were mentioned 5 times in relation to 'good' places, and only once in relation to 'bad' places.

'Bad' elements for Japanese visitors. The following factors negatively affected the evaluation of places (in order of importance): The presence of many cars and particularly, cars parked on the streets; the presence of rubbish bins, their number and size, and dirty state; the lack of people; the narrowness and dirtiness of the pavement; the presence of closed shops; and, finally lack of activity. In the category 'other', "graffiti" was mentioned 9 times as an element of 'bad' places, but never mentioned as a component of good places.

'Good' elements for Spanish locals. In order of number of responses, the top 5 selected elements were "activity" of people in first place. Many Spaniards mention the diverse activities, the possibility to stay in a place, and everyday life activities such as eating lunch or sitting in front of people's houses. The pavement was also often selected, but there were no clear comments describing it as something that improves space. Benches were also mentioned, highlighting the importance of places to sit in urban space. Restaurants were also selected as positive. Finally, the

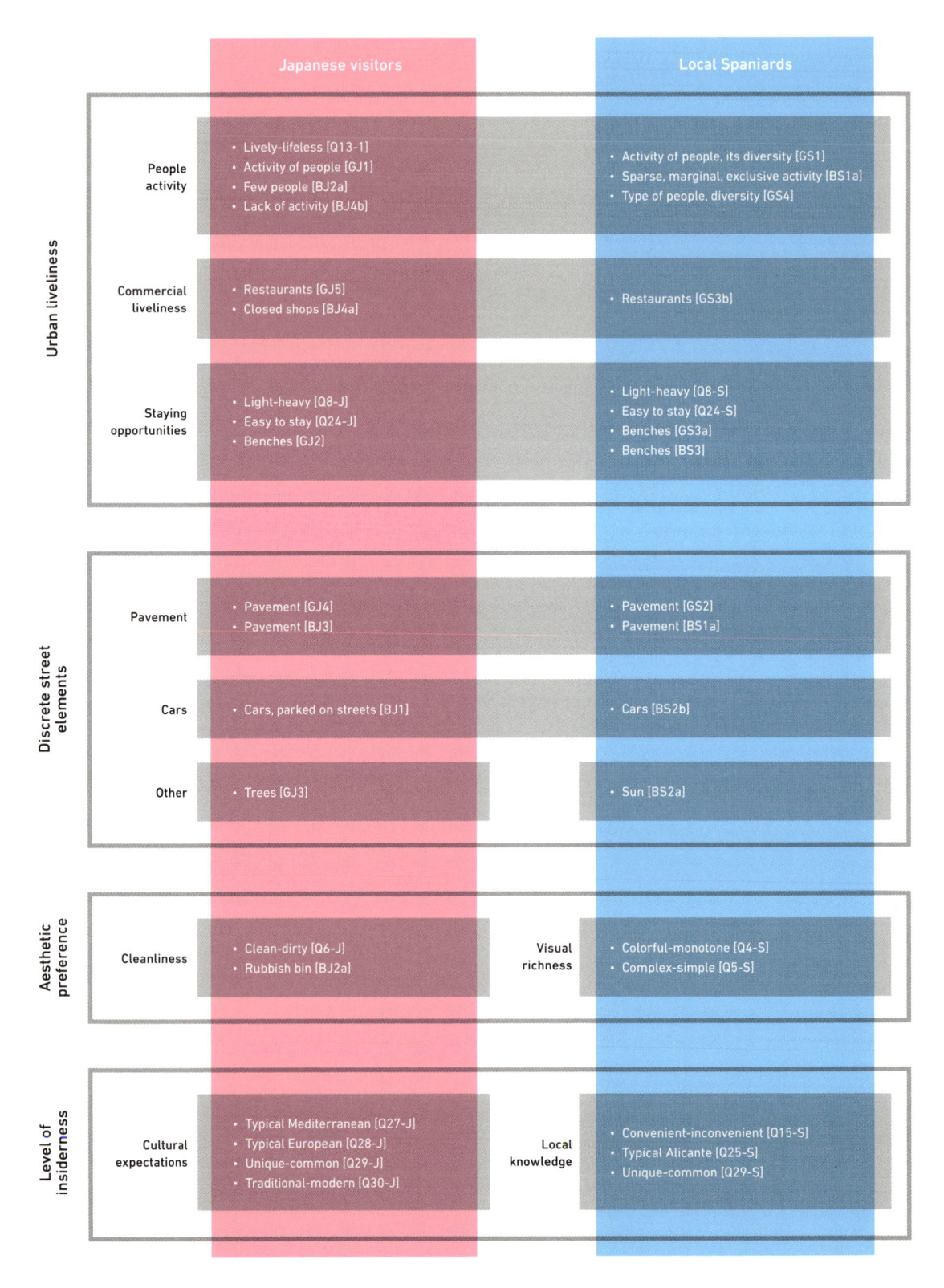

	Japanese visitors		Local Spaniards
Urban liveliness			
People activity	• Lively-lifeless [Q13-1] • Activity of people [GJ1] • Few people [BJ2a] • Lack of activity [BJ4b]		• Activity of people, its diversity [GS1] • Sparse, marginal, exclusive activity [BS1a] • Type of people, diversity [GS4]
Commercial liveliness	• Restaurants [GJ5] • Closed shops [BJ4a]		• Restaurants [GS3b]
Staying opportunities	• Light-heavy [Q8-J] • Easy to stay [Q24-J] • Benches [GJ2]		• Light-heavy [Q8-S] • Easy to stay [Q24-S] • Benches [GS3a] • Benches [BS3]
Discrete street elements			
Pavement	• Pavement [GJ4] • Pavement [BJ3]		• Pavement [GS2] • Pavement [BS1a]
Cars	• Cars, parked on streets [BJ1]		• Cars [BS2b]
Other	• Trees [GJ3]		• Sun [BS2a]
Aesthetic preference			
Cleanliness	• Clean-dirty [Q6-J] • Rubbish bin [BJ2a]	Visual richness	• Colorful-monotone [Q4-S] • Complex-simple [Q5-S]
Level of insiderness			
Cultural expectations	• Typical Mediterranean [Q27-J] • Typical European [Q28-J] • Unique-common [Q29-J] • Traditional-modern [Q30-J]	Local knowledge	• Convenient-inconvenient [Q15-S] • Typical Alicante [Q25-S] • Unique-common [Q29-S]

fig.7: Discussion: interpretation of combined results (outer characteristic elements and inner psychological elements)

"type of people" item was highlighted, especially in the sense of "diverse ages and types", contact with local people, and contact with foreigners owning shops. 'Other' elements provided in the free response were fountains (3 times), chairs (3), the castle (2), stairs (2), playgrounds (2), advertisements (2), and finally graffiti (2), which for some locals seemed to be a positive element.

'Bad' elements for Spaniards. The first element was "activities": The lack of activity, the activities of marginalized people (homeless persons, prostitutes), touristic activity, or its exclusivity (activities for only the rich). The second was the pavement, especially the lack of appropriate pavement for walking. The third was the "sun" in the sense of lack of sunlight. The fourth was "cars" as a problem, especially poorly solved parking problems, heavy traffic, and insecurity. However, there was also an annotation indicating bad access for cars as a problem. The last item was "benches" in the sense of lack of places to sit, their poorly maintained state, the lack of people using them, or their bad location in urban space. 'Other' elements provided in the free response were fences (3), neglected buildings (3), and the casino (2) located on the seafront.

6.3 Analysis 3: Psychological preference through SD method

The second part of the questionnaire (Step 7) is an SD survey. The adjectives and clauses (henceforth called items) employed in the SD survey aimed to cover a wide range of parameters that seem to affect the character of a place. The questionnaire survey consisted of 40 items, divided into 4 groups: a) physical condition group (total 12 items, Q1 to Q12); b) behavior group (total 12 items, Q13 to Q24); c) place identity group (total 8 items, Q25 to Q32); and d) preference group (total 8 items, Q33 to Q40). Feelings toward urban spaces were measured on a 7-point scale (see figs.5 and 6).

A multivariable analysis using the SD questionnaire survey data was conducted to determine the difference in urban space preferences between Japanese visitors and local Spaniards. Multiple regression analysis was conducted using the average value of items from the preference group as response variable and all other items in the physical condition, behavior and place identity groups (except Q1, Q14) as explanatory variables. Q1 was excluded from the analysis because the authors identified the question as being prone to misinterpretation, which might have misled the respondents. Q14 was also excluded from the explanatory variables because it seemed to be related more closely to the preference group, and therefore it was re-categorized into the preference group when conducting the factor analysis.

Figures 5 and 6 show the average ratings by local Spaniards and Japanese visitors. Tables 6 and 7 show the results of the multiple regression analysis for Japanese and Spanish participants, respectively. As a result of the analysis, 8 items (Q6, Q8, Q13, Q24, Q27, Q28, Q29, Q30) suggested a relationship with Japanese visitor preference, and 7 items (Q4, Q5, Q8, Q15, Q24, Q25, Q29) have suggested a relationship with local Spaniard preference.

7. Discussion

The results obtained about outer tangible elements and inner psychological elements are discussed in this section regarding the commonalities and differences for Japanese visitors and local Spaniards. The top five outer elements from each category (good and bad, Japanese visitors and local Spaniards) are organized together with the inner elements from the multiple regression analysis. By grouping the elements with a similar meaning (see fig.7), it is possible to discuss them according to the following four categories.

7.1 Urban liveliness

Both groups coincide in appreciating the role of *urban liveliness*. This liveliness can be understood as composed by three factors: human activities, commercial vitality, and staying opportunities in public space.

Human activities. Visitors and locals coincide in appreciating spaces that seem lively (Q13-J), and with activity of people (GJ1, GS1). Local Spaniards, particularly, stressed the appeal of diverse activities, such as walking, eating, and playing, happening simultaneously and by people of different ages. Lack of liveliness was also among the main reasons for negatively judging a place: few people (BJ2b), and lack of activity (BJ4b, BS1a). Spaniards, with a deeper knowledge of the place, were also able to identify the negative impression created by marginalized people, such as prostitutes, and the homeless. These differences can also be seen in the free annotations of the survey sheet. Japanese described that they like a place where local people gather and that looks lively, while Spanish students described that they like places that they can use for multiple activity or to communicate with many people. It is obvious that there are more deep descriptions of daily life from the perspective of the user in the responses of local Spaniards. While there is a slight difference between Japanese and Spanish perspectives, there is a consensus that places where many people gather for various kinds of activities are preferable.

Commercial liveliness. Visitors and locals coincided in appreciating the need for commercial liveliness in urban spaces. Both identified restaurants (GJ5, GS3b) as

Elements related to 'good' places

Photographs by **Japanese visitors**

[GJ1] Activity (sitting, talking, eating, etc.)

[GJ2] Benches (many, in open space)

[GJ3] Trees (palm trees, many)

[GJ4] Pavement (wide, unique)

[GJ5] Restaurant (many, terrace cafes)

Photographs by **local Spaniards**

[GS1] Activity (diverse, staying, everyday life)

[GS2] Pavement

[GS3a] Bench (place to sit, outdoor space as bench)

[GS3b] Restaurants (presence of restaurants)

[GS4] Type of people (diverse ages and types, foreign shop owners, local people)

important urban elements, especially those with outdoor seating space. Japanese visitors highlighted the presence of closed shops (BJ4a) as negative, an appreciation that does not emerge from the results of local Spaniards. One possible explanation is that locals are used to the presence of closed shops, especially due to the negative impact of the international and domestic financial crises, which is dramatically affecting family-run, small business such as the small shops along the streets of Alicante.

Staying opportunities. Common results between Japanese visitors and local Spaniards are "light" (Q8-J, Q8-S) and "easy to stay in" (Q24-J, Q24-S), IS5), which suggests that a place that is not oppressive, and that it is likely to offer opportunities to spend more time is recognized as comfortable for both groups. This idea is supported also by the selection of benches (GJ2, GS3a, BS3) as a prominent outer element by both groups. A comfortable place to stay and to sit seems to be a fundamental parameter that contributes to quality of urban space.

7.2 Discrete street elements

There were some outer elements that seem to play a decisive role in the evaluation of space. For both groups it was the pavement, both as something that can contribute to the quality of space (GJ4, GS2), and something that spoils it (BJ3, BS1b). This attention to pavement can be understood if we consider that it is an element with which city users are in continuous contact, and on which their safety depends to a great extent. Japanese visitors also highlighted the aesthetic qualities of pavement.

Cars were also an important element, in this case in a negative sense. Both groups coincided in the negative impact of cars on public space and security (BJ1, BS2b). Japanese were negatively surprised by the number of cars parked on the streets. This can be explained by the fact that in Japan this kind of street parking is rare. Cars in Japan are parked within private land lots or in parking structures, and to buy a car it is necessary to prove that one owns or rents a parking space. Most Spaniards, when asked, would agree that the presence of many cars parked along the street is also problematic, but probably participants in the survey did not write any such comments because, again, they are used to it.

As for other discrete elements, trees (GJ3) were frequently chosen as positive by Japanese. In the case of Spaniards, the lack of sun (BS2a) was a decisive element to negatively judge a place.

7.3 Aesthetic preference

There were significant differences at some points, which can be considered as aesthetic preferences. Japanese visitors tended to highlight the negative impact of places considered "dirty" (Q6-J) and the presence of rubbish bins (BJ2a) on the streets. There were many free descriptions stating that they dislike dirty places with rubbish on the ground, while they like neatly kept streets. There was also a difference in the perception of graffiti. The majority of Japanese visitors considered it as "dirty" and felt "unsafe", whereas local Spaniard wrote comments regarding it as a form of art, and even associating it with good places. This might be explained because graffiti is less common in Japanese cities, and because the longer background of architectural studies in the Spanish participants (5 years older in average than the Japanese) might have influenced their perception of graffiti as desirable urban art.

Local Spaniards were also concerned about the lack of cleanliness, but it did not appear as prominently as in the Japanese results. On the other hand, impressions such as "colorful" (Q4-S) and "complex" (Q5-S) showed a significant relationship with local preference. Locals seem to prefer the rich visual stimulation of a colorful and complex urban experience. The prominence of cleanliness for Japanese can be understood culturally because Japan is a well-known case in which cities are extremely clean, to the extent that, for example, many smokers carry portable ashtrays to avoid disposing of ashes on the pavement.

7.4 Level of insiderness

Finally, a clear difference emerges between both groups in the items related with "place identity" of the SD method survey, which can be explained as a different level of insiderness or familiarity in relation to Alicante. Japanese visitors preferred spaces seen as "typical Mediterranean" (Q27-J), "typical European" (Q28-J), "traditional" (Q30-J), and "unique" (Q29-J). On the other hand, Spaniards tended to appreciate space perceived as "convenient" (Q15-S), "typical Alicante" (Q25-S), and "unique" (Q29-S). Convenience is a quality learned only from the experience of residing in a place, and accordingly it was only highlighted by Spaniards.

The term "unique" seems to be understood in a different way between Japanese visitors and local Spaniards. Japanese students as visitors capture this feature from a broader framework. They seem to show more positive impressions about places where they can feel a different "unique" culture, as compared with their own cities and urban landscapes, and to satisfy expected images formed before visiting the place. Spanish students as local residents capture features from a more detailed framework. They can distinguish their own uniqueness from other neighboring cities and prefer places where they can feel their own identity. It is relevant that locals showed a clear preference for what is typical of Alicante (and not broader categories, such as European or Mediterranean). This shows the positive effect on urban space appreciation when local people feel identified with a place that they see as possessing a distinctive identity.

8. Conclusions

The urban identity of Alicante, as a "selective way of imaging, acting and communication" (Hague 2005:10) has been explored through a Japan-Spain cross-cultural survey, which included selection of places, tangible outer elements, and psychological inner elements. The results show commonalities and differences in the appreciation of urban space. Liveliness, the presence and activities of people, commercial vitality, and opportunities to stay outdoors were considered as positive qualities by both sides, together with a particular attention to pavement and car management as fundamental street elements influencing spatial quality. Differences were clear in the aesthetic appreciation of places: Japanese visitors highlighted the importance of cleanliness, while local Spaniards show preference for complexity and visual richness. Finally, the level of knowledge of the place determined important differences, since, for example, local Spaniards tended to prefer convenience. As for place identity, Japanese visitors preferred "unique" and "typical" places in a broad sense, while locals prefer places that they could identify more specifically as unique and typical of Alicante.

The appreciation of the above-mentioned qualities, which are not only specific to Alicante, but present in almost any urban space, seem to depend on cultural background (e.g. cleanliness) and on different knowledge levels of the place (e.g. convenience). But there are urban qualities, like liveliness for the case of Alicante, that seem to have a strong cross-cultural appeal and make places attractive for locals and visitors. The problem of loss of urban identity is complex and needs to be considered from multiple angles. Further analysis on other nationalities, an examination of current urban design policies in Alicante, together with a detailed examination of each plaza, boulevard, and street appearing in this survey is necessary to properly address the problem of urban identity and future studies will be necessary. From the present research it is fair to say that street liveliness, as a clear cross-cultural urban quality that seems to satisfy both locals and visitors, seems to be one of the important viewpoints to be considered in those further studies.

Acknowledgements

This study was originally published as Cross-cultural evaluation of public space qualities: Re-imaging the Urban Identity of Alicante City. *Journal of Architecture and Planning* (Transactions of the Architectural Institute of Japan), No. 680 (Oct. 2012). Reprinted by kind permission of the publisher.

References

Carmona, M. 2010. Contemporary Public Space, Part Two: Classification. *Journal of Urban Design* Vol. 15, No. 2 (2010.5):157–173.

Hague, C. 2005. Planning and place identity. In C. Hague and P. Jenkins, eds. *Place identity, participation and planning*. New York: Routledge.

Oishi, H., S. Murakawa, and D. Nishina. 2007. An analysis on the psychological evaluation for preferable landscapes by the subjects. *J. Environ. Eng.*, AIJ, No.618 (2007.8):101–108.

Sepe, M. 2009. PlaceMaker Method: Planning 'Walkability' by Mapping Place Identity. *Journal of Urban Design* Vol. 14 (2009.11):463–487.

Tabata, E. and Nishide, K. 2007. Analysis of form, elements and evaluation of collective form in Harajyuku, J. Archit. Plann., AIJ, No.620 (2007.10):89–94.

Yamamoto, K., H. Oishi, S. Murakawa, and D. Nishina. A study on the regional characteristics of the inhabitants' preference for regional landscapes in Higashi-Hiroshima City. *J. Environ. Eng.*, AIJ, No. 587 (2005.1):53–61.

Elements related to 'bad' places

Photographs by Japanese visitors

[BJ1] Cars (parked on the street, many)

[BJ1a] Rubbish bins (many, large, dirty)

[BJ3] Pavement (narrow, dirty)

[BJ4a] Shop (closed)

[BJ2b+BJ4b] Few people, no activity

Photographs by **local Spaniards**

[BS1a] Activity (lack, marginalized, touristic, only for rich)

[BS1b] Pavement (lack of pavement appropriate for pedestrians)

[BS2a] No sun (dark, dirty)

[BS2b] Cars (bad spatial solution of parking, unsafe)

[BS3] Bench (no users, poorly maintained, bad urban situation)

Cross-cultural Debates

Debates transculturales
異文化間討論

Jorge Almazán, Yukino Tairako, Mio Suzuki, Milica Muminović,
Gaku Inoue, Shun Kawakubo
ホルヘ・アルマザン、平子雪乃、鈴木美央、
ミリッツァ・ムミノヴィッチ、井上 岳、川久保 俊

Como en otras ciudades turísticas, en Alicante se percibe una polarización entre lugares turísticos o usados mayoritariamente por turistas y los lugares preferidos por los residentes. Este estudio aborda esta segregación identificando espacios públicos específicos y las razones por las que estos espacios son valorados por una muestra de residentes y de visitantes japoneses. Empleamos grupos mixtos (españoles y japoneses) de debate estructurado y diagramas de afinidad como metodología participativa. Los resultados muestran que en muchos casos, cuando los residentes y los visitantes coincidían en valorar un espacio concreto, las razones que aducían para fundamentar esta valoración diferían claramente entre residentes y visitantes. Esto sugiere que una forma de compartir áreas urbanas entre locales y turistas en ciudades turísticas puede consistir en propiciar el carácter inclusivo y diverso del espacio urbano, de forma que pueda contener diversas cualidades y estímulos que respondan a preferencias tan diversas como las encontradas en este estudio entre los participantes locales y japoneses.

本論文はスペインのアリカンテ市における公共空間の異文化間研究に関するパート2である。他の観光都市と同様に、アリカンテ市の多くの場所は観光客のための場所と現地住民のための場所に二極化している。この二極化は、場所のアイデンティティの喪失と現地住民にとっての都市の質の低下をしばしば引き起こす。本研究ではKJ法を応用し、現地住民と日本人観光客の参加による集団討議を通じて、具体的な公共空間について現地住民、日本人観光客のそれぞれからどのように好ましいと思うか、その理由を明らかにした。その結果、現地住民と日本人観光客の両者が好んだ場所の多くでは、それぞれ理由が異なることが明らかになった。このことから、日本人とスペイン人のように異なる嗜好に対応できる十分な多様性を育成することが、観光都市において現地住民と観光客が同じ公共空間を共有するための方法のひとつであると言えよう。

1. Purpose

In the first phase – *Collective Urban Drift*– local Spaniards and Japanese visitors expressed their evaluations on public space individually. The first phase constitutes a record and an analysis of the first impressions of the Japanese and the opinions of the Spaniards before they met. The results suggested general qualities of public space, some seemingly related to cultural background (e.g. cleanliness for Japanese, colourfulness for local Spaniards), others to different levels of familiarity with the place (e.g. convenience for locals), and finally qualities like "liveliness" that seem to have a strong cross-cultural appeal. For these results, obtained through individual questionnaires, there was no discussion or exchange of ideas between local Spaniards and Japanese visitors.

In this second phase, Japanese and Spaniards met and formed mixed groups. Within each group participants were asked to discuss about public spaces in Alicante. Thus, the second phase reproduces the effects on evaluation of public spaces as a result of cross-cultural communication. The purpose is to identify public spaces that, through cross-cultural understanding, can be enjoyed and shared by two types of users: locals and visitors – in this case from Japan – and the reasons that could explain this coincidence in preference. The key research questions that was posed to each group is: *Which places are preferred by locals, by visitors, and in particular, by both? Why is this so? Which qualities make those places attractive?*.

2. Methodology

This second phase – *Cross-cultural Debate* – is a study of urban space employing affinity diagrams, which are based upon the KJ method, named after the initials of his inventor, Jiro Kawakita. Originally devised for cultural anthropological research, it is a bottom-up approach for understanding data (Kawakita 1996). It has been recognised as a research method by the Architectural Institute of Japan (AIJ 2005). Earlier research in Japan has employed it to visualise and organise the opinions of residents in regional surveys (Ushino 1979) and of municipal staff in charge of urban planning (Taniguchi et al. 1980). It has been also used to organise architects' statements to understand the historical flow of architectural thinking (Okuyama et al. 1994). In these three cases, researchers (typically two or three authors) create the affinity diagrams by themselves. However, the KJ method is also used to foster decision making, creativity and good relationships in larger groups. The affinity diagrams are often used in management and planning processes to achieve inter-subjective consensus amongst the participants (Brassard 1989, Scupin 1997). This latter method is how we use affinity diagrams in this paper, namely as a support for the mixed group of Spanish and Japanese participants to achieve inter-subjectivity.

The second phase aims to identify spaces that "epitomise" the qualities found during the group discussion. The concept of "epitome districts" was introduced by Clay (1973:38) as "Special places in cities [that] carry huge layers of symbols [and] that have the capacity to pack up emotions, energy, or history into a small space." Cybriwsky (1991:151) develops the concept in his study on Tokyo, as places where "one can see the bigger place in compression or miniature", and as the places one needs to write about "in order to be representative and reasonably complete about the city". The substantiation of abstract qualities in these "epitome places" or spatial exemplars can be considered an essential step to link research to practice, theoretical categories to real phenomena.

The participants in this second phase were 42 university students of architecture and engineering, including 18 local Spanish students residing in the city (mean age: 25 years) and 24 Japanese students visiting the city for the first time (mean age: 20 years) (Table 1).

2.1 Phase 2: Group discussions

After the fieldwork of the first phase, participants were asked to engage in group discussions. The aim was not to summarise participants' opinion statistically, as in the first phase, but rather to explore qualitatively ways to evaluate public spaces by developing a cross-cultural discourse. In other words, the goal was to foster a narrative on urban identity, understood as relational and dynamic way of imagining a place. To achieve this, we asked participants to develop categories by using affinity diagrams, following methodological steps based upon KJ method. Our method was designed to allow non-specialists to achieve a rich evaluation of urban places through a participatory process. This process, as a qualitative research, has the difficulty of maintaining a certain level of validity and reliability. This difficulty was addressed by using the affinity diagram method, devised for group discussion to overcome individual subjectivity and achieve inter-subjective conclusions by systematically registering and categorising the ideas that emerge during the group discussion.

We organised five mixed groups and assigned one urban sector to each group. We gave each team all the questionnaire materials for the corresponding sector realized during the first phase (questionnaires filled during

Table 1: Composition of the discussion groups

		Group 1	Group 2	Group 3	Group 4	Group 5	Total	Mean age
Spaniards	Male	2	1	0	2	1	6	24.8
	Female	1	2	4	2	3	12	25.3
Japanese	Male	1	3	5	3	3	15	20.1
	Female	3	2	0	2	2	9	20.6

fieldwork, photographs and maps). The research question given to all groups was formulated as follows: *What makes urban space good or bad? Try to find coincidences and differences in your opinions.* Students engaged in discussion according to the following three steps, completed on 7 March 2012.

• *Step 1: Card making (9:00 to 12:00).* All groups were instructed to look through all questionnaire materials realize in Phase 1, and make as many cards (Post-it notes) as possible by transferring the annotations from the questionnaires to the cards. The aim was to use all data from Phase 1. Participants had to understand the written annotations but also check the place those annotations referred to by looking at the photographs and maps. Each card contained a clear and distinct idea and was distinguished by colour, with yellow cards for annotations from Japanese participants, red cards for the cards from Spanish participants, green cards for newly added opinions, and blue cards for other open comments. The participants were asked to thoroughly describe all data on public spaces without judging whether the comment is useful for the discussion.

• *Step 2: Revisiting places (12:00 to 16:00).* Time was given for participants to revisit the places and refresh their understanding of the sector, which also informed participants who did not visit or remember all places described in the annotations from the individual survey.

• *Step 3: Categorising and titling (16:00 to 20:00).* All groups were instructed to look over each card written in the step 1, to make small groups of cards by affinity by gathering annotations with similar content, and to give a title to each group. Participants were instructed to repeat this process, and create additional overarching groups (i.e., intermediate and upper categories). Participants were allowed to add new cards (opinions, viewpoints etc.) and use them together with the cards from step 1. They were expected to maintain an objective attitude and not to deviate from the theme of the discussion. The instructions also emphasised that they needed to discuss thoroughly and move forward after achieving consensus, with the aim of coming to a valid conclusion.

• *Step 4: Formulating and connecting (20:00 to 21:00).* All groups were instructed to find the connections between the categories and arrange all cards for the final diagram.

They were told to complete the diagrams by gluing the cards on an A1 sheet of paper, drawing the frames, titles and connections with lines and arrows indicating relationships between categories such as opposition, influence and contradiction (see example in fig. 1).

2.2 Place selection

After completing the affinity diagrams participants were instructed to select 'good urban spaces', based upon the conclusions of their discussions. As already clear from the results of the *Collective Urban Drift* survey, there were difference of opinions on 'what makes a good urban space' between the Spaniards and the Japanese. There were also areas of agreement, and the group discussions helped both groups to understand each other's opinions and to modify their own opinion based upon this understanding. Participants were asked to select at least three places: one good for Spaniards (a place considered good according to the opinions of the Spaniards recorded in the affinity diagram), one good for Japanese and a third one good for both (Japanese visitors and local Spaniards). Although the affinity diagrams also included reflections on negative urban characteristics, for the selection of places we focussed on the 'good' urban spaces to simplify the task. Negative qualities were addressed by implication. This focus on good qualities is also a way to connect this study with design practice, which relies on positive examples as design models. The places selected as "good for both" Japanese and Spaniards have been represented as "urban files" in the following section of this book.

The affinity diagrams serve to develop abstract concepts from a myriad of opinions recorded during fieldwork. Now those concepts had to be mobilised to look back retrospectively at actual spaces in the city. It is reasonable to assume that participants gained a better understanding through the group discussions, especially of the difference reasons and expectations between locals and visitors. In a final presentation, each group explained their thought process and the reason for their choices by using both text and graphics such as architectural drawings, diagrams and photographs. These verbal and visual explanations were video recorded.

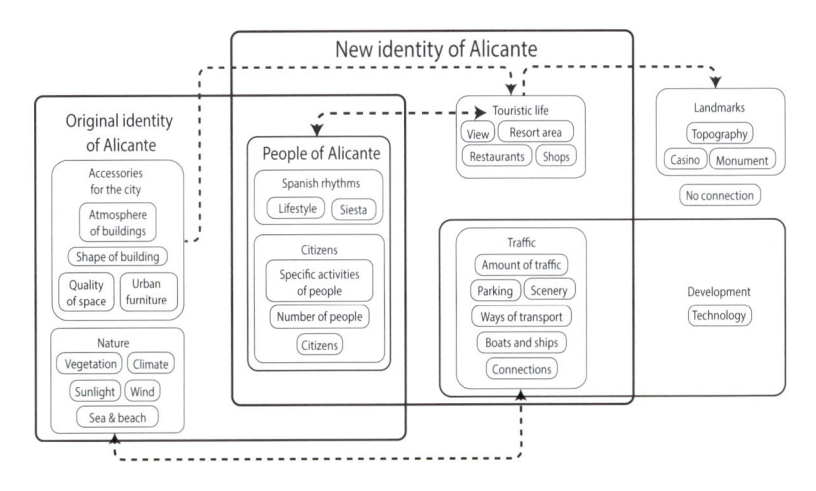

fig. 1: Example of resulting affinity diagram (group 3)

3. Results

What follows is a compilation of the explanations given by each group about the affinity diagram and the selected places during the final presentation. The participants chose a series of places (see location in fig. 3) and provided oral explanations on those places, including objective descriptions (such as the use, or shape of the place) and subjective explanations on preference (features considered positive or negative). In fig. 2 we show photographs of the selected places and keywords of the positive features. Since our focus is on the positive evaluation of place, in fig.2 we have excluded other comments such as descriptions and negative evaluations. In the explanation below, we have extracted all the positive features as keywords from the narrative explanations, and these are indicated as underlined words. As for the affinity diagrams, we will refer to a group of cards as a 'subcategory,' and groups of subcategories are called just 'categories'.

3.1 Group 1: Mercado-San Antón

The affinity diagram showed that the annotations about the physical characteristics (e.g., physical appearance of buildings) were mostly negative. There was a lack of positive comments on the physical features of the sector, but the group found many positive annotations about more intangible elements under the category of people. The following places were selected considering those elements, especially the role of place in facilitating social interaction, and the importance of knowledge or familiarity with the place.

• *For Spaniards: Eight and Half.* This is a bar with several spaces that functions as a cultural centre. Spanish members characterised it as a public house and appreciated its multifunctional character, the fact that the bar can be rented for events organised by users, and also the relationship with its charismatic owner. The Japanese did not share the enthusiasm for the place, due to the language barrier, and also because they had the impression that the place is only welcoming for specific people. Besides, Japanese did not find the building façade particularly welcoming or friendly, but rather hidden and difficult to enter.

• *For Japanese: Panteón de Quijano*. The Japanese selected this place as good because they considered it full of sunshine, trees and vegetation, and they viewed it as open and welcoming. In contrast, Spaniards stated that the park was occupied by homeless people, and therefore, it was difficult for them to use this park.

• *For both: Mercado Square*. This square was chosen by both Japanese and Spaniards. The Spaniards chose the place for its multi-functionality (shopping in the market, eating in the terraces outdoors, resting, chatting), and the possibility of social encounter. Japanese liked it because it was full of sunshine and they could participate in and enjoy local activities.

3.2 Group 2: Casco Histórico

Through the affinity diagram this group found that the urban qualities of the district converge into two topics, 'view' (related to the subcategories 'good view/visual') and 'activity' (related with the subcategory 'inactive'). They further explored the details of the card annotations grouped under those subcategories, and found that view and activity were interpreted in slightly different ways by Japanese and Spaniards. Both understood activity to mean liveliness and the presence of shops, but Spaniards included comments about spontaneity and the appropriation of public space. Good view for both meant wide, clear and bright space, but Japanese added nuances about tidiness, calm and peacefulness, which appeared in the affinity map as well. Those ideas guided both groups in their selection of the following 'good places'.

• *For Spaniards: Barrio de Santa Cruz*. This residential precinct is located on the slope of Mount Benacantil, close to the castle. It is characterised by narrow streets, small one or two-story houses. The Spaniards appreciated the appropriation of the public space by the expressions of everyday life (such as outdoor seating as an extension of the living room or private flower containers on the street).

• *For Spaniards: Mayor Street*. This is a pedestrian street, characterised by numerous cafés and restaurants that expand their seating space with terraces. Spaniards considered it as lively space with the possibility for numerous interactions between different users.

• *For Japanese: City Hall Square*. This plaza, connected with Mayor Street, was viewed by the Japanese as an open, wide space, and as a calm, clean and well-organised plaza.

• *For both: Ereta*. This park, located on the slope of Mount Benacantil, was appreciated for its spectacular view of the sea, and its recreational areas with fountains and urban furniture.

3.3 Group 3: Seafront

This is the sector that most clearly shows the polarisation of places, between tourists and locals. The places selected by this group reflect the perception suggested in the affinity diagram that there are 'original' and 'new' identities of the city and an opposition between locals and tourists.

• *For Spaniards: Camon*. This public cultural centre was selected as a good place by Spaniards, who explained that it works both as a cultural and social hub. It provides access to film, music, photography, multimedia art, equipment and software. In addition to creative activities, this place was appreciated because it offers a web system for members, where people can create online communities that can be linked to major social networking sites.

• *For Japanese: Explanada*. This promenade runs along the marina. For the Japanese it had an open and welcoming atmosphere created by a wide palm-lined boulevard paved with neatly designed tiles, and terraced cafés on one side facing the sea. Although this boulevard was built in the mid-19th century and is probably one of the most iconic places in Alicante, locals did not select it. They said that they use this place, but that they do not consider it special. They felt that this place has fallen in the realm of touristic Alicante, and they do not identify with the place.

• *For both: Postiguet*. Located at the slope of Mount Benacantil, the beach offers diverse activities such as playing sports, running along the beach, having walks on the pedestrian paved side, eating and drinking at terraced cafés. Both sides evaluated this place as good, but with differences in their focus of preference. Spaniards appreciated multi-functionality itself, as well as the historical background of the location as a place that has been always important for local people and used for festivals. Japanese were attracted by its atmosphere of sunshine and a relaxed lifestyle.

3.4 Group 4: Ensanche-Diputación

This group particularly focussed on the patterns of these colours and found clear differences in the approach of each side. For the selection of places they could not take any category as the most relevant, since each category contained cards about both good and bad characteristics. Instead, they refined the subcategories and identified the criteria mentioned below.

• *For Spaniards: Jorge Juan Stairs*. This location has public stairways connecting a boulevard with a high school located on a hill. Spaniards chose it because of its wide open space, the view, its iconic presence in the city and the number of activities conducted by young people day and night.

• *For Spaniards: Chinese area*. This area has several shops run by Chinese residents. Although not particularly impressive, Spaniards found it interesting because of the exotic products and food they can see in the area, and the small billboards written in Chinese characters. The reasons stated for selecting this place were cultural exchange, multicultural atmosphere, providing new relationships between the foreign and the domestic, and a different shop style.

• *For Japanese: Diputación*. This is open public space with greenery and places for relaxing. However, since the garden is walled and it is part of the grounds of a provincial administration building, it is not commonly known as public garden by locals. Good characteristics of this place were described as easy access (well connected to the main street and the Alicante train station), iconic building (the historical administrative building), park, sunlight, European atmosphere, and in particular, comfort from being protected from the street.

• *For both: Marvá-Soto-Gadea*. This boulevard, which follows the topography of the city and connects the sea and the hills, is one of the main streets in the city, and was chosen because it is multifunctional, is an active pedestrian space, and has much greenery and places to stop and rest.

3.5 Group 5: Centro

In this group, Japanese and Spanish members easily came to select the same places as 'good for both'. However, when they explained the reasons for selecting the three places, the Japanese and Spaniards provided differing reasons. Besides the three places (selected by both sides) they also identified two additional places where it was more difficult to find consensus.

• *For Spaniards: Muntanyeta Square*. Spaniards reported good memories of this square, which was the local gathering point for the political demonstrations that swept Spain in 2011 known as the 'indignados' (which gained visibility when it reached the United States and was re-coined as 'Occupy Wall Street'). The Japanese, lacking these associations, did not find the square particularly preferable, since it is surrounded by narrow streets packed with parked cars and was not easily accessible.

• *For Japanese: Gabriel Miró Square*. This square was selected by the Japanese for its greenery, as it is surrounded by tall trees that create a comfortable leafy shade. However, Spaniards did not choose this place because they retained bad images from the past, when the trees were not maintained, which gave the square a dark atmosphere, and contributed to its use by marginalised people.

• *For both: New square*. The Japanese selected this place because of its characteristic open space, enclosed by buildings in traditional pastel colours, and the presence of a modern aquarium in the middle. The Spaniards selected this place because they can see people from all ages gathering and relaxing, chatting or drinking.

• *For both: Castaños-San Ildefonso*. The Japanese selected this street crossing because of its characteristic appearance with historical colourful buildings and urban furniture. The Spaniards selected this place because they can feel comfortable, as it is an attractive place to hang out and provides a traditional link with their history. For both, this area was also attractive as it is only for pedestrians and people can enjoy the street without traffic noise.

• *For both: Calvo Sotelo Square*. Japanese selected this place because it provides a place both for adults and for children by putting a café and small parks together. They

Cross-cultural Debates | Almazán, Tairako, Suzuki, Muminović, Inoue, Kawakubo

	Good for **Spaniards**	Good for **Japanese**	Good for both **Spaniards and Japanese**
Group 1: Mercado-San Antón	**Eight and Half** Public house, multifunctional, events organized by users, charismatic owner	**Panteón de Quijano** Sunshine, trees, vegetation, open, welcoming	**Mercado Square** Multifunctionality, social encounter Span.: Jpn.: Sunshine, enjoy local activity
Group 2: Casco Histórico	**Barrio Santa Cruz** Appropriation of the public space, everyday life **Mayor Street** Lively, interaction between different users	**City Hall Square** Open, wide, calm, clean, well-organized	**Ereta** Both: Spectacular view, recreational areas **Postiguet** Span.: Multi-functionality, historical background, important for local people, festivals Jpn.: Sunshine, relaxed lifestyle
Group 3: Seafront	**Camon** Cultural and social hub, creative activities, web system for members	**Explanada** Open, welcoming, wide palm-lined boulevard, neatly designed tiles, terraced cafés, facing the sea	**Marvá-Soto-Gadea** Both: Multifunctional, active pedestrian space, greenery, places to stop and rest
Group 4: Ensanche Diputación	**Jorge Juan stairs** Wide, open, view, iconic presence, activities conducted by young people **Chinese area** Exotic products, billboards written in Chinese characters, cultural exchange, multicultural, different shop style	**Diputación** Easy access, iconic building, park, sunlight, European atmosphere, protected from the street	**New Square** Span.: People from all ages gathering and relaxing Jpn.: Open, buildings in traditional pastel colours, aquarium **Castaños-San Ildefonso** Span.: Comfortable, hang out, link with history Jpn.: Historical colourful bld. urban furniture Both: Only pedestrian, no traffic noise
Group 5: Centro	**Muntañeta Square** Good memories, gathering point, political demonstrations	**Gabriel Miró Square** Greenery, tall trees, comfortable leafy shade	**Calvo Sotelo Square** Span.: Large, sunny open, meeting point Jpn.: Place for adults and children, inter-generational exchange, lively, attractive

fig. 2: Views of places selected and reasons for selection in the group discussions

found this kind of place, which enables inter-generational exchange, lively and attractive. The Spaniards selected this place for having a large, sunny open space, and being a well-known meeting point.

4. Discussion and conclusions

This study focused on urban public spaces in Alicante to respond to the research question: Which places are preferred by locals, by visitors, and in particular, by both? Why is this so? Which qualities make those places attractive? This section discusses the methodology, and summarises and discusses the results.

4.1 On methodology

This study contains intrinsic limitations because of its methodological design. First of all, the participants from both nationalities were all young people, whose perspective also needs to be contrasted with that of people from other generations. This generational bias will be discussed in next section. Similarly, all of the participants were students of architecture and engineering, but not experts, urban planners or architects. They lack the awareness of the technical or political constraints operating in urban spaces. Finally, not only age, nationality, professional and cultural background, but also gender and gender roles need to be considered in relation with urban space, but also in relation with the interpersonal dynamics in methodologies based on group discussions, such as the one used in this paper. Because of these limitations, the results need to be considered as partial and not exhaustive.

Within these limitations, the bottom-up participatory evaluation presented here was appropriate for the research goal of finding narrative ways to identify preferable spaces and the reasons within a cross-cultural framework. From previous similar investigations (Almazán et al. 2008) we consider it successful in terms of the speed and depth in which participants could engage in discussions, particularly the Japanese students. The Spaniards, who know the city better, who are used to an open and confrontational discussion style, and whose mother tongue is closer to English (the lingua franca employed for the discussions) could have easily dominated the process. The visual and participatory character of the affinity diagrams, nevertheless, helped to facilitate cross-cultural inter-subjectivity.

We could identify possible ways for improving the method. The explanations of the final results, verbal and recorded in video, were not clear enough sometimes. We believe that asking the participants for a written explanation would have helped them to better organise their ideas. Also, several participants expressed the sentiment that the step between the affinity diagrams and the selection of places was difficult. The goal was to develop abstract ideas about 'what makes an urban space good or bad?' to help select specific places. The idea was not just to organise information according to a mere logical affinity, but to introduce inter-subjective criteria. We believe that this could have been partly avoided if we found ways to make the original data collected during the urban drift survey more subjective. This means, for example, asking participants in the survey to express their values ('trees make a very nice space') rather than just provide descriptions ('there are trees').

In any case, as a qualitative tool, affinity diagrams can never claim to provide as firm results as formal or numerical logic. They are part of a narrative structure whose strength lies in facilitating understanding within its context. In that sense, the affinity diagrams served as a useful trigger for discussion, a map to explore ideas, zooming in for detailed annotations or out for broader categories, and as a physical record of a collective thinking process. Although participants had to follow the rules of the affinity diagrams, the groups managed to innovate and find ways to enhance the method, such as groups 1 and 5 using different ink colours to distinguish positive and negative features. The extensive coverage given to some of the preliminary results of the overall process in the provincial newspapers (Información 2012) shows the potential interest that this study can trigger amongst local residents and policy makers.

4.2 On urban places in Alicante

The results obtained can be summarised according to the three preferences: places preferred by Spaniards, by Japanese and by both. The first and second group show tendencies that could be expected and that partly coincide with the results of Phase 1 (*Collective Urban Drift*).

Therefore, the most relevant finding was about the places preferred by both sides. What follows is a summary and a discussion of these results, graphically organized in fig.2.

Preferences of Japanese visitors. The places selected by Japanese participants showed a tendency that could be expected in first-time visitors. They seemed to prefer historical and traditional places, which can be considered as 'exotic' from their cultural perspective. Examples are the positive descriptions on the "European atmosphere" of the Diputación, or "historical buildings" of the New Square and Castaños-San Ildefonso. On the other hand, there were also often reasons for selection that the authors did not expect, such as a recurrent preference for "greenery" and places to "relax" (e.g. Panteón de Quijano, Gabriel Miró Square, or Diputación gardens). Knowing Japanese architecture and its meditative, calm gardens, such a tendency might seem a cultural stereotype. However, the tendency emerged freely from Japanese participants. This tendency to look for relaxing peaceful spaces might also relate to a desire for rest from the numerous stimuli encountered in a foreign country.

Preferences of local Spaniards. The places chosen by the Spaniards showed a deeper understanding that could also be expected. Their evaluations are entangled with the experience of the everyday life and historical memories (e.g. the "good memories" evoked by the Muntañeta Square). Some of their preferences correspond to the interests of a younger and educated population (the cultural centres of Eight and Half and Camon), and we could easily expect slightly different results from other types of participants. Other preferences, like a preference for multifunctional spaces full of activity and people, seem to correspond to a cultural tendency that can be clearly identified in the lively streets of South European countries (e.g. the "street life" of Mayor Street or the "social encounter" of the Mercado Square). The polarisation of places, best represented by their dislike of the iconic Explanada boulevard, which Spaniards did not select in this survey (Phase 2) nor in the previous one (Phase 1), seems also to be unrelated to age and occupation, but rather to a more general lack of identification by locals with the current state of the place.

Preferences of both. The most unexpected finding was found in the places preferred by both sides. At the beginning of the research, we aimed to find particular qualities that could satisfy both sides, and therefore indicate ways to avoid the negative consequences of urban polarisation. Such cross-cultural urban qualities were found in three places: Ereta, Marvá-Soto-Gadea, and the pedestrian character of Castaños-San Ildefonso. However, we found that in most cases when both sides preferred the same place, it was for different reasons (e.g. Mercado Square, Postiguet, New Square, Castaños-San Ildefonso and Calvo Sotelo Square). For example, the Postiguet beach is appreciated by Spaniards for its "diverse activities, history and festivals", while Japanese enjoy "sunshine and a relaxed lifestyle".

In conclusion, the results show a range of criteria for which some urban places are preferred over others. The visitor preferences confirmed those of tourists, although they also showed tendencies that could be considered as Japanese cultural preferences. The local preferences demonstrated a deeper understanding of the place and a rejection of places considered touristy. As for the places preferred by both the Japanese and Spaniards, the places were very often selected for different reasons. This finding suggests that a way to avoid polarisation between local and touristic places, and the loss of identification of locals with some areas of their city does not depend only upon particular shared preferences, but also upon the capacity of a place to nurture enough diversity so as to enable different qualities that can stimulate and respond to the preferences of different people, including preferences as different as those of the Japanese and Spaniards.

The public spaces identified by both sides, and the reasons offered, suggest urban characteristics and actual spaces through which the coexistence of locals and visitors can be achieved, and therefore tourism, rather than damaging and polarising the identity of the city, can instead contribute to the enhancement of local economic and social capital.

Acknowledgements

This study was originally published as *Cross-cultural participatory study on preferred public spaces: Re-imaging the Urban Identity of Alicante City* (Part II) Journal of Architecture and Planning (Transactions of the Architectural Institute of Japan) No. 686, Vol. 78 (April 2013) Reprinted by kind permission of the publisher.

fig. 3: Location of places selected in the group discussions

References

AIJ (Architectural Institute of Japan) ed. 2005. Survey and Analysis Methods for Architecture and Urban Planning (in Japanese). Tokyo:Inoue Shoin.

Almazán, J., L. Galán, and Yoshihiko Ito, eds. 2008. Link Tokyo-Madrid. ISBN 978-4-9904160-0-3.

Brassard, M. 1989. The Memory Jogger Plus. Methuen, MA: GOAL/QLP.

Clay, G. 1973. Close-Up: How to read the American City. Chicago: University of Chicago Press.

Cybriwsky, R. 1991. Tokyo: The Changing Profile of an Urban Giant. London: Belhaven Press.

Información (newspaper). 2012. Así nos ven los japoneses. March 10. On-line version at http://www.diarioinformacion.com/alicante/2012/03/10/ven-japoneses/1232353.html

Kawakita, J. 1996. KJ Method: Creating Ideas From Chaos (in Japanese). Vol. 5 of Kawakita Jiro Collected Works. Chuokoronsha.

Okuyama, S., F. Yamada, and K. Sakamoto. 1994. Spatial conceptions of architects on contemporary houses in the articles: study on design theories of architects in Japan. Journal of architecture, planning and environmental engineering (Transactions of the Architectural Institute of Japan), No. 456 (1994.2.28):123–134.

Scupin, R. 1997. The KJ method: A technique for analyzing data derived from Japanese ethnology. Human Organization, Vol. 56, Issue: 2:233–237

Taniguchi, H., Y. Moriyasu, and W. Yashiki W. 1980. Toshi kikaku tantou yori mita, toshi no tekisei kibo ni kansuru kenkyuu: Toshi shūseki to toshi kankyō shigen ni kansuru kisoteki kenkyū sono 5 (Research into appropriate city size as seen by urban planners: Basic research into urban concentration and urban environmental resources, No. 5). Summaries of Technical Papers of Annual Meeting, Architectural Institute of Japan, 1980.9

Ushino, T. 1979. Comprehensive District Plan by Inhabitants and the "Kande method": Studies on making a comprehensive district plan in rural areas by inhabitants (I) (in Japanese). City planning review, extra number, No. 14 (1979.11). City Planning Institute of Japan.

114 | 115   Cross-cultural Debates

Urban file 01
Mercado Square

Also known as the Flower Plaza, or the "25th May Plaza". Located at the rear of a market building, it recently became an all-age place for gathering and eating fresh appetizers from the market, especially as a social warming up for lunch and "tardeo," the Saturday afternoon going out.

Labels: Capitán Segarra St.; Central market rear façade; Flower shop; People eating appetizers; Bench; Bar terrace; Calderón de la Barca St.

Urban file 02
Ereta Park

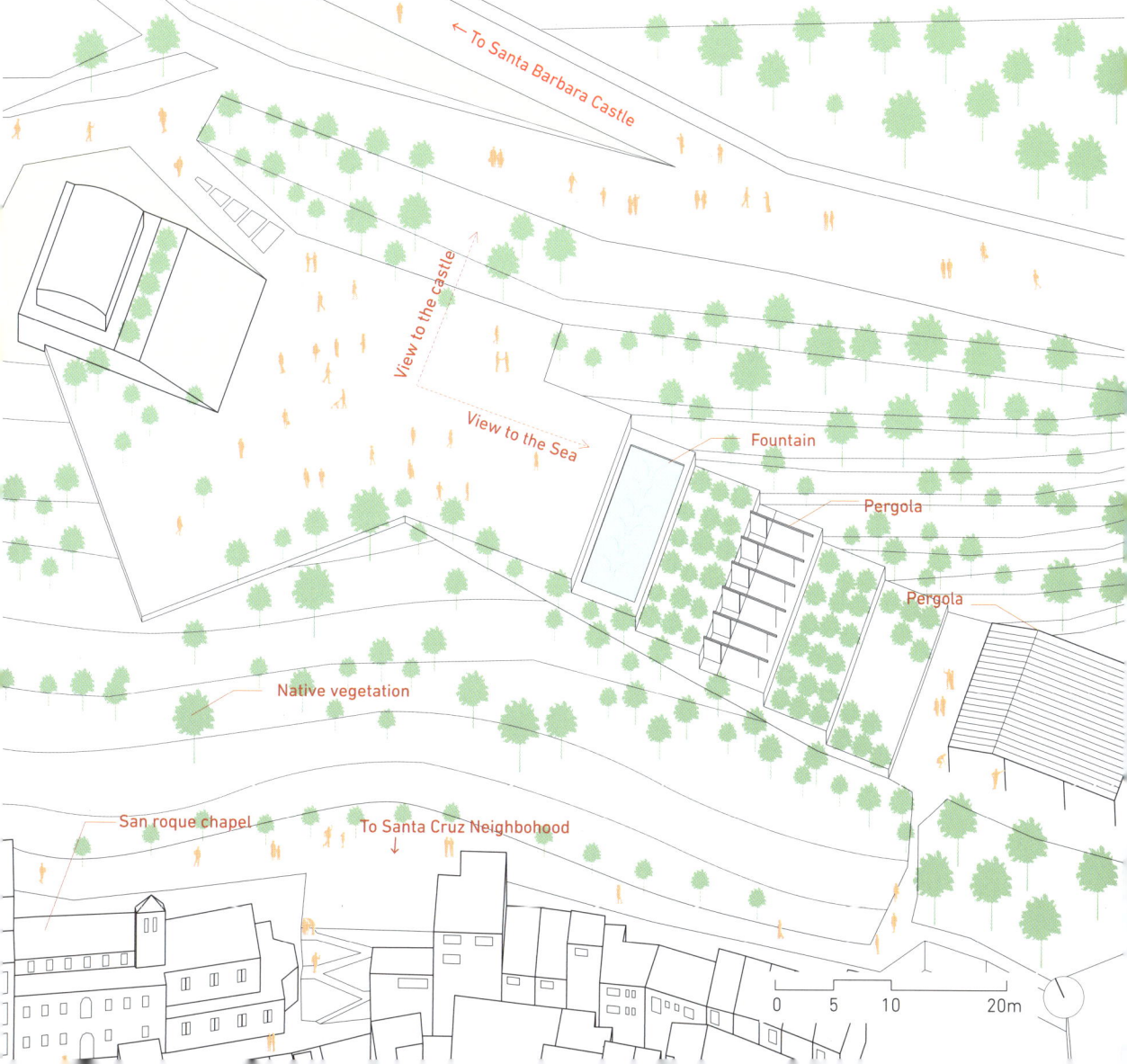

Designed by Bigarnet & Bonnet, and opened in 2003, this park appropriates for the city the hillside of the Benacantil Mount. Its design makes exclusive use of native vegetation, respects the original topography, and offers privileged views to the sea, the city and the castle.

← To Santa Barbara Castle

View to the castle

View to the Sea

Fountain

Pergola

Pergola

Native vegetation

San roque chapel

To Santa Cruz Neighbohood

0 5 10 20m

116 | 117   Cross-cultural Debates

Urban file 03
Postiguet Beach

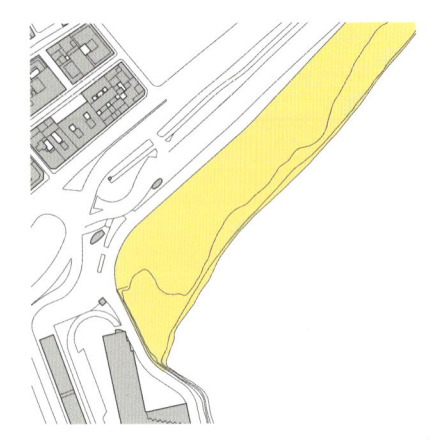

Reknowned for the quality of its sand and its palm tree boardwalk, Alicante's urban beach is a highly urbanized space with an intensive infrastructural equipment including car parking spaces, a tram-train station, cafés, children playgrounds, sports zones and public showers.

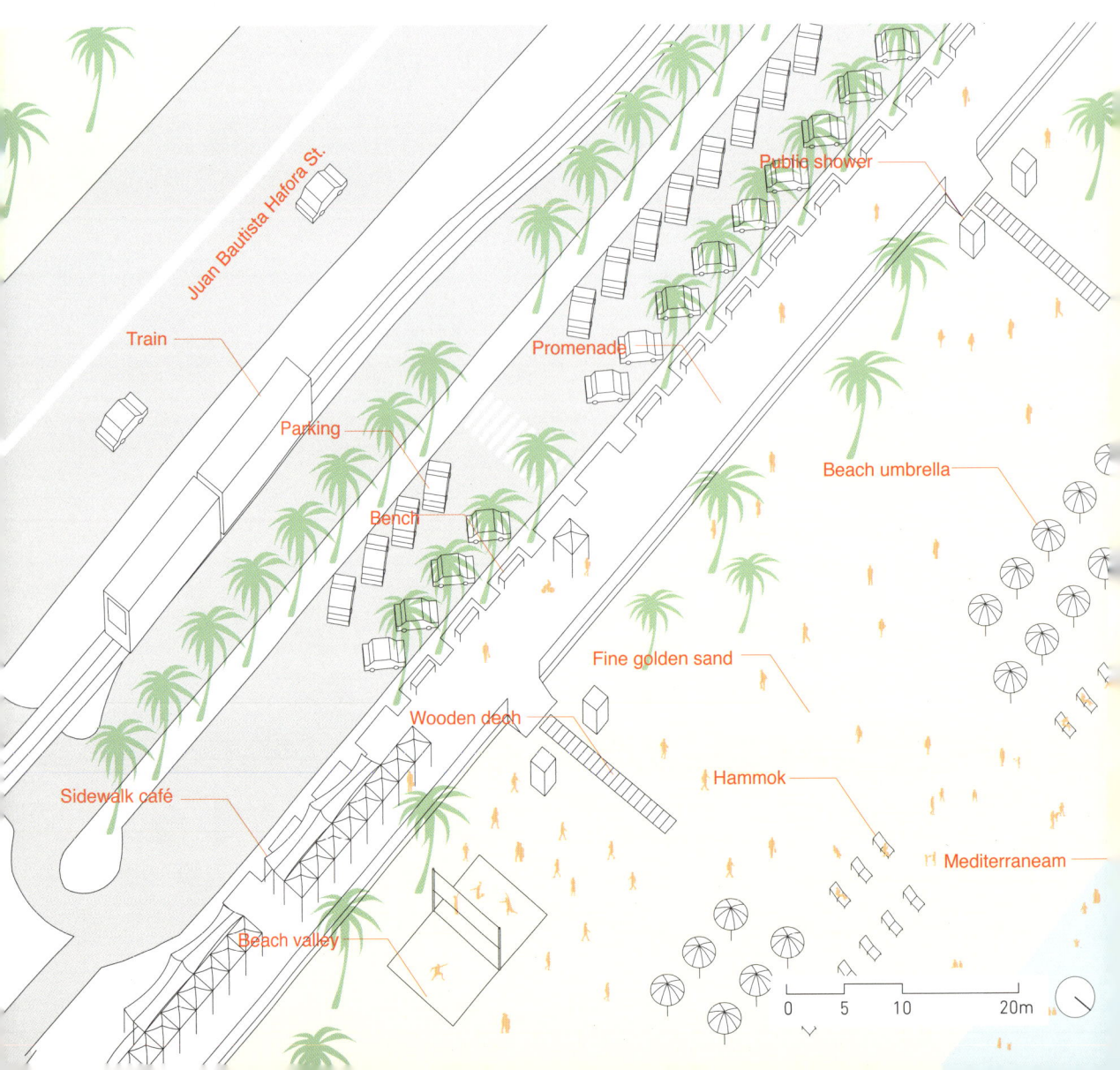

- Juan Bautista Hafora St.
- Train
- Parking
- Bench
- Sidewalk café
- Beach valley
- Wooden deck
- Promenade
- Public shower
- Beach umbrella
- Fine golden sand
- Hammok
- Mediterraneam

Urban file 04

Marvá, Soto and Gadea Boulevards

The main North-South boulevard of the "ensanche," the sector corresponding to the 19th century city expansion, is a gently sloped urban promenade with children playgrounds, benches and kiosks, that connects the Tossal Mount with the sea.

Cross-cultural Debates

Urban file 05
New Square

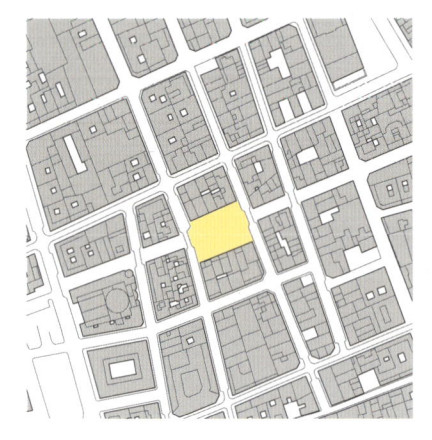

The tiny "Plaza Nueva" is continuously animated by the flow of passers-by created by the two adjacent pedestrian streets. The outdoor aquarium, much liked by children, and the bar terraces under pergolas, where their parents often sit, foster a place where different generations can enjoy together.

- Pedestrian street
- Felipe Bergé St.
- Navas St.
- Bar terrace under pergola
- Aquarium
- Bars in ground floor
- Colón St.
- Camarada César Elgueza St.
- Pedestrian street

Urban file 06
Castaños, San Ildefonso Crossing

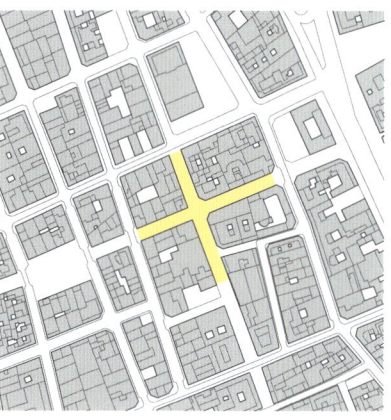

Restaurants, pubs and cafés, all extend their sitting spaces to the outdoors at this crossing of two pedestrian streets. The crossing and its surroundings become a continuous and densely occupied urban living room where chance encounters often happen.

- San Ildefonso St.
- Ground floor restaurant & shops
- Bench
- Bar terrace
- Parasol
- Castaños St. — To Teatro Principal
- To New Square →

0 5 10 20m

Urban file 07
Calvo Sotelo Square

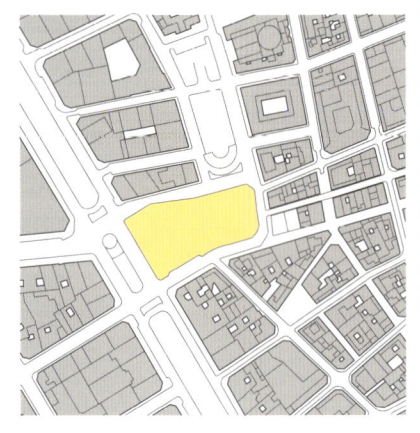

Also known as the "Pigeon plaza". The birds, together with the playgrounds become one the attractions for children, while adults can watch over them sitting from the adjacent café terraces. The central location and open spaces make this plaza a famous meeting point.

Extroduction
Toward a Post-Souvenir City?

¿Hacia una ciudad post-souvenir?

ポスト・スーヴェニア・シティをめざして？

Jorge Almazán ｜ ホルヘ・アルマザン

El *turista participativo*, un nuevo tipo de turista que busca la experiencia cultural real, puede convertirse en un incentivo de revitalización urbana. En el caso de la provincia y la ciudad de Alicante, los modelos turísticos previos propiciaron un desarrollo fordista de bloques de apartamentos y urbanizaciones de baja altura desparramados por el paisaje. El *turismo participativo*, sin embargo, valora los centros urbanos consolidados y potencia la reapreciación de la vida cotidiana. Junto a monumentos e iconos arquitectónicos, la vitalidad urbana cotidiana pasa a ser también un activo turístico. En lugar de la polarización espacial tan característica de las ciudades turísticas, en las que residentes y foráneos usan espacios segregados, el nuevo turismo propicia lugares públicos donde visitantes y residentes coinciden e interactúan. Estos lugares pueden potenciarse mediante un diseño inclusivo, en el que diversos usos, intereses y expresiones coexistan. Aprendiendo de la psicología ambiental y de corrientes artísticas recientes, se pueden proponer *escenarios urbanos relacionales*, lugares caracterizados por una congruencia entre un orden visual distintivo, y la vitalidad desordenada propia del uso social activo de la ciudad. Más allá de los tradicionales lugares de "sol y playa", se propone aquí potenciar estos escenarios urbanos que posibilitan una polinización creativa entre residentes y visitantes. El centro urbano de Alicante, cuya compacidad y diversidad propicia encuentros espontáneos, las infraestructuras de transporte, la presencia de instituciones de investigación como la universidad, y la propia calidad de vida urbana que la ciudad ofrece, son algunas de la precondiciones que permiten imaginar esta nueva ciudad turística, más inclusiva y creativa.

真の文化体験を探求する「参加型ツーリスト」という新しいタイプの観光客は、都市再活性化の起爆剤となる可能性を秘めている。従来型の観光モデルがアリカンテ県や市にもたらしたまち並みは、大量に建設された画一的なアパートメント群や、秩序なく点在する低層の分譲住宅地であった。しかし「参加型ツーリズム」は、既存の市街地を評価し、日常生活の再興を促す。モニュメントや建築的アイコンとともに、日常的な都市の活力もまた、観光資源に変容させる。さらに、この新しいツーリズムは、観光都市に典型的に見られる空間的二極化、すなわち住民と外部者が別々の空間を使用するという状況に代わって、公共空間でツーリストと住民がめぐり会い互いに刺激し合う場へと変容させる。

こうした出会いの場所は、さまざまな用途・関心・表現の共存を可能にする包括的デザインにより、さらなる活性化が可能となる。環境心理学や近年のアートの潮流をヒントに、明確な視覚的秩序と、アクティヴな都市生活特有の雑然とした活気との結合を特徴とする「関係型都市景」を、そこに提案することができよう。「太陽と砂浜」という伝統的なイメージを超え、住民と訪問者同士の創造的な結合を促すような都市情景を活性化するのである。

コンパクトながら多様性を包含したアリカンテ市中心部は、自然発生的な出会いを促す。また交通インフラが充実し、大学をはじめとする研究機関を備え、豊かな都市生活の基盤が確立しているのもアリカンテの特長である。より包括的で創造的な、新しい観光都市。その創造に必要な条件は、十分に備わっているといえよう。

A loose speculative approach to a fundamental area of conduct is better than a rigorous blindness to it.
—Erving Goffman, *Behavior in Public Places*

Potentials

What will the *post-souvenir city* be like? The emergence of more sensible tourism practices has been explored in the form of essays (Part I) and urban experiments (Part II) for the case of Alicante. It is too early to foresee specific consequences, but here we can pose questions and propose concepts that might guide future debate and actions.

The essays revealed a scenario of potentials for Alicante and other tourist regions. The process of urbanization in Alicante, as in other *sun, sand and sea* Spanish destinations, results from a development model that treats the city and the territory as a commodity for mass tourism consumption. The initial Fordist phase of the model targeted the package tourist and built for him standardized facilities and transport infrastructure. The second phase, supported by neoliberal policies, targeted the second-house owner and led to a sprawling occupation of the territory by low-rise holiday houses. Intimately connecting tourism and the construction industry, both phases developed new urban spaces outside of or neglecting the existing urban cores.

Coexisting with the package tourist and the second-house owner, a new profile of the tourist has emerged. He looks for urban authenticity, organizes his own trips, makes full use of information technology, and does not depend on tour operators. Rather than staying at standardized hotels or investing in stereotyped "Spanish style" holiday houses, he searches for real cultural experiences. The neglected existing urban cores now come to play an essential role in providing opportunities to participate in local everyday life. The infrastructural consequence of this re-appreciation of the urban nodes could create a demand to connect them, as Oliver reminds us in his essay, an incentive to develop the coastal territory as a hyper-connected metropolitan area.

The emergence of this *participatory tourist* is coupled with a generalized social awareness of the limits of Fordist and neoliberal developments. If the regular complaints about environmental damage and political corruption were not convincing enough, the bursting of the Spanish property bubble in 2008 has finally triggered a generalized debate on the urgent necessity for a different economic model. In the meantime, amid a generalized economic crisis and record-high unemployment, the so-called "manna" of tourism stills flows, and even increases. In the summer of 2013, revenues from tourism and the number of foreign tourists hit record highs (see the news report in Sánchez-Silva 2013). The good news was followed by discussions in Spanish media on the weakness of this apparent success. It was often mentioned that the increase in visitors can be attributed to political instability in other tourist destinations in North Africa and Turkey, which are not perceived as safe, rather than any qualitative improvement in the offerings of Spanish tourism. Also that the Spanish tourism industry relies too heavily on the *sun, sand, and sea* model, and that the tourism offer needs to diversify its offerings and raise its cultural profile to attract a wider range of tourists. Although this weakness is widely acknowledged, it should not overshadow the reasons why tourism is a sustained industry that has managed to support local economies for over 60 years. And most importantly for our focus here, how urban space has contributed to this sustained economy. There are cases of early touristic urbanization that can be defended as models, even from the contemporary point of view of sustainability. One clear case is Benidorm, explained by Mesa in his essay, which has managed to create a place with distinct character, a social laboratory, and an ecological model of compactness that avoids the uncontrolled sprawl that unfortunately became so common along Alicante's shores.

The call for a *post-souvenir city* is therefore not a rejection of the past. The scenario proposed in the essays points rather to acknowledging the social complexity of landscapes that are not "resorts" but living cities and territories, the limited repertoire of urban planning instruments to cope with that complexity, and the changing role of the tourist. A conception of the city as a multi-scale assemblage of different dimensions – physical, social, and environmental, as Nieto explains – seems more relevant today. A city in which its users, residents and visitors, become actors that materially transform the city through their spatial practices.

Liveliness and inclusiveness

The scenario described in the essays has been tested through an urban experiment in two phases. Designed in collaboration with psychologist Yukino Tairako, this experiment suggests some concrete urban qualities and spaces, taken from the study case of Alicante. Both the first phase (*Collective Urban Drift*) and the second (*Cross-cultural Debates*) were designed to find urban qualities that facilitate the coexistence of visitors and locals. Alicante is one of the many cases in which areas for tourists seem segregated from the everyday life of locals, creating a polarization that impoverishes both the experiences of tourists and also the range of places available to locals. Aiming to reproduce a hypothetical *participatory tourist*, we discover in the *Collective Urban Drift* phase that the appreciation of the urban experience for both visitors and locals depends heavily on the liveliness of its streets, the vitality of its public spaces, the presence of people, opportunities to sit in public space, and the presence of commerce. This conclusion undermines architects' reliance on the visual aspects on the city and the tendency to design visually iconic spaces to attract visitors, and supports the conclusions of authors like Alexander, Whyte and Gehl, who since the early 1960s have been vindicating the importance of the social use of urban space.

Secondly, the *Cross-Cultural Debates* suggest that the specific public spaces that actually attracted both visitors and residents had the capacity to provide different stimuli to different users rather than a singular urban quality that can satisfy both visitors and residents. Urban vitality seems to be one of the most important factors, but only from a statistical point of view. When the focus is on particular spaces other factors can be equally relevant. Rather than a "consensual" or mean urban quality, it is fair to say that there is a certain inclusive character that makes the coexistence of multiple and diverse stimuli, visual expressions, and activities possible at the same time in one place. This multiplicity of stimuli does not necessary mean a chaotic urban landscape without scenic "unity". Rather it points towards the necessity of developing a beauty of inclusiveness. This capacity of an urban setting to accommodate diverse spatial configurations and aesthetic values was already advocated by Venturi, Scott Brown and Izenour (1977) in their examination of Las Vegas: "The emerging order of the Strip is a complex order. It is not the easy, rigid order of the urban renewal project or the fashionable "total design" of the megastructure." The seemingly incongruous buildings of Las Vegas "show the vitality that may be achieved by an architecture of inclusion or, by contrast, the deadness that result from too great a preoccupation with tastefulness and total design" (Venturi et al. 1977: 52–53). Since the Las Vegas manifesto, complexity and diversity have become accepted aesthetic values. However, too often architects end up "designing" the appearance of diversity itself, rather than creating the conditions to allow diversity to emerge spontaneously from the citizens' practice of urban space.

Even inclusive overlapping might create controversies over the values that public space should foster. Rather than avoiding them, these controversies are desirable in the development of an urban identity as a relational and dynamic participatory process of building a collective narrative. Graffiti for example, as Suzuki explains in her essay, are often rejected as vandalism. But in East London they came to be seen as public art, and have even become an attractor for visitors. Managing controversies of this kind and integrating them proactively in the design of public space, instead of trying to ignore or suppress them, can play a decisive role in the process of building identity, and it can lead to urban innovation and the transformation of neglected aspects into positive urban assets.

Relational settings

From the *Collective Urban Drift* phase, as mentioned above, urban liveliness appeared prominently as a cross-cultural urban quality, confirming a long tradition of urban criticism that calls for more attention to be paid to the social use of space. Architects and urbanists traditionally relied on the visual dimension of the built environment, and the Modern Movement, with its intimate relation with the avant-gardes of the visual arts, continued this tradition.

This predominance of the visual has come in for criticism since the 1960s and the beginnings of post-modern thinking. Jarvis (1980) identifies two currents which since then have polarized the theory of architecture and urbanism. The "artistic tradition," which addresses the built environment as three-dimensional artistic objects, Jarvis explains, has its source in Sitte (1889) and his compositional principles for plazas, streets and monuments, induced from the study of medieval, renaissance and baroque urban space, and in clear opposition to 19th-century urbanism. According to Jarvis, Le Corbusier continues this visual tradition, although with a geometric aesthetic opposed to Sitte's picturesque compositions.

As a criticism against this tradition, a new tradition of "social use" has emerged since the 1960s. Jarvis cites Lynch, Jacobs, and Alexander as its pioneers. Instead of addressing the material form of the city, Lynch (1960) turns to examining the mental image that people have of the city. Jacobs (1961) makes detailed observations of everyday use of public space to build her critique of modern planning. Alexander starts his investigations in the same period, culminating in *A Pattern Language* (1977), where he describes the relation between specific spatial designs and their positive effect for social interaction and the well-being of users. To these authors cited by Jarvis we can add the studies on urban public space by Gehl (1971) in Scandinavia and Whyte (1980) in New York.

The "social use" tradition stems from researchers directly related to architecture and urbanism. In parallel since the 1960s, environmental psychology emerges with on-site – and not in laboratory – studies of human behavior. Within that current, the work by Roger Baker and his concept of behavior setting is especially relevant. The concept implies the unitary and simultaneous study of the interaction between physical environments and human behavior. Lang (1987) defines these behavior settings as "a stable combination of activity and place". He notes its four basic components: "A recurrent activity – a pattern of stable behavior; a particular configuration of the environment – the milieu; a congruent relation between both – a synomorphism; and a specific period of time."

In the field of aesthetics a similar approach has emerged. In his book *Relational Aesthetics*, the art critic and curator Nicolas Bourriaud describes a series of artistic practices which have emerged since the 1990s as an "aesthetic theory that consists of judging art works on the basis of the inter-personal relationships that they represent, produce or unfold" (Bourriaud 2002:112). He cites artists whose artistic production is based on

fig.1: Tsukiji Market, Tokyo

fig.2: Shibuya Crossing, Tokyo

"encounters, events, different types of collaborations between persons, games, festivals and places of conviviality" (Bourriaud 1998:28). The most immediate critique of the sociability modes described would be their artificiality. These events do not spontaneously emerge from everyday life, but within the controlled context of art galleries. Borriaud insists that this critique does not appropriately judge the value of "relational art", since it should be judged from a formal, even visual, point of view: "The goal is not conviviality, but the product of conviviality, in other words, a complex form which combines a formal structure, a series of objects available to visitors, and the ephemeral image that emerges from the collective behavior. In a sense, the use value of convivialty intermixes with its exhibition value within a visual project" (Bourriaud 2002:83). From the art world, there is thus a visuality that not only interacts with the spectator, but that makes him take part as a formal element of the project. From the field of aesthetics a synthesis is suggested between the "artistic" (visual) tradition and the "social use" tradition. Social behavior, specifically festive and convivial interaction, is treated as a visual element.

The congruency of social and visual or aesthetic qualities in a specific space has been theorized as *behavior setting* by environmental psychology, and as *relational art* by aesthetic theory. Architecture and urbanism, given its synthetic character, become the natural field of application of these notions, the field where aesthetics and psycho-social well-being can become congruent. These congruencies or *relational settings* found in public spaces can become one of the assets of the *post-souvenir city*.

Monumental everydayness

After the enormous success of the Guggenheim Museum in Bilbao, almost all Spanish provincial capitals aimed at creating a similar immediate "Bilbao effect". Iconic buildings with astronomic budgets were proposed, many even built. They seemed to be the magic solution to put a city on the international map of tourism. And during the flamboyant Spanish bubble period they seemed also financially possible. The bursting of the bubble in 2008 unveiled the political corruption and economic disasters left behind these megalomaniac projects. The success of Gehry's Bilbao, as in Utzon's Sydney Opera, came then to be seen in a more realistic way, as exceptional exemplars of ingenuity and truly iconic architecture made possible under equally exceptional conditions.

This exaggerated attention to the iconic and the spectacular has further neglected the potential of everyday life and ordinary urban spaces. Tourist pamphlets and guidebooks highlight monuments and popular yearly festivals, but too often neglect the space between monuments and the time between festivals. Those spatio-temporal interstices are equally important for the image of the city. The post-souvenir city finds a new potential in this everyday urbanism, which, far from a fetishism of ordinariness, represent an interest in moments of quotidian festivity, and spontaneous urbanism of remarkable ingenuity, beauty and inventiveness. It is a movement towards a different kind of monumentality, a monumental everydayness. Tokyo, a city famous for its lack of icons, nevertheless has places like the Tsukiji market, the Shibuya crossing, or Yasukuni Street. These emergent involuntary urban monuments are intensively lived and used spaces that nevertheless have become

fig.3: Yasukuni Street, close to Shinjuku Station (Tokyo)

fig.4: Mercado Square on Saturday, noon. A relational urban setting in the city of Alicante.

some of the city's most iconic places, even internationally, often appearing in foreign movies on Tokyo.

On Alicante's shores, the Levante beach of Benidorm, explained by Miguel Mesa, could be added to this list of sites of everyday monumentality. In the city of Alicante proper, the places selected in the *Cross-cultural Debates* could be also seen as possessing this everyday monumentality. The Mercado Square could be one example (see the *Urban Files* section). Every Saturday around noon, the plaza becomes full with people standing in small groups, drinking, chatting and eating the fresh products from the market. Most of them, in their 30s to 50s, are dressed up as if they were going to an evening party. In fact, after the appetizers on the plaza, the gatherings continue as many of them move to the adjacent streets (especially the area of the crossing of Castaños Street with San Ildefonso Street), where pubs and night clubs are fully open from the early afternoon. These people collectively create a "Saturday night" atmosphere at the brightest time of the day. This recent social phenomena might be explained by the increasing population of mature singles who want to have an active social life but need to go home early or cannot afford late-night activity that would waste their Sundays or affect their biorythms. Also by young parents who leave their children with relatives for a few hours in order to enjoy some time out with friends (Alberola, 2012). The parties end around the time for dinner, when mature singles go back home and young parents pick up their children, have dinner with them, and prepare to spend Sundays with their families. This event, and the plaza and streets that support it, are remarkable *relational urban settings*. Not only for its casual festivity, and its participatory openness, but as it happens in heritage buildings or monuments, for its anthropological interest as a visualization of a unique local culture.

The creative tourist city

Through his interest in everyday life and living authenticity, the *participatory tourist* can incentivize urban imagination. He can become a force towards a more *creative city*, a notion that has been extensively explored in the field of economy by what we can call the "creative economy" movement, basically represented by the work of Howkins (2001), Florida (2002), and Landry (2000). Their concepts point out the necessity to adapt cities to a new competitive environment in which creativity and innovation become the essential economic resources. They emphasize the importance of places, both as social and physical settings, as physical incubators of creativity.

Unlike the critical approach that underpins much research in geography and urban studies, the "creative economy" movement offers business advice and management slogans. They call on managers and policy makers to foster "tolerance" and "diversity" as an entrepreneurial strategy to achieve a "creative city" in order to improve the competitive position of the city in the market of cognitive capitalism. Their research brings into focus for the business world elements of society that have been considered marginal or subversive, like Florida's famous "bohemian index" or the "gay index" indicators, as key factors for creativity.

The "creative economy" school can be criticized for promoting bourgeois urbanism and gentrification, superficial versions of the urban movements that since the 1960s recognize the value of street life, festivity, avant-garde cultural practice, sexual diversity and multiculturalism. However, they must also be acknowledged for their systematic and statistics-based research that links economy and creativity and by doing so establishes bridges between two worlds that often despise each other, due to the prejudices of the "bohemian" world of cultural production and the "pragmatic" world of business and management. Widely recognized contemporary artists like Koons, Hirst and Murakami are equally or even more famous for their financial skills. Also, many private enterprises have become centers of aesthetic and social innovation. Beyond romantic images and prejudices, the relevant point here is to acknowledge the importance of the urban setting to foster creativity. Landry (2000) calls it the "creative milieu": "clusters of buildings, a part of the city, a city as a whole or a region – that contains the necessary preconditions in terms of 'hard' and 'soft' infrastructure to generate a flow of ideas and inventions." It is beyond the scope of these concluding remarks to analyze those preconditions, but at least we could mention five aspects or preconditions in Alicante that could support a cultural turn towards a *creative tourism city*.

The first is related to the value of *human diversity* to trigger flows of ideas. The multiple and varied visitors – the short-term tourist, the yearly university exchange student, the long-term pensioner – act as cultural cross-fertilizers. The second aspect is the *infrastructure*, mainly built for tourism, which can be equally be used to facilitate the mobility of creative talent. The third aspect is the *urban public space*. In spite of the endless opportunities for telecommunicating, the importance of face-to-face encounters has not changed. The city center of Alicante acts as a neutral territory where people from different social class and ages mingle in unplanned ways, facilitating opportunities for encounter and interaction. The compactness of this center, with its concentrated commerce and services, is an asset that could be promoted even further. For example, by creating small spaces in the city center where small, young creative businesses could have an opportunity to gain visibility and the social exposure they need to prosper. The fourth is the presence of *research and education facilities*, specifically the University of Alicante, which could play a much more relevant role in urban life. Finally, the *quality of life* – the good weather, gastronomic traditions, and night life – are qualities that attract not only tourists but also creative talent.

These preconditions are supported by the intensity of urban life found in Alicante and many other Mediterranean cities. Often taken for granted by local residents, this intensity is nevertheless an invaluable urban quality that can play a relevant role in the project of overcoming an excessive dependence on the *sun, sand and sea* model. The role of everyday urbanism, a shift from designing icons to setting the conditions for nurturing *relational urban settings*, recognition of monumental everydayness, and an exploration of the creative potential triggered by tourism are possible ways to imagine this *post-souvenir city* in Alicante.

References

Alberola, Pino. 2012. A las diez en casa. *Diario Información* [Available at: http://www.diarioinformacion.com/alicante/2012/03/26/diez-casa/1237657.html]

Alexander, C., S. Ishikawa and M. Silverstein. 1977. *A Pattern Language: Towns, Buildings, Construction*. Oxford: Oxford University Press.

Bourriaud, N. 2002. *Relational Aesthetics*. Dijon: Les Presses du reél, 1998.

Florida, R. 2002. *The Rise of the Creative Class: And How It's Transforming Leisure, Community and Everyday Life*. New York: Basic Books.

Gehl, J. 1996. *Life Between Buildings: Using Public Space*. 3d ed. Skive: Arkitektens Forlag, 1971.

Howkins, J. 2001. *The Creative Economy*: How People Make Money from Ideas. London: Penguin.

Jacobs, J. 1984. *The Death and Life of Great American Cities: The Failure of Modern Town Planning*. London: Peregrine Books, 1961.

Jarvis, R. 1980. Urban environments as visual art or social setting. *Town Planning Review* 51 (1), 50-66.

Landry, C. 2000. *The Creative City: A Toolkit for Urban Innovators*. London: Earthscan.

Lang. J. 1987. *Creating Architectural Theory: The Role of the Behavioral Sciences in Environmental Design*, New York: Van Nostrand Reinhold.

Lynch, K. 1960. *The Image of the City*, Cambridge: MIT Press.

Sánchez-Silva, Carmen. 2013. El turismo bate otro récord en agosto. *El País*. [Available at http://economia.elpais.com/economia/2013/09/23/actualidad/1379921562 _131605.html]

Sitte, C. 1889. *City Planning According to Artistic Principles*. Translated by G R Collins and C C Collins. London: Phaidon Press, 1965.

Venturi, Robert, Denise Scott Brown and Steven Izenour. 1977. *Learning from Las Vegas*. Cambridge: MIT Press, 1972.

Whyte, W. H. 1980. *The Social Life of Small Urban Spaces*. Washington DC: Conservation Foundation.

Contributors

Jorge Almazán, editor
Jorge Almazán is a practicing architect and academic. He graduated from the School of Architecture at the Polytechnics University of Madrid and completed the Doctoral Degree at the Tokyo Institute of Technology. He has collaborated in several projects for SANAA and Atelier Bow-Wow. In 2008 he was Invited Professor at the University of Seoul. Currently he teaches architecture and leads a research laboratory at Keio University (Tokyo).

Miguel Mesa del Castillo
Miguel Mesa del Castillo graduated from the School of Architecture at the Polytechnics University of Madrid and completed the Doctoral Degree at the University of Alicante. Professional experience includes collaborations with Francisco Alonso de Santos, José María Torres Nadal and Massimiliano Fuksas in Rome. In 1996 he spends a year as a researcher assistant at the University of Rome "La Sapienza". Currently he teaches architecture and leads the Fab lab at Alicante University.

Rosario Navalón
Rosario Navalón, PhD in Geography (University of Alicante) and Master in Land Planning, is professor of Regional Geographic Analysis at the University of Alicante since 2001. Member of the Institute of Tourism Research, she currently chairs the group dedicated to Tourism, Leisure and Recreation. Her research focuses on planning and management of tourism territory, and on the diversification and differentiation of mature destinations by making use of the cultural heritage.

Jose M. Torres Nadal
Jose M. Torres Nadal, PhD Architect, Associate Professor of the Barcelona School of Architecture 1978-1990. Professor and Chair of Project Design in the Alicante School of Architecture since 1997. Active as a professional in ARQUITECTURAS TORRESNADAL. Invited in 2006 to the "On Site: New Architecture in Spain" exhibition in the MOMA. Numerous lectures, books and publications. See work and cultural projects in the book ARQUITECTURAS TORRES NADAL: UN TRABAJO, Ed. Rueda.

Enrique Nieto
Enrique Nieto graduated from the School of Architecture at the Polytechnic University of Madrid and completed the Doctoral Degree at University of Alicante, where he is currently Tenured Associated Professor of Architectural Design, and Director of Master Studies: *Sustainable Architecture and Urbanism*. His built work has been prized and showed in several places as: 12th Spanish Architecture and Urbanism Biennial, Awards of Architecture of Región de Murcia, and FAD Awards.

José Oliver
José Oliver graduated from the School of Architecture at the Polytechnic University of Valencia, Master in Architectural Rehabilitation, and Ph. Doc. Degree at the same institution. Professional experience in Europe and other countries like Brazil, Costa Rica, Israel, etc. Currently Professor in the University of Alicante, Spain, working since 1999 in Bachelor, Master and Doctoral levels. Invited professor in other European universities in Berlin, Amsterdam, Delft or Aachen.

Darko Radović
Head of the Mn'M project, a Professor of Architecture and Urban Design at Keio University, co-director of International Keio Institute for Architecture and Urbanism–IKI, and a Visiting Professor at the United Nations University, Tokyo. He is also a member of the Philips Center for Health and Well-being Livable Cities Think Tank. He has taught, researched and practised architecture and urbanism in Europe, Australia and Asia, and held senior academic positions at the University of Belgrade, University of Melbourne, University of Tokyo and at Keio University (current). His research focuses at the nexus between environmental and cultural sustainability, public-private interface and - loveable cities.

Mio Suzuki
Mio Suzuki studied at Waseda University, Japan, and received her Bachelor in Architecture, Science and Engineering. From 2006 to 2011 she worked for Foreign Office Architects in London where she enjoyed success in various large scale projects including a number of high-rise buildings projects. In 2011, she moved back to Japan and worked at Keio University. Currently she is Research Assistant and PhD candidate at Keio University.

Yukino Tairako
Yukino Tairako, master's degree in psychology, is a doctoral candidate at the Graduate School of Human Sciences, Department of Psychology, Sophia University. She is also a professional clinical psychotherapist, and has been trained in psychoanalytic psychotherapy, cognitive behavioral therapy, and psychological assessment. Her fields of expertise are psychological assessment and treatment for psychosomatic disorder.

Translators

Elizabeth Chamberlain Polli
Elizabeth Chamberlain Polli (Ph.D. Columbia University, 1997) has been translating from Spanish into English off and on since the 1980s. Publications include translations of poetry, prose and essays by Sergio Chejfec, Felix de la Concha, Fritz Glockner, Wendy Guerra, Ana Merino, José María Merio and Luis Muñoz. Polli has directed the Spanish Language Program at Dartmouth College since 1998.

Yoshihiko Ito
Yoshihiko Ito completed his doctorates at the Graduate School of the University of Tokyo. Architectural historian specializing in Spanish Architecture, he also studied at the Polytechnics University of Madrid and the Autonomous University of Madrid. He is currently working as a research fellow at the Tokyo University of Science. He has engaged in research and teaching at Keio University, Hosei University, Autonomous University of Madrid, and others.

Post-Souvenir City : Mediterranean Urban Intensity and New Tourism Practices in Alicante

First Published by	IKI (International Keio Institute)+flick studio co., ltd.
Supervised by	Darko Radović / IKI (International Keio Institute for Architecture and Urbanism)
Edited by	Jorge Almazán / IKI (International Keio Institute for Architecture and Urbanism)
Technical Editor	Shinya Takagi and Takako Ishida (flick studio), Mie Arioka (Studio SETO)
Technical Assistance	Keio University Jorge Almazán Laboratory:
	Motoo Chiba, Gaku Inoue, Nozomi Shimizu, Shota Takayama, Yuri Oikawa, Ken Tamura, Maho Sugiyama
Book Designed by	Tomofumi Yoshida (9P)
Cover Illustration	Sae Ohno
Production Coordinator	Kumi Aizawa (silent voice)
Japanese Translation	Yoshihiko Ito
Japanese to English Translation and English Proofreading	Thomas Donahue
Spanish to English Translation	Elizabeth Polli
Published in Japan by	flick studio / Shinya Takagi
	2-28-6 Higashiazabu Minato-ku, Tokyo Japan 106-0044
	tel : + 81 (0)3-6229-1501 / fax : 03-6229-1502
Printed in Japan by	Fujiwara Printing Co., Ltd.

Copyright for publication ©2014 IKI – International Keio Institute for Architecture and Urbanism, Darko Radović and flick studio Co., Ltd.
Copyright for each chapter belongs to the author of that chapter. Copyright for photos and drawings, unless stated otherwise, is held by individual authors.
All rights reserved / Copyright@2014 for first edition of the book by Keio University

IKI / International Keio Institute for Architecture and Urbanism
co+labo, Keio University, Department of Systems Design Engineering,
3-14-1 Hiyoshi, Kohoku-ku, Yokohama, 223-8522, Japan, tel: +81 (0)45-566-1675